# Contents in brief

# Full contents

# Contributors

**Steven B. Emery** is an anthropologist working as a Lecturer in the School of Geography at Birmingham University, UK. The School aims to deliver interdisciplinary research to advance understanding of the social, economic, environmental and technological challenges faced by rural areas and the relationship between them. Steven holds a BSc (Hons) in Environmental Management from Lancaster University, an MSc in EU Environmental Management from the same institution, and a PhD in Anthropology from Durham University. He has good connections to Keele University via his interest in rural work and sustainability.

**Steve French** completed both his undergraduate degree and MA in History and Politics at the University of East Anglia and subsequently worked in the Inland Revenue, where he was active in the IRSF union (now the Public and Commercial Services Union, PCS). He then moved to Birmingham University to complete a PhD (examining German collective bargaining after unification) in 1999. Steve joined the staff at Keele University in September 2000, after working as a Research Assistant at the LSE and as a Lecturer in Industrial Relations at the University of Warwick. He sits on the advisory board of Migrant Workers North West and the Regional Refugee Employment Group of the West Midlands Strategic Migration Partnership.

**Lindsay Hamilton** has been a Lecturer in Management at Keele University since 2009, having previously taken a scholarship at Keele University to carry out ethnographic research for her PhD thesis on veterinary surgeons. Since 2010 she has been an editor of the Sage journal, *Ethnography* with Paul Willis (Princeton). She is a member of the Research Institute for Social Sciences at Keele University and has a book in print called, *Animals at Work: Identity, Politics and Culture in Work with Animals* (Brill Academic Press). Lindsay's interests lie in the research method of ethnography, a technique that is used to examine the cultural worlds in which people live and work. Her main research focus lies in the co-creation of cultures with and around non-human animals, the networks and the relationships that form between humans and 'other than humans'. Theoretically she is influenced by the possibilities of Actor–Network thinking, and particularly its application in scientific contexts such as veterinary medicine. She enjoys reading books which lie at the interface between philosophical and ethnographic research, especially by Anne-Marie Mol, John Law and Bruno Latour.

**Phil Johnson** is a Teaching Fellow in Keele Management School. He joined Keele in 2005 after a career with Marks & Spencer, where his principle roles included store and third-party contract management, and global supply chain strategy. His academic CV includes visiting roles at the Universities of Cranfield, Warwick and Leeds, amongst others. Highlights of current teaching include Operations & Quality Management (year 2), and a number of Strategy modules across MBA, MSc and Undergraduate programmes. He is also Programme Director for the Postgraduate Certificate in Leadership and Management. Phil is a fluent French speaker, has a BA in European Studies, and an MSc in Logistics and Supply Chain Management from Cranfield University.

**Mihaela Kelemen** is Professor of Management at Keele University. She holds a PhD in applied economics from the Academy of Economic Studies, Bucharest and a DPhil in Management Studies from Oxford University. She came to Keele in 1996 and was promoted to Chair in 2006. Her current research focuses on community leadership, innovation and volunteering. She is also interested in exploring the contribution that American Pragmatism has made and could make to organisational knowledge and management practices. Along with Anita Mangan, Mihaela has recently been awarded several Arts and Humanities Research Council (AHRC) Connected Communities grants to explore the role of volunteering processes in the construction of personal communities. She is the author of five books including the seminal *Managing Quality: Managerial and Critical Perspectives* (London: Sage, 2003). Her most recent publication, edited with Nick Rumens, is *American Pragmatism and Organization: Issues and Controversies*, (Ashgate: Gower, 2013).

**David Knights** is Professor of Organisational Analysis at Swansea University School of Management, Lancaster University and the Open University. He also holds a visiting post at Stockholm University Business School. He was previously a professor at Manchester University where in 1994 he co-founded the international refereed journal: *Gender, Work and Organization* on which he continues as co-editor in chief. Recent journal publications include: 'Myopic Rhetorics: Reflecting on the demand for relevance in organisational and management research', *Academy of Management Learning and Education*, 7/4, 2008, pp. 537–552; 'Making and Mending your Nets: The management of uncertainty in academic/practitioner knowledge networks', *British Journal of Management*, 20, 2009 pp. 125–142, and 'Managing Masculinity/

Mismanaging the Corporation', *Organization*, 19/4, July 2012, pp. 385–404. You can email David at the following address: david.knights11@btinternet. com.

**Anita Mangan** has been a Lecturer in Management at Keele University since 2009, having previously worked in Cardiff Business School and University College Dublin, Ireland. She is a member of the Research Institute for Social Sciences at Keele University. With Professor Mihaela Kelemen, she is the holder of two current AHRC awards as part of the AHRC's Connected Communities programme. Both awards stem from an initial AHRC study entitled *'Exploring personal communities: A review of volunteering processes.'* Anita's theoretical perspective is informed by her interest in post-structuralist theories (in particular, the work of Michel Foucault and Judith Butler). She is broadly interested in issues of identity and subjectivity, power and control, discourse analysis and critical management studies. Her fieldwork is qualitative and longitudinal, focusing on volunteers and volunteering processes, non-profit modes of organising and community. As part of her current AHRC research awards, she is working with New Vic Borderlines, an award winning national theatre, using dramaturgical techniques and experiential drama exercises to capture the untold stories of volunteering.

**Darren McCabe** is Professor of Management at Lancaster University. He has published widely on a number of workplace innovations including Total Quality Management, Business Process Reengineering and Teamwork. He has a broad interest in the cultural conditions of work, power, resistance, identity and subjectivity. He is generally interested in qualitative/ ethnographic research and has conducted research in the Financial Services and Manufacturing sectors.

**Laura Mitchell** joined Keele University as a Lecturer in Human Resource Management in January 2011. Before this, she worked as a Graduate Teaching Assistant and Tutor at Lancaster University. Laura holds an MA in HRM and Knowledge Management from Lancaster University as well as a BA (Hons) in Organisation Studies and HRM from the same institution. She completed her PhD at Lancaster in 2011. She is now a member of the Research Institute for Social Sciences at Keele University and an active member of the British Sociological Association. Laura's interests lie in the social and cultural issues that impact upon organisations as well as the politics of dignity, membership and belonging at work. She is currently involved in ethnographic fieldwork in the sub-cultural context of live action role play and is particularly interested by the ways that those participating in this activity are able to create shared values, meanings and identities through the pursuit of 'fantasy'. She is particularly interested by the applications and theoretical possibilities of Erving Goffman as well as a wide range of post-structural organisational theorists such as Rolland Munro.

**Teresa Oultram** is a Lecturer in Management at Keele University and has extensive experience in industrial settings both as a manager and latterly as a researcher. Her primary research focus is youth employment and apprenticeship, a subject which formed the basis for her PhD and more recent publications in the field of policy, education and youth work. She works as an assistant editor on the *Journal of Organizational Ethnography* (Emerald).

**Gordon Pearson** completed twenty years in industrial management before joining academia. His line management experience included most management functions as well as general and strategic management. His specialist experience in mergers and acquisitions were the basis of his first book, *The Strategic Discount*, a critique of accounting's short termism. His first degree was a BSc in Management Sciences at Warwick University. He subsequently completed a PhD in Strategy, Innovation and Culture at Manchester Business School, published as 'The Competitive Organization'. His academic career has included heading up the Department of Management and MBA programmes at Keele University. His critical analysis of theory's impacts on practice is evident in all his books, which also include *Strategic Thinking, Integrity in Organizations, Strategy in Action*, and most recently *The Rise and Fall of Management* and *The Road to Co-operation*. *The Rise and Fall of Management* views the current plight of management practice and theory in its long term context, drawing some conclusions regarding the dysfunctional impact of economic theory on management practice. *The Road to Co-operation* highlights the dangers of using unreal mathematical models to guide policy prescriptions, showing the damage done to real economies, markets, firms and people, and proposing realistic changes in policy and practice, which would be prerequisite to recapturing real long term economic success on a co-operative, and non-exploitative foundation. Further information is located on the internet at www.gordonpearson.co.uk.

**Barry Schofield** is a Research Fellow at Keele University and has extensive experience in political marketing, journalism and public affairs. For 19 years he worked as a newspaper journalist and later joined Newcastle-under-Lyme Borough Council where he became the Head of Policy Review and Communications. He is currently employed as a constituency assistant to the Member of Parliament for Newcastle-under-Lyme. After completing his undergraduate degree at the Open University, he became a member of the Centre for Social Theory at Keele University where he completed an MA in

Social Theory and Organisation, and a PhD. His primary research interests are in the philosophy of organisation. He is a lifelong fan of Port Vale FC.

**Emma Surman** is Lecturer in Marketing at Keele University. Her current research interests lie in two broad areas. These have both been explored through empirical studies into the experience of call centre operators who telework from their own homes. The first is emotion in the workplace and how this particularly relates to gender, technology and the playing out of power relations and identity. This work has focused on the amount of unseen and unvalued emotional work that takes place both in the workplace and in the home, which is essential to ensure its smooth functioning. The second area of research relates to the ways that people both construct and consume social spaces. This work has looked at how, in the absence of their staff from the workplace, call centre supervisors seek to manage the homes of their staff as a work space in an attempt to retain control and compensate for their invisibility.

**Nik Taylor** is Senior Lecturer in Sociology at Flinders University in Adelaide, Australia. She has co-authored the research monograph, *Animals at Work: Identity, Politics and Culture in Work with Animals* with Lindsay Hamilton. Nik received her PhD 'Human-Animal Relations: A Sociological Respecification', from Manchester Metropolitan University in 1999. Since then she has researched issues such as links between human and animal directed violence, and humane education and animal assisted therapy. Nik is the Managing Editor of *Society & Animals*; a charter scholar of the Animals and Society Institute; a participant in the Australian Animals Study group, and an Associate Member of the New Zealand Centre for Human-Animal Studies. Nik is also an editorial board member of *Anthrozoos, Sociology,* and *Sociological Research Online*. She has published numerous works on human–animal relations, the latest of which include, 'Animal Abuse and Criminology: The contribution and the challenge' in *Critical Criminology* and 'Can Sociology contribute to the emancipation of animals?' in a co-edited volume entitled *Theorizing Animals: Re-Thinking Humanimal Relations* (Brill, 2011).

# Introduction from the editors

*Lindsay Hamilton, Laura Mitchell and Anita Mangan*

This book is an unashamedly radical collection of critical voices, assembled here to explore and illuminate the context of management today. We strongly feel that this book has been needed for two purposes: first, to provide us with a repository of alternative perspectives to orthodox studies of workers, organisations and their management and, second, to bring together a variety of authors whose dissenting voices, when taken together, present a significant commentary on the oversimplification of the world often presented to students in management schools. Drawing on a broad collection of studies and perspectives, this book challenges accepted wisdom. It challenges everything from theories in mainstream textbooks to our reliance on mediated information and even our frameworks for ethical behaviour. As such, this book does not present clear problems and clear answers but instead explores a range of philosophical and applied ideas about organisation in order to shed light on the complexities of contemporary work. What emerges is not a mirror image of organisational life in perfectly ordered sections, but a range of different ideas and opinions that show how distinctly 'messy' business and management really is.

Despite its critical and challenging approach to such issues, we maintain that this is a hopeful text nonetheless. Its optimism lies in the very fact that we are trying to evade the limiting constrictions of simplification by helping readers to ask the right questions. No easy answers are suggested in this text. Instead readers are encouraged to draw their own conclusions and to create their own puzzles and dilemmas. Read carefully, then, this book will give hope to those seeking new ideas about organising and work; hope that stems from the idea that things could be different if we choose to manage differently.

The tone of this book is predominantly aimed at undergraduate students, yet scholars and the wider practitioner community may also find perspectives here of interest. Attempts have been made to avoid academic jargon where possible, and where it has been necessary to maintain it, a useful guide is given in the topical glossary at the back of the book. The chapters are also kept brief, presenting the crux of their material or argument to the reader and allowing them to draw their own conclusions, rather than attempting to persuade the reader through lengthy analysis. As a provocative aide to debate on matters evident in organisations today, readers will bring their own perspectives and histories to the book and will likely find much to reflect upon. In the epilogue, Phil Johnson presents a personal reflection on his own experiences as a manager and the corresponding or dissenting themes that this highlights from his own career in industry. This epilogue offers a valuable counterpoint to the theoretical and empirical material, by offering students another way of thinking about applying the ideas in this book.

For students and tutors, then, we would suggest that this book offers a useful counterpoint to standard or orthodox texts, presenting a 'dark mirror' that evokes and outlines the shadowy corners of messiness that are so often concealed by conventional managerial teaching tools. On that basis, we think that the text can be read in any order; the book is intended to provoke different meanings in different readers and at different times. Theoretically, methodologically and ethically heterodox, the textbook is not written in one tradition; it is polemic, theoretical and often ethnographic. Chapters draw on a variety of fine-grained empirical studies embedded in a particular context as well as theoretical discussions presenting illustrative examples and we make no attempt to force these into convenient sections or types. Thus, the book has not been laid out as a conventional textbook; students should not feel that the material presented in these chapters encompasses the totality of knowledge on any topic. We strongly recommend that all readers engage creatively with the references to other texts and materials presented at the end of each chapter. These bibliographies are the starting point for readers to explore new topics, philosophies and theories about the world of work.

Although the book presents a wide-ranging collection of contributions there are, nonetheless, a number of small connections which unite a variety of works from different backgrounds as similar stories emerge. Primarily, our collection emphasises the 'mess' of everyday life in the detail of working; it encompasses so much more of our lives than the fictional nine-to-five and it is something of a mistake to presume it can be defined neatly by time, place or task. Yet the dedication of so many people to hard work and the value to be found in it of itself is a solid continuity in several chapters, regardless of the grime, stigma or lack of pay attached to it. It is also clear that despite the rise of the service sector, we are not all 'clean and tidy' office workers in the contemporary world as many textbooks might imply. In fact, a sanitised representation of workers as 'clean and tidy' units of production presents confusing spectres of what constitutes 'real work' and how workers' identities are constituted.

This particular issue matters immensely to students of business and management studies. It matters because the global nature of labour and relations of production are no longer a unique phenomenon, but an everyday matter of business practice informing many aspects of managing and undertaking work. It is taken as a starting point that such contextual factors are crucial to any reading of an individual workplace. No business operates in a vacuum; in fact, it is often the case that 'macro' or global factors impact upon small groups and individuals at the local level. With this in mind, the book also highlights the extent to which many classic concerns and theories of work and its management are still present and relevant in the contemporary world. The book engages with the history of ideas, showing how contemporary concepts have roots in other disciplines such as philosophy, sociology, history, literature and anthropology. We argue that there is no clear 'one best way' or model answer when looking at contemporary issues in management. Instead, we argue that students need to have an appreciation of context, lived experiences and the ability to consider (if not agree with) multiple perspectives. Investigating some of the continuations between 'old' and 'new' ideas, we reflect and revisit old ideas in new ways. Thus we show how apparently new ideas often draw on long histories. In the next section of this introduction, we present a guide that outlines the key themes and ideas that each chapter presents.

## Guide to the chapters

The book opens with a chapter by Gordon Pearson on 'The corruption of business: A statement of a contemporary problem'. Pearson offers an overview of the current crisis in Western business practice. He is particularly interested in the role that classic economic theory plays in business today, arguing that much of the corruption, amoral practice and abuse of power in big business stems from the theory of shareholder primacy. He argues that business schools are complicit in maintaining the status quo because the classic management theories taught to students promote a Darwinian vision of big business, where companies compete for survival with little interest in wider social issues of equality, fairness and sustainability. Pearson's chapter offers a statement of a problem in the sense that it identifies significant moral, political and social failures in classic management theory which, he argues, leads to the corruption of business. The chapter finishes by calling for a change in business school programmes so that graduates can help to reduce corruption in business. This chapter acts as a clarion call for change and, as such, sets the tone and agenda for the rest of the textbook.

If Pearson is arguing that classic management theories over-simplify the world and lull practitioners into a narrow, decontextualised worldview, then the chapter by Mihaela Kelemen offers a redress to classic theory. 'Ambiguity as organisational practice: An American Pragmatist perspective' draws on philosophy, in particular the work of the American Pragmatists, to explore ambiguity in organisational life. While classic management theory tries to contain ambiguity or manage it away, Kelemen argues that ambiguity is endemic and a central feature of organisations and their wider society. Her chapter highlights the messiness and indeterminate features of organisations and questions whether we can ever 'solve' these issues. Drawing on the idea of a 'wicked problem' that is intractable, evolving and multi-faceted, Kelemen argues that we should learn to live with ambiguity. Rather than defining it as a problem to be solved, we should embrace the messy, uncertain and ever-changing qualities of life. The philosophical perspective adopted in this chapter is a welcome addition to thinking about management. One of the central themes of the book is to encourage students to view the world from multiple perspectives, moving beyond a single fixed point of reference to a broader more inclusive view. American Pragmatism, with its focus on our *embodied* experience of the world, reminds us that we can never adopt a purely rational response to situations; we have emotional, as well as intellectual responses to events and we need to acknowledge our confused, angry or joyous responses to situations even in spaces so (apparently) rational and organised as our workplaces.

Continuing with a philosophical perspective, Laura Mitchell's chapter concentrates on the issue of dignity. Her chapter on 'Dignity and meaningful work in organisations' focuses on the individual, rather than the organisation, and considers what we might mean when we refer to an individual's value, worth and rights. Although the argument draws on philosophical debates from the 18th century, this is a topical and important chapter given the current employment landscape. Graduates and school leavers enter a world where the idea of a 'job for life' has been abandoned, part-time working and zero-hours contracts are becoming the norm and previously secure 'white collar' jobs are also being undermined by outsourcing, waves of redundancies and the unanticipated consequences of the financial crisis of 2008. In this world of work, how does a worker find dignity? How is his or her work made meaningful and how is the value of the work to be decided? Like Kelemen's chapter on ambiguity, Mitchell highlights the 'messiness' of organisational life and argues that it is difficult to understand concepts such as dignity without having the conceptual tools to interpret them.

From dignity and meaningful work, we move to a case study by Darren McCabe and David Knights ('Is paternalism still relevant? Changing culture in a mutual UK insurance company') which offers an in-depth reading of a particular management style: paternalism. Having originally been associated with the caring capitalism of 19th century family run businesses, paternalism fell from favour in the 20th century although in recent decades, it is beginning to be revived. McCabe and Knights explore paternalism in a mutual UK insurance company (mutuals are where the insurance policy holders are also members of the company), charting the ways in which paternalistic management styles have evolved in the organisation, questioning whether the old ways still persist and whether paternalism is as caring and concerned for employees as its advocates suggest. Using rich data drawn from a longitudinal case study, the chapter demonstrates the ambiguity and 'messiness' inherent in organisational life; paternalism in both its current and historic forms is shown to have both positive and negative outcomes. Moreover, it shows how difficult it is to talk about paternalism in isolation because, as the chapter demonstrates, it cannot be separated from the effects of gender, class and race.

Our argument in this textbook is that management ideas have a long history; contemporary issues in management have roots in other disciplines and – as management scholars – we need to find new ways of engaging with these issues. Thus, in her chapter on 'Youth Employment, Masculinity and policy', Teresa Oultram offers an up-to-date empirical case study of apprentices, a form of training that has a history dating back to medieval times. Echoing Mitchell's concerns about dignity and meaningful work, Oultram looks at the ways in which people enter the world of work, focusing in particular on NEETs (young people not in education, employment or training). Drawing primarily on the work of Michel Foucault, a French philosopher and historian, Oultram theorises apprenticeships as a disciplinary technique, whereby responsibility for the citizen is shifted away from the state and on to the individual. In this sense, apprenticeships can be read as part of an *enterprise discourse* that promotes neo-liberal values of aspiration, acquisition, self-fulfilment and self-regulation. The chapter shows the political and class-based tensions between UK government policy, which promotes lifelong learning and the idea of a 'career', and the actual lived experiences of young apprentices, whose responses to and experiences of apprenticeships vary considerably from that promoted by official government policy.

Unexpected responses to official policy also feature in Steven Emery's chapter on 'Hard work, productivity and the management of the farmed environment in anthropological perspective'. While the chapters thus far position the world of work in an urban environment, Emery shifts our focus from urban concerns to rural issues. Like Oultram, he is interested in how workers respond to policy initiatives (in this case, political and social incentives to adopt environmental, sustainable practices). His ethnography of farmers offers a subtle account of how lifelong farmers measure and judge their life's work, highlighting the tensions between farmers who work within an existing tradition over a lifetime and newer farmers with no previous connection to the local land. While a chapter on rural farming practices might not seem like an obvious choice for a book on contemporary issues in management, Emery's ethnography addresses some very modern concerns. First, like Mitchell, Emery is concerned with dignity and meaningful work; ideas which he explores through a discussion of the work ethic. His careful presentation of the tensions between two farming families, the Colleys and the Spuhlers, shows that relatively straightforward concepts such as 'hard work' are in fact deeply ambiguous and contextual; what looks like a 'field full of thistles' or a 'jungle' to one farmer is a source of pride to another. Like the ambiguous account of paternalism offered by McCabe and Knights, Emery's analysis alerts us to the existence of multiple perspectives and interpretations of the world. As managers, we may think that we have a clear overview of events, but as this case study shows, our interpretations of events may not be accepted by other audiences and can always be contested. Second, like Oultram, Emery offers an empirical example of how 'abstract' policies and initiatives impact on real lives in the workplace, home or 'natural' environment. Echoing Pearson's concerns at the start of the book, Emery shows the practical effects of theory.

The questions of value and worth are also explored by Lindsay Hamilton and Darren McCabe. Here, however, focus shifts from rural food production to the opposite end of the agricultural process, as this chapter ('Disjointed, degraded and divided? A tale of dirty work at the chicken factory') offers an ethnographic account of working in a poultry factory. Drawing on classic definitions of 'dirty work' and in particular Ackroyd and Crowdy's (1990) study of the culture of an abattoir, Hamilton and McCabe argue that it is a misnomer to think of dirty work as one single thing; there are degrees of dirty work on the factory line, as well as a blurred definition between 'clean' and 'dirty'. Dignity is an underlying concern in any discussion of 'dirty work' and crops up here too. After all, this is work that the majority of the population do not want to engage in; 'dirty workers' allow the rest of society to ignore the work or pretend that it does not exist. How, then, do the line workers, butchers, vets and inspectors create and maintain a sense of dignity and self-worth in this workplace? In Ackroyd and Crowdy's case study, this was achieved by the creation of a culture which glorified the dirt (blood and guts) through a noisy display of masculinity. In contrast, Hamilton and McCabe suggest that the chicken factory condemns workers to silence; the speed of the production line requires intense concentration and the predominantly migrant workforce are also silenced by the lack of a common language or cultural background. This ethnography gives us an insight into the darker sides of organisation and society, showing us a side to management and wider society that we might prefer to ignore.

Highlighting another community of workers often marginalised and ignored, Steve French's chapter ('Migration into the United Kingdom: Employers and the *function* of migrant labour') queries the frequent assumptions regarding migrant workers often presented by the media in the United Kingdom. Taking an in-depth look at the data available in historical context, French highlights that simple assumptions about migration based upon rational economic perspectives are not sufficient to explain the impact of the many political and regulatory influences on migrants. Focusing on the types of work migrants undertake in the UK today in comparison with data from the 1970s, this chapter presents some complex truths about the exposure of particular migrant groups to insecure employment and 'dirty work', such as the vets discussed by Hamilton and McCabe. Furthermore, French presents a compelling picture of structural patterns of inequality affecting not only migrant populations, but also native workers, through the provision of a wealth of skilled and unskilled labour. This not only has significance for students of work and migration, but also highlights key questions regarding the provision and cost of education and training and the externalisation of those costs by the state. Such research implicitly and explicitly critiques the political discourse on the deregulation of markets, and emphasises the significance of such ideologies for everyday workers.

While the previous chapter dealt with migrants who leave home in search of work, Emma Surman explores the world of teleworkers; those who use technology to enable them to work from home. 'Interpreting technology: Telework and the myth of liberation' digs beneath the optimistic rhetoric of teleworking to ask questions such as: what happens when you work from home; what are the new challenges you have to cope with; is telework the same as being in an office; is it liberating or does it collapse the distinction between home and work, thereby challenging the work–life balance? Surman begins by revisiting key texts on telework, which claimed that advanced information and communication technologies would liberate workers by eliminating the daily commute, offering more freedom and a stress-free work environment. The case study of female teleworkers offers another example of the importance of learning about real lives and lived experiences; rather than the homeworking ideal promised in the literature, these workers struggled to cope with workplace demands in an informal environment. Noise from other family members, neighbours, doorbells and pets created external distractions. In addition to this, the workers struggled to create a conducive working environment in the home, resorting to a series of symbolic gestures and practices in order to make the switch from leisure and family time to work. Moreover, the controls and surveillance they experienced in the office remained. This case study illustrates the ambiguities of new working practices and technologies, suggesting that attempts to find new ways of working are complex.

Barry Schofield's chapter 'Media as mediation: Uncertainty and representation in the construction of news' marks a break from the case studies and ethnographic material by asking us to think about what we mean when we talk about 'the truth'. Specifically, he is interested in how news is constructed (see also French, Chapter 8 this volume) and draws on personal experience as a freelance journalist to alert us to the uncertain nature of reality in printed accounts. When we read textbooks, newspapers, company reports, or any authorised text, we tend to assume that we are being presented with the 'real' version of events. Schofield encourages us to be cautious and sceptical when presented with official accounts. He argues that news is presented as a neutral by-product of actual events, but as his example shows, all texts need to be read with a critical eye. This chapter points to the political, contested nature of truth-telling; just as Pearson links the corruption of business to classic management theory, so Schofield reminds us that underneath every official version of events, there are untold stories, hidden perspectives and suppressed alternatives. As students of management, we need to be aware of multiple perspectives and the constructed nature of organisational reality. When faced with a case study, a theory or a practical management problem, remember to ask yourself: 'Is this what really happened? How do I know? Who else do I need to speak to? What information has been suppressed or forgotten in the telling of this particular story?'

This idea of 'meaning making' (how the 'facts' of an event are constructed) is also a feature of the chapter by Nik Taylor and Lindsay Hamilton. Their chapter, 'Care of the underdog: Animals, culture and the creation of moral certainty in the rescue shelter' examines human–animal interaction in an animal shelter, exploring how collusion and collective concern work to render the homeless animals manageable. Unlike the other case studies, Taylor and Hamilton uncover the workers' explicitly political approach to life. Although the workers and volunteers ostensibly draw on discourses of care and concern for the vulnerable 'other', in practice, their concern is articulated through resistance to management, judgemental attitudes to potential pet owners and a constant evaluation of their colleagues' motivations and politics. It would seem that care for the underdog is predicated on a lack of care, or exasperation, with other humans. The chapter offers an insight into post-humanism, requiring us to go beyond a traditional Western worldview that separates humans from the rest of nature. It is a challenging chapter that once again asks the reader to imagine the world from multiple perspectives. In the first chapter, Pearson asks us to think beyond classic economic and management theory; interpreting the world from a post-human perspective is one such approach.

The textbook starts with a critique of classic management education, arguing that popular economic theories have played a role in the corruption of business and in the economic problems that various economies have been suffering since the financial crash of 2008. The following chapters cast light on a variety of theoretical perspectives and case studies, all of which have been designed to illustrate the 'messiness' and ambiguity of everyday working lives. In the final chapter, Anita Mangan returns to the problem posed by Pearson by asking 'Where are the alternative organisations in Organisational Behaviour textbooks?' Mangan's argument is political throughout, highlighting the role that business schools play in training graduates to accept and reproduce capitalist values. Drawing on Foucault's concept of a 'régime of truth', she argues that mainstream Organisational Behaviour textbooks promote a narrow view of business, presenting their neo-liberal approach as 'common sense' and the 'one best way' of doing business. The second half of the chapter explores what is meant by alternative organisations and alternative modes of organising, promoting consensual, democratic and co-operative forms of work. Many alternative organisations emerged as a grassroots response to inequality and unfairness in society and Mangan argues that studying them can provoke us to ask if there is a better way of managing and organising our lives.

The book closes with an epilogue by Phil Johnson, who draws on his long experience as a manager to consider ways in which the case studies and theories in the book can be applied in practice. As Johnson notes, reality is always messier and more complicated than mainstream textbooks imply. He argues that theoretical models that seem reasonable on paper often prove to be too simplistic when applied to real life settings. Echoing the ideas expressed in this introduction, Johnson reminds the reader that there are no 'one size fits all' answers to contemporary issues in management. Our task, as students, academics and practitioners, is to engage with the messiness of everyday life by treating each other with respect and adopting a critical approach to received wisdom.

# Final note

This book is the combined effort of many contributors to draw together a collection that is more than the sum of its parts. Our goal has been to develop this book in the tradition of Keele Management School's critical past, with an eye to the challenges of management now and in the future. The book draws on our commitment to longitudinal, ethnographic approaches to fieldwork, as well as our shared interest in questioning inequality, unfairness and abuse of power. The collected chapters approach the world of work from unexpected angles, introducing subjects that do not often appear in management texts; we hope that they will help students to challenge what they read elsewhere and develop creative, lateral and critical thinking skills.

 **REFERENCES**

Ackroyd, S. and Crowdy, P.A. (1990) 'Can culture be managed? Working with "raw" material: The case of the English slaughtermen', *Personnel Review*, 19 (5), 3–13.

# 1

# The corruption of business: A statement of a contemporary problem

*Gordon Pearson*

## 1.1 Introduction

Corruption in business, especially, but not solely in the financial sector, is a continuing feature of the daily news. The late Professor Sumantra Ghoshal of London Business School suggested (Ghoshal, 2005) that the economic theory, which now underpins much of management teaching, has been a major cause of that business corruption. The purpose of this chapter is to review the contribution made by theory, and in particular identify the specific components of theory which have had the greatest impact, and to consider the possible corrective actions that might be available.

The following sections present a broad overview of business in its industrial and financial context, acknowledging that the essential focus on profitability leads inevitably to business inhabiting the boundaries of legality and acceptability. Key theories which appear to have become deeply held ideological beliefs guiding the management of business are identified and their validity is challenged. Some of the resulting impacts on business and the real economy are noted. Finally consideration is given to corrective action. Examples are quoted of relevant initiatives which have been taken by business management, while other possibilities are identified which are available to those shaping the business and governance context. Finally, a brief note is made of how changes to business school and management curricula might contribute to that correction.

## 1.2 Business amorality

The current level of criminality in business is considerable. Most of the leading banks and hedge funds, and many of the fund managers and currency and commodity traders have paid substantial fines for specific wrongdoing. These scandalous behaviours are far too many to list here. While much malfeasance occurs in the financial sector, the real economy (extraction, manufacturing, distribution and non-financial services) has its share of convicted criminal businesses, detailing of which would more than fill this chapter. Moreover, there is a twilight zone of possibly legal but nevertheless wholly unacceptable behaviours which are clearly against the common good, including those whose notoriety is based on really creative but aggressive tax avoidance. The numbers of these businesses far exceeds the criminal.

The management of any real economy business necessarily involves the pursuit of efficiency and effectiveness in identifying and supplying customer satisfactions. The survival and long-term prosperity of any such business depends crucially on the discharge of those responsibilities, which at base involves the avoidance of waste in all its forms. This managerial duty, in the face of competition, leads inevitably to businesses pushing the boundaries of what is acceptable and legal in the pursuit of efficiency and waste avoidance. This dynamic tension is intrinsic to the business concept.

Ever since the beginnings of industrialisation in the 18th century, there have been businesses which have crossed the line of acceptability and legality in their pursuit of survival and long-term prosperity. Some knowingly exploit opportunities which are only available through explicit acts of criminality. Some of those may adopt that as their standard approach to doing business. However, the vast majority of businesses surely seek, for whatever reason, to operate within the legal constraints placed on them. Some such businesses will spend large sums ensuring that they exploit every possible opportunity within the law. Some unknown proportion of such seek to do business in ways which their various stakeholders would regard as straightforward, honest and worthy of trust. The number of these appears to be influenced by the general business culture in the real economy, which Bower (1966) referred to as 'the way we do things around here'. That in turn is shaped by the relevant law and the degree of its enforcement and the theoretical underpinnings which embody the orthodox wisdom which is taught in the mainstream business schools and relevant university departments.

This mix of influences, business culture, corporate law and management theory are not independent of each other, but interact in the way they shape business practice. Moreover, they are also affected in turn by the evolving business practices to which they contribute.

Ghoshal recognised the damage being done over the past few decades by business school and management faculty promoting dubious economic theories to their students:

> [A]cademic research related to the conduct of business and management has had some very significant and negative influences on the practice of management. These influences have been less at the level of adoption of a particular theory and more at the incorporation, within the worldview of managers, of a set of ideas and assumptions that have come to dominate much of management research. More specifically, I suggest that by propagating ideologically inspired amoral theories, business schools have actively freed their students from any sense of moral responsibility. (Ghoshal, 2005: 76)

Ghoshal argued that those 'amoral theories' had become self-fulfilling prophecies. In social science and in particular in economics, a theory, whether right or wrong, if accepted by sufficient numbers, will shape behaviour. Ghoshal noted that maximising shareholder wealth, promoted and promulgated so that it had become universally accepted as the purpose of business – an essential of the capitalist system – had achieved just such self-fulfilment. Management efforts had been diverted from the survival and long-term prosperity of their firm, to focus on making or extracting as much money as possible, and as quickly as possible, for the gain of shareholders at the expense of all other stakeholders.

## 1.3    A note on historical context

The modern financial sector was brought into being by necessity to raise finance for the major infrastructural projects, such as transportation systems, that were needed to get industrialisation going in the 18th century. It took around seven hugely expensive years from starting the work on a canal to it earning the first penny. Banks, joint stock companies and widely dispersed share ownership were essential to raising that wholly unprecedented scale of liquid funding. And as industrialisation proceeded so did the supportive financial sector, raising funds for the railways and for the new factories and equipment of the Industrial Revolution.

While the practice of industrial management was also brought into existence by necessity in the late 18th century, it was not formalised as a coherent body of knowledge until the development of big business in the United States a century later. The so-called 'robber barons' developed large-scale operations, mainly through merger and acquisition, such that they were able not only to be exploitative of their employees but also to destroy competition and so control markets and fix prices. At the same time, they established undue influence over government, which was persuaded to welcome such business leaders into the upper echelons of society, where they subsequently used their immense wealth to establish their names as philanthropists.

Concurrent with American big business, a management curriculum was established by the early American business schools whose faculty had hopes of establishing management as a high profession of equal standing with medicine and the law, adopting a form of Hippocratic Oath as commitment to honourable and true performance of their managerial duties. Khurana (2007) describes the attempts to institutionalise management as a profession. However, without mandatory qualifications and a professional gatekeeper, as existed in medicine and law, management could never be so established.

Today, the 'robber barons' are better known for their latter-day acts of philanthropy, including the funding of business schools which have immortalised their names. In the contest between the early business school professionalisers and the 'robber barons', it is clear that the latter won. Government stood back from regulating business, allowing 'big business' to exploit their monopolistic power in many industries. The resulting Wall Street based financial sector inflated the investment bubble which eventually burst in the 1929 crash and subsequent 'great depression'. Over the following years, statutory regulation was progressively imposed to break monopolistic abuses and to ensure markets were made, and remained competitive with the hope that such a market crash was not repeated.

The 20th century saw management firmly established as a professional endeavour, with a growing body of knowledge and understanding based on the study of real people in real business settings. Names like Argyris, Herzberg, Jacques, Likert, March, Mayo, McGregor, McLelland, Simon, Trist, and many more, contributed a complex and rich understanding of human behaviour and human frailty in different work settings. Economic theory was then pluralistic, including some account of economic history as well as classical theory with Keynesian and monetarist contributions.

However, over the past 40 years or so, since the demise of the socialist alternative, the empirically based management curriculum has come to be dominated by the singular neoclassical ideology. This is based on mathematical modelling of human actors and their behaviour with, at its root, the crude and simplistic self-interest maximising 'economic man', from which caricature any deviation is treated as insane or at least irrational. The lessons learned from the 1929 Wall Street crash and 'great depression' have lost potency and much of the subsequent regulation has been removed or relaxed since then. Subsequently, management has been taught to organise business so that the interests of owners are maximised by any means so long as it lies within the law.

## 1.4 Economic institutional truths

Galbraith (1989) warned about the dangers of 'institutional truths'. They were not truths at all, but overarching lies which had to be bought into if an individual was to survive and prosper in a particular setting. Economic institutional truths are founded on a huge body of academic theory. Though there are much earlier antecedents going back to ancient Greece and China, modern economics could reasonably be held to have started with Adam Smith's *An Inquiry into the Nature and Causes of the Wealth of Nations* (Smith, 1776). His 'inquiry' was based on observation rather than on the abstract development of theory. He observed productivity gains from the specialisation of work, which he exampled with his pin workshop: one man making pins from beginning to end could perhaps make one a day and certainly not twenty, whereas ten men, each specialising in a different stage of production, could make up to 48,000 a day. The only problem, then, was to find a market for that scale of production and Smith held that government interference with tariffs, quotas and subsidies only served to restrict the size and growth of markets. Markets freed from government imposed quotas and tariffs were an enabling factor for industrialisation.

Those who came after Smith focused more on the development of theoretical construction to explain, rather than 'inquire'. A century after Smith, economists were keen to establish their study as a science, so turned their backs on scientific observation. Instead they focused on developing mathematical models of economic structures, processes, actors and behaviour. Chester Barnard (1938) claimed it was not until he had relegated economic theory to a secondary place that he began to understand organisations and human behaviour in them. Guy Routh (1975), one of many heterodox economists, has provided a serious critique of neoclassical modelling:

> Economics . . . ignores facts as irrelevant, bases its constructs on axioms arrived at a priori, or 'plucked from the air', from which deductions are made and an imaginary edifice created. . . . Man and society are stripped of their attributes, as if they could exist without psychological, political, legal, historical or moral dimension. Thus verification is both impossible and regarded as unnecessary. In effect,

then, orthodox economics becomes a matter of faith and, ipso facto, immune to criticism. (Routh, 1975: 26)

The departure from observed reality to focus on mathematical modelling has gathered further momentum since Routh's description. Application of mathematics necessitated the crude maximisation objective functions plus a whole array of the most unrealistic subsidiary assumptions.

Over the past few decades economics has progressed further into mathematical fantasy. Kay has pointed out in some detail the hugely improbable assumptions that have to be made to ground Lucas's highly influential 'dynamic stochastic general equilibrium model' (Kay, 2011). The primary aim of contemporary economics is to build models that can be computerised and be capable of being run to a solution. Practical reality appears to be of no concern. For contemporary economics, realism is not a serious consideration. Friedman used the instrumental argument: realism is unimportant, what matters is the ability to predict, though that ability is never tested. More recently when the Queen asked why economists had not predicted the 2007–2008 crisis, the response from Lucas was that the crisis was not predicted because economic theory predicts that such events are unpredictable (Kay, 2011).

Lucas himself credits the intelligence of earlier 'attempts to deal theoretically' with monetary issues by Hayek, Keynes and contemporaries, but notes their inability to calculate the predictions of their own theories without the 'equipment of modern mathematical economics' made possible by computerised calculation. An alternative view might be that those earlier economists were fortunate not to have been seduced by the 'equipment of modern mathematical economics' and therefore had to depend, at least to some extent, on observed reality and a degree of 'common sense'.

## 1.5 Universal belief in shareholder primacy

Despite their limited concern with practical reality in creating their mathematical models, economists have nevertheless sought to apply their theoretical conclusions to real situations. Friedman was a leading example who had a powerful impact on the real world. *Capitalism and Freedom* published in 1962 at the height of the Cold War, included the following much cited assertion:

Few trends could so thoroughly undermine the very foundations of our free society than the acceptance by corporate officials of a social responsibility other than to make as much money for their stockholders as possible. (Friedman, 1962: 133)

Friedman was writing at a time when it was uncertain whether 'our free society' would prevail. His idea was a response to perceived threats. There was then no supporting theory, nor legal statute, nor even any significant common law precedent for his argument. The world was widely viewed as being divided between the two philosophies of socialism, most of which had in practice become totalitarian, and the free enterprise society which was arguably democratic. Friedman's statement sprang from the unreasonable belief that any step towards social democracy, no matter how small, would lead ultimately and inevitably to a full-on totalitarian communist state. He clearly regarded 'corporate officials' exercising social responsibility as just such a step.

The call to maximising shareholder wealth, in denial of social responsibilities, and even of consideration of the company itself, was simple and fitted the neoclassical maximising model. Moreover it had far wider relevance than merely to 'corporate officials'. It described an objective measure of corporate performance, and by default, a system of morality which appeared to be readily quantifiable and came to be seen as a cornerstone of mainstream market capitalism. Still today, most company directors believe it is their legal duty to do what they can to maximise the wealth of shareholders. Institutions, such as the Confederation of British Industry and the Business Round Table in the United States endorse and promote this belief. Influential magazines such as *The Economist*, and think tanks such as the Institute of Economic Affairs actively propagate the idea. It is the often unstated, but almost invariably active, assumption behind finance and business reporting in the press and broadcast media. The general belief is that this is what capitalism is all about (see, for a fuller discussion, Schofield, Chapter 10 this volume).

Moreover, no less a person than Adam Smith had referred to the artisan of his day saying that

> By pursuing his own self-interest he frequently promotes that of the society more effectually than when he really intends to promote it. (Smith, 1776: 292)

The only difference between Smith and Friedman appeared to be one of maximising. But though that turned out to be quite a difference, the mainstream was settled: business existed for the exclusive benefit of shareholders. In other words, moral, ethical, ideological concerns over fairness or social responsibility were secondary to the profit motive; that is, the drive to perpetuate shareholder returns in the form of dividends and other bonuses.

The first Cadbury report on corporate governance argued that

> [S]hareholders, as owners of the company, elect the directors to run the business on their behalf and hold them accountable for its progress. The issue for corporate governance is how to strengthen the accountability of boards of directors to shareholders. (Cadbury, 1992: 6)

The many subsequent codes of practice never wavered from that perspective. After the 2007–2008 crash, the Financial Reporting Council updated its code, restating its purpose as being 'to promote high standards of corporate governance' and thus help 'a board discharge its duties in the best interests of shareholders.'

In the United States, the Business Roundtable claimed:

> [T]he paramount duty of management and of boards of directors is to the corporation's stockholders. (Khurana, 2007: 320)

Perhaps, most important of all to creating the dominant belief in shareholder primacy was the fact that mainstream business schools and university departments across the globe taught the primacy of shareholder value to succeeding generations of leaders in business, finance and government. And it is still taught by leading business school faculty, as confirmed by extracts from a July 2013 *Financial Times* report on business education:

> While there is growing consensus that focusing on short term shareholder-value is not only bad for society but also leads to poor business results, much MBA teaching remains shaped by the shareholder primacy model.
> 'The prevailing view in business schools has been that a primary function of corporations is to further the interests of their shareholders', says Colin Mayer, Professor of management studies at Oxford's Saïd Business School.
> Craig Smith, Professor of ethics and social responsibility, at Insead, agrees. 'Students come in with a more rounded view of what managers are supposed to do, but when they go out, they think it's all about maximising shareholder value.' (Murray, 2013: 12)

Not only did they teach it, but academic economists developed a theory to justify it. So, it is not altogether surprising that company directors continue to profess their commitment to maximising shareholder value; nor that the powerful and wealthy should forcefully promulgate their support for that belief. Mainstream commitment to the primacy of shareholder value remains dominant.

## 1.6   The theory of shareholder primacy

Belief in shareholder primacy is founded on a set of apparently careless assumptions derived from a theory which is clearly founded on false analysis. The original Cadbury Report's conjecture that shareholders own the company was probably the expression of a careless assumption. Shareholder ownership is quite distinct from other forms of ownership because of its essential privilege of limited liability. Shareholders actually own share certificates which grant entitlement to dividends and to capital growth, both being at risk. They do not own the company.

Cadbury also stated that shareholders elect directors to run the business on their behalf. The truth is that directors are usually appointed by internal processes and shareholders merely vote to accept or reject those appointments at subsequent general meetings, the vast majority being a matter of rubber stamping. When a company is first registered or incorporated, its directors are already in place and shareholders are invited to buy shares in the company, being persuaded, or not, by the strength of its business case, which of course includes some assessment of the apparent calibre of the people directing it. Directors precede shareholders. Cadbury was carelessly stating what had become the universal assumption.

There was no explicit theoretical support for the notion of shareholder primacy until academic economists developed agency theory, a decade after Friedman's dictum. Agency is a long established legal concept: the relationship whereby the agent is legally empowered, and obliged, to act on behalf of, and in the best interests of, the principal. The origin of this legal relationship goes back to the 16th century overseas trading expeditions which in the beginning were financed individually. Then the captain of a ship was legally enabled to represent the interests of his principals who were those who financed the expedition and stood to gain or lose on the basis of its success.

Economic models of what economists refer to as 'the firm' have been widely recognised as implausible and inadequate. However, in a widely quoted article, Alchian and Demsetz (1972) expressed the firm as a 'centralised contractual agent in a team productive process'. Their meaning, though imprecise, nevertheless depicted the firm as an agent, rather than the principal, to those centralised contracts. Four years later, Jensen and Meckling (1976) in another frequently cited paper, defined the firm in a way which enabled them to completely sidestep the inconvenient fact of the firm's existence and its position as the principal in contractual arrangements. This they did with the following statement:

> It is important to recognize that most organisations are simply legal fictions which serve as a nexus for a set of contracting relationships among individuals. (Jensen and Meckling, 1976: 309)

Attention was thereby focused on the contracting relationships, notably, in the absence of the firm as a legal fact, the relationship between directors and shareholders, making the false claim that the directors were agents of the shareholders and therefore bound to act at all times in the shareholders' best interests.

These assertions were clearly not careless assumptions like those made by Cadbury. The core of agency theory appears carefully fabricated. Economics, not being a science, presents theories including agency theory which – though demonstrably untrue – nevertheless persist as theory and continue to influence real behaviour.

Agency theory highlights what economists refer to as the agency problem: the possibility that company directors, though held to be the agents of shareholders, might not seek to maximise shareholder wealth, but being 'economic men' might seek to maximise their own self-interest. The economists' solution to this was to bribe, or 'incentivise', company directors by converting them into shareholders through the stock option incentive schemes that have created the massive remuneration inequalities experienced today.

Agency theory is the focus of a massive amount of academic publication, with more than a thousand journal articles on agency and associated topics and millions of pounds of funding to research and promote the theory and so provide the apparently solid academic foundation for the mainstream belief. But it is false. The company is not a legal fiction; it is a legal fact. That is its whole point. Company directors are appointed as the agents of the company. Their contracts of employment and service agreements are with the company, not shareholders, and are specific about the requirement to act in the best interests of the company at all times. Company law has always been specific about directors' duties to the company and its long-term prosperity, and also to have regard to the interests of the various stakeholders. Nowhere in the world is there a legal statute which confirms company directors as the agents of shareholders. And despite it being the mainstream

Loan Receipt
Liverpool John Moores University
Library Services

**Borrower Name: Alyami,Azizah**
**Borrower ID: ********

Contemporary issues in management /
31111014674699
**Due Date: 23/01/2017 23:59**

Total Items: 1
16/01/2017 15:10


Please keep your receipt in case of
dispute.

belief, a review of case law found only one item providing any support, back in 1919, and that was so weak it has only ever been cited once (Lan and Heracleous, 2010).

So Friedman's statement about the responsibilities of corporate officials is wrong on both counts: they do not have a responsibility to make as much money as possible for stockholders, but they do have moral responsibilities. This was a point that Friedman himself admitted late in his life (Friedman, 2003).

## 1.7 The impacts of false ideology

The belief in neoclassical ideology and, in particular, shareholder primacy has had two kinds of impact: internal to the business and externally affecting the whole of society. Ghoshal, as a business school academic, was himself mostly concerned with the impact on management behaviour within organisations. He explained the effect of neoclassical economics becoming dominant as freeing 'students from moral responsibility'. Thus liberated, they were led to believe it was their duty to pursue the interests of shareholders above everything else. Those students then became monstrous caricatures of corrupted leadership, he described as,

> [T]he ruthlessly hard-driving, strictly top-down, command-and-control focused, shareholder-value obsessed, win-at-any-cost business leader. (Ghoshal, 2005: 85)

It is that version of management and governance that has captured organisations, particularly in the Anglo-American economies. It is an approach to management, identified by McGregor (1960) as Theory X, which clearly assumes that people at work are only interested in maximising their own self-interest. They are lazy and will avoid work if they can; they dislike taking responsibility, prefer to be directed, have little ambition and only want security. Consequently, they must be coerced, controlled, directed and threatened in order to get them to contribute to organisational goals. Theory X is obviously self-fulfilling: intelligent people managed by such a regime would undoubtedly be likely to behave as assumed. The role of management is thus corrupted and as such is responsible for much of the corporate criminality referred previously.

However, the 'morally liberated' business school graduates go on to play leading roles not just in industrial management, but also in the worlds of finance and politics, where they multiply the negative impacts between organisations, most notably between organisations within the real economy and those in the financial sector. Since the 1986 stock market 'big bang' computerisation and deregulation, the financial sector has grown prodigiously to include all sorts of financial intermediaries, hedge funds, private equity and sovereign funds, and traders of all kinds dealing in equities, bonds, and a huge variety of financial derivatives. The purpose of the financial sector is no longer to raise finance for investment in the real economy, but simply to extract maximum value for the benefit of shareholder investors, pushing hard against the boundaries of legality to do so. The consequence is that much vitality of the real economy which is exposed to the financial sector has been extracted.

The nature of shareholding has also changed. The vast majority of quoted shares are now controlled by professional fund managers and traders, rather than the ultimate investors who in most cases are unaware of exactly where their funds are placed. It is also calculated that between two thirds and three quarters of all stock market trades on Wall Street and the London Stock Exchange are now made by automated ultra-fast systems, mostly controlled by a computer algorithm without human intervention.

Deregulation has allowed the establishment of global monopolists. One example is the company, Glencore Xstrata, who now effectively control global markets for several strategic commodities in food, metals and energy, and are able to fix prices for their own advantage at everyone else's expense. They have demonstrated their preparedness to do so by manipulating global wheat prices, at huge cost to those in poverty, so as to profit from proprietary trades (Blas and Farchy, 2011). Monopolistic auditors collude in criminality and tax evasion. Banks fix international money markets, so affecting mortgages and small business loans. Financial data providers – a $25bn market – charge ultra-fast trading clients for access to market moving information seconds ahead of the general market, so enabling insider dealing and destroying market credibility. Globalisation of markets and firms without hindrance from global regulation enables the payment of national taxes to be largely a matter of choice.

The overall effect of all these abuses is an explosion in inequality which used to be defended by the 'trickle down' argument: that the wealthy would have to invest their money somewhere and the benefits would inevitably trickle down to the real economy so that the mass of the population would benefit in due course. It no longer applies. The money extracted from the real economy is now mostly invested by professional fund managers and traders in financial 'products', swaps and derivatives, from which there is very limited 'trickle down'.

Fox and Lorsch (2012: 1) noted there has been a 'multi-trillion dollar transfer of cash from US corporations to their shareholders over the past 10 years.' The City of London has achieved similar disinvestment. Also in the past decade the number of public companies in the UK has almost halved and declined by 38 per cent in the United States. Similarly, the number of Initial Public Offerings (IPOs) has declined by over two thirds, and in the case of small and medium sized enterprises (SMEs) on which the hopes for an innovative high-tech future rests, by more than 80 per cent.

The response to these various negative impacts has so far been limited. Since the 2007–2008 crash, a few low-level individuals have been charged and imprisoned, but mostly the apparently great and good companies have settled quasi-criminal charges by payment of readily affordable fines. A number of enquiries have been set up and some have reported without any serious action being proposed, let alone taken. The publication of revised voluntary codes of practice has continued, but with no real change being achieved.

## 1.8 Reversing the corruption of business

The reversal of the impacts described above would require the abandonment of the maximising shareholder value dogma. Rather than one stakeholder having primacy over all the rest, a more balanced approach, respecting the interests of all stakeholders, would have to become the mainstream of how business is done. This is already required by law as in the Companies Act 2006 and by American state laws, but the law is ignored with apparent impunity. It needs to become both practice and the theory that is taught in universities and business schools.

When company law was first framed, it was based on the idea of democratic voting; one member: one vote, irrespective of the number of shares held. In the United States in particular, people were nervous then of businesses being controlled by small groups of wealthy individuals against the interests of the majority. But by the early twentieth century democratic control was losing out to the plutocrats; one share: one vote was becoming the norm. Despite company law stating explicitly that company directors' legal duty is to act in the interests of the company, having regard to other stakeholder interests, directors are powerless against the shareholder who controls over 50 per cent of the equity. Such a holding gives absolute control, with the company in effect reduced to the status of ordinary private property, despite the shareholder still enjoying the unique privilege of limited liability.

This anomaly is fully exploitable in the USA, UK and Anglo-American based economies. Almost everywhere else in the world, corporate governance practice provides effective support for non-shareholder stakeholders, and more protection against predatory finance, than in Anglo-America. A review of alternative governance practice in Japan, Germany, China and India is provided by Pearson (2012). In particular the European company approach, notably followed with success in Germany, moderates that discontinuity when a majority shareholding is achieved. The moderation is by the legal grant to employees of 50 per cent membership of the supervisory board in a two tier structure. Thus a hostile takeover is not so simple to execute and assets are not so easily stripped out of a European company, as they are in Anglo-America. Such an innovation would be a big step, having major implications for the internal management of the corporation as well as protecting the real economy from a predatory financial sector.

An enlightened approach to management can be profitable in the 21st century. It is feasible for big corporates to adopt a straightforward and balanced approach to the communities they serve as demonstrated at Unilever's 2010 annual general meeting. CEO Paul Polman explained the company's dedication to a 'long term value creation model, which is equitable, which is shared, (and) which is sustainable.' Challenged regarding shareholder value, Polman responded:

> If you don't buy into this . . . don't put your money in our company . . . Consumers and retailers want this sort of initiative, and the planet needs it . . . (it's) the right way to do business. (Skapinker, 2010, online)

Similarly, W.L. Gore and Associates, maker of Gore-Tex fabric and other high-tech products, are regularly voted one of the most innovative companies and among the best to work for. Gore is a private company co-owned by the Gore family and its employees, more than 8,500 people worldwide. Gore does not follow 'the ruthlessly hard-driving, strictly top-down, command-and-control focused, win-at-any-cost' style of management described by Ghoshal (2005: 85). It has created a uniquely engaging and non-hierarchical organisational culture where people can express themselves and contribute without any trace of paternalism.

> There are no titles or conventional lines of command at Gore, where the only way of becoming a leader is to attract followers – if a project can't attract people to work on it, then it doesn't get done. (Caulkin, 2009: 6)

The question arises that if businesses can be both virtuous and profitable, why are they not all like that? It was noted earlier that the corruption of business had resulted from a mix of influences, business culture, corporate law and management theory. Moreover, that those influences are not independent of each other, but interact in the way they shape business practice, and that they are also affected in turn by the evolving business practices to which they contribute. Polman and Gore are examples of practice which could be influential in the mix.

So far as theory is concerned, agency theory would have to be loudly acknowledged for what it is: an existential untruth. It would have to be totally rejected. But more than that, the conversion of economics into a quantitative 'science' unrelated to real practicalities would also need to be rejected, or the 'science' would need to be consigned to ivory tower isolation as an exercise for training of the mind, as was formally argued as the justification for teaching Latin. The focus of practical economics would need to return to observed reality, rather than mathematical fantasising. Furthermore, the law would need to be rigorously enforced as it already stands. That would be a revolutionary change from current practice. In addition, though, it would require international agreement, regulation would need to be introduced to authorise the break-up of monopolistic positions and the recreation of genuine competition. The current position is that markets are global, and leading firms are global, but regulation is still largely national, which enables firms to evade and avoid practical constraint. Effective global regulation is restricted by such widespread adherence to the neoclassical ideology.

## 1.9   Conclusion

The corruption of business is clearly a topic which demands more than a single chapter, or even a single book, for its adequate consideration. Nevertheless this chapter has highlighted some important issues and some potential correctives have been identified. The general business culture is shaped at least in part by the orthodox wisdom taught in business schools, which Ghoshal (2005: 75) argued actively frees students from 'any sense of moral responsibility'. There are daily reminders that this truth is still applicable. At the time of writing (August 2013), J.P. Morgan Chase agreed to pay $410m to settle the US regulator's charges of energy price fixing. While the bank did not admit wrongdoing, it accepted payment of $410m as an affordable business expense which absolved individuals of any personal guilt. Considerations of moral responsibility appear to have played no part in Morgan's processes. This is just one example, of course.

Ghoshal was greatly concerned that business school faculty should first stop teaching the neoclassical dogma, agency theory, economic man and the rest. He argued that it had done, and continued to do, great damage. And it clearly still does. Business schools and management faculty could play a decisive role in changing the status quo by changing the taught curriculum and thereby changing the organisational culture. Management could be taught as a professional endeavour, with a technical curriculum based on the substantial existing body of knowledge and rich understanding of business and human behaviour. Students so educated might then play their part in reducing the corruption of business.

 **REFERENCES**

Alchian, A.A., and Demsetz, H. (1972) 'Production, information costs, and economic organisation', *American Economic Review*, 62(5), 777–795.

Barnard, C.I. (1938) *The Functions of the Executive*, Cambridge MA: Harvard University Press.

Blas, J. and Farchy, J. (2011) 'Glencore reveals bet on grain price rise', *Financial Times Commodities Section*, 24 April. Accessed at: http://www.ft.com/cms/s/0/aea76c56-6ea5-11e0-a13b-00144feabdc0.html#axzz2cJUGT4fS (retrieved 15 September 2013).

Bower, M. (1966) *The Will to Manage: Corporate Success through Programmed Management*, New York: McGraw-Hill.

Cadbury, A. (1992) *The Committee on the Financial Aspects of Corporate Governance*, London: Gee and Company.

Caulkin, S. (2009) 'Individuality can banish the downturn blues', *The Observer, Business & Media*, 24 May, 6.

Fox, J. and Lorsch, J.W. (2012) 'What good are shareholders?' *Harvard Business Review*, 90(7/8), 48–57.

Friedman, M. (1962) *Capitalism and Freedom*, Chicago, IL: University of Chicago Press.

Friedman, M. (2003) Interviewed and discussed in Bakan, J. *The Corporation: The Pathological Pursuit of Profit and Power*, New York: Free Press.

Galbraith, J.K. (1989) '*In pursuit of the simple truth*', Commencement Address to women graduates of Smith College, Massachusetts.

Ghoshal, S. (2005) 'Bad management theories are destroying good management practices', *Academy of Management Learning & Education*, 4(1), 75–91.

Jensen, M.C. and Meckling, W.H. (1976) 'Theory of the firm: Managerial behaviour, agency costs and ownership structure', *Journal of Financial Economics*, 3(4), 305–360.

Kay, J. (2011) 'The map is not the territory: An essay on the state of economics', in Coyle, D. (ed.), *What's the Use of Economics? Teaching the Dismal Science after the Crisis*, London: London Publishing Partnership. Accessed at: http://ineteconomics.org/blog/inet/john-kay-map-not-territory-essay-state-economics (retrieved 20 December 2011).

Khurana, R. (2007) *From Higher Aims to Hired Hands: The Social Transformation of American Business Schools and the Unfulfilled Promise of Management as a Profession*, Princeton, NJ: Princeton University Press.

Lan, L.L. and Heracleous, L. (2010) 'Rethinking agency theory: The view from law', *Academy of Management Review*, 35(2), 294–314.

Lucas, R.E. Jr (1995) 'Monetary neutrality', Prize Lecture, 7 December, University of Chicago. Accessed at: http://www.nobelprize.org/nobel_prizes/economic-sciences/laureates/1995/lucas-lecture.html (retrieved 20 April 2013).

McGregor, D. (1960) *The Human Side of Enterprise*, New York: McGraw-Hill.

Murray, S. (2013) 'MBA teaching urged to move away from focus on shareholder primacy model', *Financial Times, Business Education*, 7 July.

Pearson, G. (2012) *The Road to Co-operation: Escaping the Bottom Line*, Farnham, Surrey: Gower Publishing.

Routh, G. (1975) *The Origin of Economic Ideas*, London: Macmillan.

Skapinker, M. (2010) 'Corporate plans may be lost in translation', *Financial Times, Comment*, 22 November. Accessed at: http://www.ft.com/cms/s/0/78cf6070-f66e-11df-846a-00144 feab49a.html#axzz2cJUGT4fS (retrieved 20 September 2013).

Smith, A. (1776) *An Inquiry into the Nature and Causes of the Wealth of Nations*, Oxford: Oxford University Press.

# 2

# Ambiguity as organisational practice: An American Pragmatist perspective

*Mihaela Kelemen*

## 2.1 Introduction

It is widely recognised that ambiguity is an incontestable feature of all forms of organisation. Ambiguity refers to the idea that events, words and behaviours in organisations might have more than one meaning for those seeking to interpret them. In organisations, then, ambiguity is the state of affairs in which people are required to 'make sense' of the organisational milieu; the multiplicity of different ideas and viewpoints they encounter in their daily working lives. Opinions are, however, divided on the nature and role of such multiplicity in organisations. Ambiguity is sometimes seen as confusing or dysfunctional and, therefore, necessitates calls for immediate intervention to ensure its containment or removal. Consider, for example, a manager who wishes to make things clear by being explicit about how and why a certain task should be performed in a particular way. There appears to be an implicit assumption in many existing studies that ambiguity is an organisational input, a resource that requires careful management. At other times, however, ambiguity is seen as a positive and enabling feature of organisational life, to be preserved and nurtured rather than eradicated.

As a way of thinking through the implications and possibilities of ambiguity in organisations, this chapter advances a three dimensional perspective that considers ambiguity as: (1) a resource to be 'organised', (2) an (intended or unintended) consequence of organised activity and, (3) a practice that makes processes of organising possible in the first instance. I start by commenting on these three perspectives and the ways in which they are intertwined. I then suggest that the 'organisational ambiguity as practice' dimension could benefit from insights offered by American Pragmatism, a philosophical school of thought which has placed 'ambiguity' at the heart of its agenda.

Organisational ambiguity arises when too much information is floating around and individuals are confused by the multiplicity of ideas, concepts or initiatives going on at the same time. Unlike uncertainty, which can be solved by collecting more information in order for people to be able to make predictions about future events, ambiguity cannot usually be solved by an increase in the amount of information available to individuals in the organisation. This is not solely a matter of instruction or communication of data. It is not unusual for authors to speak about linguistic ambiguity and experiential/ pragmatic ambiguity as distinct domains. Levine (1985) views ambiguity both as a literary affair, in that words and sentences may have more than one interpretation, and as experiential ambiguity which refers to the ambiguous consequences that stimuli may have upon practices. Indeed, if your line manager asks you to be more committed to your work, this could give rise to both linguistic and experiential ambiguity. Commitment could mean to work harder, work longer, or work smarter depending on the circumstances in which these words have been uttered. The message is ambiguous and it is for you to decipher it. Let's say you opt to work longer hours: this action could also lead to ambiguous outcomes that may be interpreted differently by you and your line manager. You may appear more successful in that you are present at work longer, but your health or family life may suffer.

## 2.2    The role of ambiguity in organisations

Organisational theorists have been preoccupied with ambiguity for over four decades and have viewed it mostly as a resource (input into the organisation) or as an outcome of organised work. Seminal work by Cohen and March (1974) discusses the ambiguities relating to the role of leadership in colleges and universities, organisations which are seen to follow the pattern of 'organised anarchies'. In such organisations, the role of leadership is highly ambiguous to the extent that it is impossible to establish any relationship between decisions at the top and organisational outcomes. Thus, while the expectation may be that leadership will handle ambiguity, one cannot be sure about the consequences of this process. Cohen et al. (1972) proposed a model of decision making which went beyond the taken for granted rational worldview of the time, arguing that all choices and decisions in organisations are made under some form of ambiguity. The authors discuss three forms of ambiguity: ambiguity relating to authority when there is no clear leadership role or structure, ambiguity relating to goals when there are divergent interpretations of what the organisation should aim for, and ambiguity relating to technology when there is a lack of clarity about the relationship between means and ends. The emphasis in their work is on how individuals make sense of ambiguity and how they alter their behaviour in light of their new interpretations, thus enforcing the view that ambiguity is a resource to be managed (both individually and collectively).

Karl Weick also refers to the pervasive nature of ambiguity in organisations, a state arising from the richness and multiplicity of meanings attached to the same event or process (Weick, 1979). For Weick, ambiguity is a resource and organisations are a means of managing it, while the perpetual task of leadership is to make sense of it in order to ensure the survival and adaptation of the organisation. Other scholars have acknowledged the relationship between ambiguity and the context in which it arises (Martin and Meyerson, 1988). Hatch (1997) argues, for example, that one can only assess the meanings and consequences of ambiguity in relation to organisational culture. Furthermore, ambiguity is itself a cultural phenomenon being 'subjectively perceived when a lack of clarity, high complexity or a paradox makes multiple (rather than single or dichotomous) explanations plausible' (Martin, 1992: 93). Thus, ambiguity enhances the need for symbolic management and makes more central the role of leadership in providing meaning and guidance to the subordinates. The 'ambiguity as resource' view came to prominence with the work of Eisenberg (1984) and the advancement of the concept of 'strategic ambiguity'.

Strategic ambiguity is defined as the purposeful use of ambiguity for particular ends in organisations. Eisenberg's work emphasises mainly the benefits of strategic ambiguity. He suggests that organisational conflict could be reduced in organisations if goals are kept broad and ambiguous to the extent that they could be espoused by everyone while at the same time allowing for different interpretations. Thus, the task of leadership is to provide a level of abstraction at which general agreement can occur without limiting specific individual interpretations (Eisenberg, 1984: 231); a scenario referred to as 'unified diversity' (Eisenberg, 1984: 230). Meyerson (1991) uncovered such unified diversity in her study of the experiences of the hospital social workers whose effective performance depended on the acceptance and use of ambiguity.

Ambiguity is also seen to facilitate organisational change since it provides the means to move gradually from one interpretation to another and as such reduces friction and resistance to change (Chreim, 2005). Previous work (Kelemen 2000) on the implementation of Total Quality Management documents the way in which ambiguity is downplayed or nurtured, depending on the situation at hand, in order to ensure the smooth implementation of quality improvement programmes.

This brief overview of the literature on organisational ambiguity identifies three ways in which ambiguity is presented as a strategic resource for organisations. First, the existence of ambiguity permits the *maintenance of vital organisational tensions* such as between centralisation and decentralisation (Hatch, 1997) allowing organisational members to make sense of organisational values in personalised ways that offer opportunities for creativity and innovation. Martin and Meyerson (1988) suggest that in certain environments which thrive on ambiguity, individuals have greater freedom to act, play and experiment and are at less risk when they do so because the organisational culture in question depends heavily on individual autonomy and resulting creativity rather than on standardised routines and procedures.

Second, ambiguity may also *foster deniability* which is a key element of saving face or preserving status when things go wrong or when decisions must be reversed (Giroux, 2006). When managerial initiatives fail, for example, managers can always blame esoteric factors for their lack of vision and commitment or simply invoke the ambiguity of the current environment (Munro, 1995). Employees, themselves, in order to save face, could invoke ambiguity as the reason for poor performance (Zbaracki, 1998).

Finally, ambiguity could also act as a *social lubricant*, reducing potential friction between different points of view (Giroux, 2006). For example, when subordinates do not understand what is going on at the top, they stick together and find comfort in the meaning of survival, rather than openly resisting or challenging the views from the top. Indeed ambiguity may facilitate the translation of various interests and the formation of networks and alliances necessary for organised action (Star and Griesemer, 1989).

However, the strategic use of ambiguity may also lead to unintended consequences, some of which may be riddled with ambiguity (the ambiguity as consequence perspective). For example, an increase in ambiguity diminishes the credibility of managerial initiatives and their utility, thus increasing the level of ambiguity in organisations. Nohria and Eccles (1998) argue that the increase in the number of meanings for the same concept/initiative makes the concept questionable over time to the point that people lose faith in its usefulness and its ability to provide solutions to problems.

Ambiguity could also create problems with regards to measurability, which is crucial in certain industries and requires a certain amount of conceptual rigour. High reliability industries which operate in highly ambiguous environments must exhibit cultural flexibility but also rigour in terms of their systems and procedures in order to avoid catastrophic accidents that lead to death and destruction (Bigley and Roberts, 2001; Weick and Sutcliffe, 2001).

Linguistic ambiguity may lead to ineffective action. Feldman's (1991) case study on the ambiguity of intention and expression in the US Department of Energy demonstrated that ambiguous goals and multiple interpretations led to ineffective action and undermined organisational self-esteem. Therefore 'unified diversity' did not appear to have positive consequences on day-to-day practices and in fact lead to more ambiguity.

Ambiguity could lead to the formation of spaces for resistance by the subordinates (Knights and McCabe, 1998; 2002) and to an open questioning of the dominant rationality. A study by McCabe (2009) suggests that ambiguity could be used as a smokescreen to cloak both the exercise of power and resistance. Ambiguity can amplify conflict and resistance because individuals can interpret situations in different ways. Finally, opposing interests that might have coexisted peacefully for a while under ambiguous initiatives and goals could resurface violently, especially when the interests of groups such as subordinates, managers, customers or investors are not met to a sufficient degree. Therefore, the network of interests and related alliances created around ambiguous goals may not be as stable as initially thought and could dissipate overnight (Giroux, 2006), thus generating more ambiguity.

So far I have shown that ambiguity can be understood as a *resource* for organised action to take place as well as a *consequence* of such organised action. The third perspective posits that ambiguity is a *practice* central to any process of organising. In what follows I trace the turn to practice in organisation studies and introduce American Pragmatism as a practice approach that could inform our understanding of ambiguity as organisational practice.

## 2.3 The turn to practice in organisation studies: American Pragmatism

We regularly talk about the routines and practices in organisational life, without giving the term any further thought. Practice, if we think about it at all, seems to be simply those things which occur in the repeated day-to-day life of organisations. The 'turn to practice' in organisation studies has encouraged scholars to ask if the term 'practice' is as a simple as it initially seems. For example, Schatzki et al. (2001) argue that the concept of practice spans many disciplines such as philosophy, cultural theory, sociology, history, anthropology, and technology studies. Although disagreement over its meanings reigns, Schatzki et al. view practice as a solution to existing dualisms and problematic dichotomies in social science theory, and as providing new impetus for reconceptualising meaning, language, power and organisation. It is beyond the remit of this chapter to offer a full review of the 'turn to practice' in organisation studies. Suffice to say that only a few organisational theorists interested in practice have inspired themselves from American Pragmatist philosophers (see Cohen, 2007; Simpson, 2009; Watson, 2010; Kelemen and Rumens, 2013).

American Pragmatism is a theory of meaning developed in America at the end of the 19th century which asserts that concepts are only relevant in as much as they are relevant for action. Charles Peirce, William James and John Dewey established American Pragmatism as an alternative to Western rationalism, which prioritises logic and rational thinking. A key criticism of Western rationalism is that it separates the mind from the body, meaning that emotions and lived experiences are downplayed or ignored. Broadly, American Pragmatists argue that the body, emotions and people's lived experience cannot be ignored when considering how we make sense of the world. As we will see in the next section, this perspective is important when discussing ambiguity. In its day, American Pragmatism attracted much criticism from other philosophers. However, its proponents did not consider pragmatism an attack on philosophy as such, only a tool to help philosophy become more practical and effective.

The progenitors of American Pragmatism listed above held various and loosely connected concerns about philosophy, truth, human experience and meaning. For example, Charles Peirce (1839–1914) trained as a scientist and, as such, was keen to apply scientific principles to philosophical problems. For Peirce, meaning was established by direct interaction with the sensible effects of one's actions. On a slightly different tack, William James (1842–1910) was troubled by the precarious place of humans in the new scientific world. His scholarly interests shifted from logic to moral and psychological matters. The pursuit of truth was less a matter of scientific endeavour and more to do with the 'here and now'; in other words, the context and the individual. John Dewey (1859–1952) affirmed Peirce's inquiring critical spirit and logical methods but, like James, his interests were moral, aesthetic, and educational, and his notion of the truth was pluralistic and tolerant of diversity (Kelemen and Rumens, 2008).

American Pragmatism challenges the dualistic relationship between knowledge and experience and argues that reality can and should be changed through reason and action. As such, pragmatism goes beyond the short-comings of positivism and certain versions of postmodernism by insisting that there is a reality out there (however fragile and disputed it might be). Further to this, Pragmatism suggests that reality can be changed for the better by applying reason. While subjective interpretations are important in this endeavour, not all of them are equally useful. Usefulness becomes a central concern for the pragmatists, which is defined primarily on two counts: (1) epistemologically, in terms of whether the information or knowledge is credible, well founded, reliable and relevant; (2) and normatively, in terms of whether knowledge/theory helps to advance one's cause/project and improve one's immediate circumstances (Wicks and Freeman, 1998).

Insights from American Pragmatism could lend more credibility to the view that ambiguity is an organisational practice, indeed a practice that is necessarily reflexive. While philosophy has grappled for centuries with the notion of ambiguity and has designed strategies for how it should be removed from scientific inquiry, American Pragmatism is the first Western philosophy to accord ambiguity a central place, viewing it in positive terms, as a productive and essential resource for achieving human betterment and scientific progress and as a practice central to human existence.

## 2.4 The place of ambiguity in American Pragmatism

We hardly speak about ambiguity on its own, but mostly in relation to the concept of clarity. Of course, neither term is self-sufficient; either depends on each other for its meaning, they embrace and reject each other in a dynamic and continuous, reciprocal and antagonistic flux. Therefore, to understand ambiguity we must acknowledge its rather antagonistic and asymmetrical relationship with clarity.

To the ancient Greeks, exemplars of Western Rationalism, the tension between ambiguity and clarity was reflected in the famous Sorite paradoxes, a series of philosophical conundrums posed in question and answer format. These are also known as little-by-little arguments which arise due to indeterminacy. Let us take the question 'what is a heap'? The vagueness of the term 'heap' puts us in a situation of saying that one grain of corn is not a heap, two grains are not a heap and so on. It appears that no one extra grain of corn makes the difference between a heap and not a heap, and we are faced with a situation where no amount of grains (however large) makes up a heap. This is a paradox for we have followed logical reasoning and we have arrived at a false conclusion. It is obvious that someone might look at a heap of corn and recognise it as such in practice, though the ambiguity of the statement of the pile as a 'heap' may confuse their expectations; it may be too small, too large, or too orderly to fit with what they interpret a 'heap' to be.

But clarity, for rationalists, was more than just the mechanism for resolving epistemological uncertainty: it was the principle by which knowledge could be made useful. As the principle of clarity became elevated on the grounds of usefulness ambiguity was treated as something to be denied and disavowed. That is until American Pragmatism sought to convince us otherwise.

Charles Peirce was perhaps the first philosopher who believed that ambiguity needed to be tolerated or at least deferred until the end of the inquiry rather than banished at the beginning. While acknowledging the need for clarity for logical expression, Peirce considered the impatient pursuit of simplicity and clarity equally harmful, becoming a negative condition that could hamper open-ended inquiry. Clarity, for him, was an impossible dream since concepts could only be expressed in an imperfect language.

It was William James who went on to treat ambiguity in distinctive positive terms. He equated ambiguity with richness, vitality and pluralism. His advocacy was rooted in a conception of the universe as ever-changing, multidimensional and forever changing, part of the vibrancy of primal experience. For James ambiguity was a positive rather than a negative force within our social and cultural experience. He interpreted ambiguity as a desire to avoid conclusive certainties and instead to celebrate the multiple possibilities inherent in every situation.

According to James, naming is at the heart of our endeavours to cope with ambiguity. Naming is a process rooted in struggles over meaning which are only resolved in practice whereby some interpretations, definitions and descriptions are privileged over others. Such processes necessarily mean that we neglect, marginalise or denigrate other subtleties of experience and shades of meaning that are left obscure. For James, the achievement of any identity, however contingent, comes at a heavy cost whose price is the exclusion of the richness and vitality that constitutes the true multiplicity of any and every cultural experience. Such richness always exceeds the capacity of our linguistic systems to re-present it fully. The desire to reduce experience to words represents a crude attempt to express the inexpressible. The pluralistic nature of experience is forever uncertain and unfinished, in a state of flux and open possibility and something that always exceeds our best endeavours to capture it logically in words.

This position was embraced by John Dewey and is most evident in his treatment of scientific inquiry. Dewey argues that modern philosophy has deferred too easily to the authority of knowledge in the name of science without questioning this authority. Diversity, plurality of experience and ambiguity have thus been assimilated into a non-empirical concept of knowledge. This, according to Dewey, is unsatisfactory for we can only appreciate the value of knowledge when it is viewed as part of the larger context of experience. Knowledge and experience cannot be separated in a dichotomous fashion for knowledge is part of experience and contributes to the enhancement of that experience while reflection is necessary to comprehend and manage experience successfully. Dewey sees reality as ambiguous and processual rather than static and formed by ready-made elements. For him, the world exhibits: 'an impressive and irresistible mixtures of sufficiencies, tight completeness, order, recurrences which make possible prediction and control, and singularities, ambiguities, uncertain possibilities, processes going on to consequences yet indeterminate' (Dewey, 1925: 47). It is this day-to-day ambiguity that triggers the need for inquiry and the creation of organisational forms. Without ambiguity there would be no inquiry, no organisation and no progress for humankind.

Organisation is therefore fuelled by the existence of ambiguity. Ambiguity arises when our normal ways of doing things are disrupted because of surprises, unusual events or words that are difficult to comprehend and deal with. Dewey (1938 [1991]) referred to such disruptions as indeterminate situations in which habits and routines are not enough to explain what is going on and to offer a way out. It is only when such a situation is identified as a problematic situation that inquiry/organisation begins and experience turns it into the cognitive mode.

It should be noted that there is no absolute end to inquiry/organisation. Inquiry/organisation does not remove doubt by returning to a prior equilibrium, but by the transformation of the current situation into a new one. It institutes new environing conditions that occasion new problems. There is no final settlement, because every settlement introduces the conditions of some degree of a new unsettling and ambiguity (Dewey 1938[1991]). As special problems are resolved, new ones tend to emerge, and the cycle repeats itself *ad infinitum*.

In this section we have seen that American Pragmatism accords a central place to ambiguity defined as a practice of organising/inquiry. I conclude by highlighting the need for a more nuanced understanding of ambiguity in organisation, beyond the traditional views that it is a resource or a consequence of organised life.

## 2.5 Conclusion

Although it is difficult to predict the trajectory of our utterances, how they will be received and interpreted, the practical context in which we find ourselves will provide certain possibilities for interpretation while limiting others. For ambiguity does not simply reside in words but also in the interpretive practices sanctioned by a particular community of actors. Giroux (2006) argues that pragmatic ambiguity, defined as 'the condition of admitting more than one course of action', is 'realised linguistically, rhetorically, textually and inter-textually, and supported by a variety of factors, both social and textual' (Giroux, 2006: 1228).

The existence of linguistic and experiential ambiguity as separate conceptual domains is a reflection of the division between words and facts, between thinking and doing, between knowledge and practice that has shaped Western philosophy for centuries. The American Pragmatist perspective helps un-divide such divisions arguing that theory and practice are the two sides of the same coin and knowledge does not have a superior hold over experience. Indeed, according to American Pragmatism, theory is a practical act of applying judgement to a problematic situation and as such, ambiguous experience is the starting point of any process of organising.

The pluralistic nature of experience is forever ambiguous and unfinished in a state of flux and open possibility and something that always exceeds our best endeavours at capturing it logically in words. Ambiguity, therefore, is at the heart of organisational practice and is itself a practice of organising. Embracing the practice perspective on organisational ambiguity may make us aware of the alternative options and possibilities that are always latent within any sphere of organising. We tend to privilege the results of organising but these outcomes result from the prior condition of ambiguity. Thus we need to begin any analysis by exploring the conditions of possibility prevailing in any situation or context rather than focusing on their results. The ambiguous operates as a quasi-practical potentiality with a rich capacity for re-shaping and re-imagining acts of organisation. When understood in these terms, the ambiguous becomes a malleable condition, one that invites new ways to imagine social relations that can be realised through acts of organisation.

## REFERENCES

Bigley, G. and Roberts, K. (2001) 'The incident command system: High-reliability organizing for complex and volatile task environments', *Academy of Management Journal*, 14(6), 1281–1299.

Chreim, S. (2005) 'The continuity–change duality in narrative texts of organisational identity', *Journal of Management Studies*, 42(3), 567–593.

Cohen, M.D. (2007) 'Reading Dewey: Reflections on the study of routine', *Organization Studies*, 28(5), 773–786.

Cohen, M. and March, J. (1974) *Leadership and Ambiguity: The American College Presidency*, New York: McGraw-Hill.

Cohen, M., March, J. and Olsen, J. (1972) 'A garbage can model of organizational choice', *Administrative Science Quarterly*, 17(1), 1–25.

Dewey, J. (1925[1981]) 'Experience and nature' in Boydston, J.A. (ed.), *Later Works 1*, Carbondale and Edwardsville: Southern Illinois University Press.

Dewey, J. (1938 [1991]) 'Logic: Theory of inquiry', in Boydston, J.A. (ed.), *Later Works 12*, Carbondale and Edwardsville: Southern Illinois University Press.

Eisenberg, E.M. (1984) 'Ambiguity as strategy in organizational communication', *Communication Monographs*, 51(3), 227–242.

Feldman, M. (1991) 'The meaning of ambiguity: Learning from stories and metaphors' in Frost, P.J. et al. (eds), *Reframing Organizational Culture*, Newbury Park, CA: Sage Publications.

Giroux, H. (2006) '"It was such a handy term": Management fashions and pragmatic ambiguity', *Journal of Management Studies*, 43(6), 1227–1260.

Hatch, M.J. (1997) 'Jazzing up the theory of organizational improvisation', *Advances in Strategic Management*, 14, 181–191.

Kelemen, M. (2000) 'Too much or too little ambiguity: The language of total quality management', *Journal of Management Studies*, 37(4), 483–498.

Kelemen, M. and Rumens, N. (2008) *An Introduction to Critical Management Research*, London: Sage Publications.

Kelemen, M. and Rumens, N. (eds) (2013) *American Pragmatism and Organization: Issues and Controversies*, Ashgate: Gower.

Knights, D. and McCabe, D. (1998) 'What happens when the phone goes wild?: BPR, Stress and the Worker', *Journal of Management Studies*, 35(2), 163–194.

Knights, D. and McCabe, D. (2002) 'A road less travelled: Beyond managerialist, critical and processual approaches to total quality management', *Journal of Organizational Change Management*, 15(3), 235–254.

Levine, D. (1985) *The Flight from Ambiguity – Essays in Social and Cultural Theory*, Chicago and London: University of Chicago Press.

Martin, J. (1992) *Cultures in Organizations: Three Perspectives*, New York: Oxford University Press.

Martin, J. and Meyerson, D. (1988) 'Organizational cultures and the denial, channeling and acknowledgment of ambiguity', in Pondy, L.R., Boland, R.J. and Thomas, H. (eds), *Managing Ambiguity and Change*, Chichester: Wiley.

McCabe, D. (2009) 'Strategy-as-power: Ambiguity, contradiction and the exercise of power in a UK Building Society', *Organization*, 17(2), 151–175.

Meyerson, D. (1991) '"Normal" ambiguity? A glimpse of an occupational culture', in Frost, P.J., Moore, L.F., Reis Louis, M., Lundberg, C.C. and Martin, J. (eds), *Reframing Organisational Culture*, Newbury Park, CA: Sage Publications.

Munro, R. (1995) 'Managing by ambiguity: An archaeology of the social in the absence of management accounting', *Critical Perspectives on Accounting*, 6(5), 433–482.

Nohria, N. and Eccles, R.G. (1998) 'Where does management knowledge come from?', in

Alvarez, J.L. (ed.), *The Diffusion and Consumption of Business Knowledge*, New York: St. Martin Press.

Schatzki, T., Knorr Cetina, K. and von Savigny, E. (eds) (2001) *The Practice Turn in Contemporary Theory*, London and New York: Routledge.

Simpson, B. (2009) 'Pragmatism, Mead and the practice turn', *Organization Studies*, 30(12), 1329–1347.

Star, S.L. and Griesemer, J.R. (1989) 'Institutional ecology, "translations" and boundary objects: Amateurs and professionals in Berkeley's Museum of Vertebrate Zoology, 1907–39', *Social Studies of Science*, 19(3), 387–420.

Watson, T.J. (2010) 'Critical social science, pragmatism and the realities of HRM', *International Journal of Human Resource Management*, 21(6), 915–931.

Weick, K.E. (1979) *The Social Psychology of Organizing* (2nd edition), Reading, MA: Addison-Wesley.

Weick K.E and Sutcliffe, K.M. (2001) *Managing the Unexpected: Assuring High Performance in an Age of Complexity* (1st edition), San Francisco: Jossey-Bass.

Wicks, A. and Freeman, R.E. (1998) 'Organization studies and the new pragmatism: Positivism, anti-positivism, and the search for ethics', *Organization Science*, 9(2): 123–140.

Zbaracki, M.J. (1998) 'The rhetoric and reality of TQM', *Administrative Science Quarterly*, 43(3), 602–636.

# 3

# Dignity and meaningful work in organisations

*Laura Mitchell*

> "The government has given us no alternative to this [illegal] work, so (this is the only way) we can live a normal life in dignity," he complains . . . Palestinian youth unemployment stands at 40 percent . . . [a young farmer says] "I have a university degree in political science, but there are no jobs out there."
>
> Browning (Reuters) Jun 2013

## 3.1 Introduction

In the context of economic crisis, matters of dignity and worth in employment have been thrown into stark relief. The quotation at the start of this chapter emphasises the awareness that work, in many kinds, is central to our sense of value and purpose in contemporary society. Even if the forms of such labour are exploitative, the need and desire for subsistence drives those who participate. Yet work and dignity are seemingly in tension, for the very activity that appears to be so central to dignity too often offers circumstances reprehensible to it.

The contemporary concern over the dignity of work is also implicitly present in classical works of the Victorian period in sociology and organisation studies, works which reflect the changing nature of life during the Industrial Revolution. Durkheim's (1893) focus on the division of labour in society stressed the way in which the changes wrought by industrial capitalism increased the dependence between individuals as they became connected to strangers through the need for their labour and expertise. This new form of solidarity, Durkheim argued, was characteristic of the change to a new form of society arranged around production. Similarly, he argued that morality was not given, but emerged from society, and consequently the greater dependence among individuals gave rise to a greater respect for individual dignity. Yet Durkheim also admitted to the possible anomie, or normlessness, that may emerge from a shift away from life dominated by connections of family and tradition rather than industrial function. Marx's (1844) declarations were more stringent, for as mankind became separated from his natural capacities he was in turn made alien to himself, estranged from his works and his very nature. The relation between dignity and work has thus been recognised as a paradoxical one since the very emergence of a society dominated by mass employment for a wage.

This chapter examines two contemporary frameworks (Bolton, 2007; Hodson, 2001) which attempt to outline what dignity at work might look like, and considers how useful they are in evaluating empirical circumstances of dignity highlighted in quotations from current events. These frameworks are described in the context of their philosophical basis, and their identification (along with other literature in the field) of autonomy, identity and abuse as key concerns for the study of dignity and work. Brief discussion of the context highlighted by each quotation explores the limited applicability of these frameworks, and argues the need for a broader understanding of autonomy and dignity which recognises the importance of social relations and context. Finally, the chapter suggests a radical alternative to these frameworks for understanding dignity and work, instead suggesting a perspective which shifts away from a focus on universal frames.

## 3.2 What does dignity mean? Two 'contemporary' frameworks

> In a knowledge economy, it can feel embarrassingly retro to talk about the dignity of labour . . . the economic downturn is forcing a reassessment of the quality of life offered by cog-in-the-wheel office life, where employees see neither daylight, their families, nor the end product of their labours. And this is an ethic that challenges directly the disposability of the consumer age. (Brooks, 2010)

> 'Today in the world this slavery [in the poor work conditions of garment factories] is being committed against something beautiful that God has given us – the capacity to create, to work, to have dignity', the Pope said at a private Mass. 'Not paying a fair wage, not giving a job because you are only looking at balance sheets, only looking to make a profit, that goes against God', he was quoted as saying by Vatican radio. (BBC, 2013)

Dignity, though a contemporary concept, has been claimed as a matter of historical relevance to studies of work and organisation (see Bolton, 2007; Hodson, 2001). The topic draws on a long history of intellectual thought, dating back further than the field of organisation studies, which can locate its origins in the Renaissance period of the 15th century (notably Pico della

Mirandola, 1486). People in organisations today, as inheritors of this legacy, are conceptualised as reasoning beings 'born free and equal in dignity and rights' (United Nations, Declaration of Human Rights Article 1). Yet as workers or employees they are also seen as no more than a factor of production, an unpredictable and unreliable cost to be managed and controlled. The key conceptual basis of such tension lies in the conflict between views on the intrinsic worth versus relative value of human persons. Such discussions draw heavily on the work of the Enlightenment (18th century) philosopher Immanuel Kant, who argued that human uniqueness and innate worth was located in free will; the capacity for independent reason. Kant argued that through the exercise of reason alone, morality or the judgement of worth could be deduced.

Contemporary work on dignity often refers to the following passage from Kant's work on morality:

> Whatever has reference to the general inclinations and wants of mankind has a market value; whatever, without presupposing a want, corresponds to a certain taste, that is, to a satisfaction in the mere purposeless play of our faculties, has a fancy value; but that which constitutes the condition under which alone anything can be an end in itself, this has not merely a relative worth, that is, value, but an intrinsic worth, that is, dignity. (Kant, 1790, translated 1949: 51)

In this passage, Kant reflects on the economic relations of society at the time. Price, as any student of economics would recognise today, is set by the demands (inclinations and wants) of the market. Equally, the identification of particular trends or 'fancies' among groups of consumers is manifest in the higher price of popular brand items. Yet Kant identifies a disconnection between the value of such objects of exchange, which are only worth something relative to their scarcity or popularity, and things which are intrinsically valuable of themselves. Dignity from a Kantian perspective is thus in opposition to price, and work, as the sale of labour for wages, places dignity in conflict. Instrumental organisations providing contemporary employment opportunities are examples of such a conflict, often understood as overlooking the intrinsic worth of persons and overly focused on market valuations, the financial and efficiency costs of 'human resources'. Such a biased orientation is a challenge to the realisation of individual human dignity in contemporary society (see Sayer, 2007; 2011).

Definitions of dignity in today's context of work and organisation have drawn on Kant through concentration on two aspects; indignity through an excessive focus on instrumentalism (price), or dignity through practices which acknowledge the capacities and worth of persons. This focus reiterates the Kantian opposition of price and worth, but although price is relatively simple to define, the matter of worth is more complex. Hodson's (1996: 722) definition draws further on Kant's ideas to focus on defining worth as based on the capacity for reason located in autonomy:

> Dignity is contingent not only on protecting oneself from abuse, but also on having personal space for one's individual identity . . . worker strategies are attempts to defend or regain dignity in the face of work organizations that violate worker's interests, limit their prerogatives or otherwise undermine their autonomy.

Autonomy, for Kant, was the 'freedom of the will', and based on the understanding that given such freedom, individuals would be self-regulating in their actions and rational in developing moral rules of behaviour. Autonomy, the freedom to make your own rules and determine your own actions, is also a difficult concept to define and its relations to the concepts discussed above are disputed (e.g., Horton, 1964). Hodson (1996; 2001), however, identifies greater degrees of autonomy in the workplace as an indicator that dignity can be realised by workers. In this context, Hodson's use of the term autonomy is limited to freedom from control over the activity of work or from interference by managers. Thus the practices which promote dignity (in this case autonomy) are identified as the opposite to those which promote indignity (excessive control). Although such autonomy may be considered a necessary condition for persons to be treated with dignity, freedom from excessive management interference or technological direction may not alone be enough to bring it about. Complimentary studies have devoted significant work to identifying a wealth of additional broadly connected or related factors (see Sayer, 2007; Bolton, 2007).

Opinions on which matters are of most relevance to dignity differ and as such the connected topics or factors are many and varied, though the themes of abuse in the workplace, identity and autonomy in work remain strong. Dignity is discussed in close relation to resistance and resentment (Lamont, 2000; Hodson, 2001; Scheff, 2006), alienation (Hodson, 1996; Doherty, 2010), bullying (Lutgen-Sandvik, 2008; Peyton, 2003), poor pay and conditions of work (Berg and Frost, 2005; Bolton, 2007; Lutz, 1995; Rayman, 2001; Westwood, 2006), national cultures (Ijzerman and Cohen, 2011; Kim and Cohen, 2010), identity (Byars-Winston, 2011; Hill, 2009; Lucas, 2011; Wierenga, 2011), inclusion and exclusion (Lamont, 2000; Purser, 2009; Woolhead et al., 2006), and justice (Cotterrell, 2011; Pritchard, 1972). Yet this is only a small selection of works which engage with the concept. The term dignity also appears more casually in discussions critical of instrumentalist practices that promote a corporate agenda without concern for the broader consequences.

Common to much of this body of knowledge is the idea that contemporary employment settings may place dignity at risk. But what dignity means and how it might be promoted through practices which incorporate a view of individual worth is still unclear, and it is rarely a discussion you will find in management textbooks. Where discussions of dignity attempt to present a more detailed definition, the discussion over worth becomes a complicated one informed by philosophical debate. Sensen (2011) and Rosen (2012) outline a significant paradigm shift between traditional and contemporary conceptualisations of dignity. Importantly, such shifts emphasise that it may not simply be our understanding of dignity that is at fault; instead, the meaning of the concept may itself be unstable. The historical shift marks a movement away from religious texts as the basis for understanding dignity, towards secular viewpoints. Notably Sensen (2011) explains that in current interpretations there is a decline in an aristocratic understanding of dignity expressed in hierarchical rank or nobility, discarded in favour of a belief in universal equality expressed in human rights. This requires that the criteria for dignity based on worth need to be universally applicable, rather than located in differentiated qualities. Such universalism draws strongly on Kant and informs frameworks of dignity such as Bolton's (2006) attempt to identify universally necessary criteria for working with dignity.

Bolton's (2006) framework lists ten components as part of two 'dimensions' of dignity; dignity *in* work and dignity *at* work (see Figure 3.1). This framework implies that dignity can be identified through the presence or absence of subjectively experienced and objectively comparable criteria. Autonomy, job satisfaction, meaningful work, respect, learning and development comprise the components of dignity *in*, while well-being, just reward, voice, security and equal opportunity comprise dignity *at*. Yet both such 'dimen-

| **Dignity in Work** | **Dignity in Work** |
|---|---|
| Autonomy | Wellbeing |
| Job Satisfaction | Just Reward |
| Meaningful Work | Voice |
| Respect | Security |
| Learning & Development | Equal Opportunity |

**Figure 3.1** Bolton's *Dimensions of Dignity* (2006)

sions' focus on criteria for dignity that are themselves complex, debated, and difficult to specify in empirical settings. Instead of one concept that is difficult to define, the framework offers several.[1] Furthermore, this primarily concerns itself with matters of dignity that apply to settings of formal employment in large organisations. The application of the same criteria to a professional worker engaging in unpaid overtime, a student in a summer job, an independent Palestinian tobacco farmer, a garment manufacturer with few alternatives in Bangladesh, or a minimum wage care assistant is difficult. Those who are self-employed or who work as volunteers are also hard to account for. However, the framework does offer a useful benchmarking tool to compare large organisations where many people find employment.

Hodson (1996; 2001), primarily draws on the concept of autonomy as the redress to alienation in work. Identifying the primary risks to dignity at work as overwork, contradictory attitudes to employee involvement in the organisation, reduction of autonomy and mismanagement or abuse, Hodson (2001) argues that dignity nonetheless is not simply a matter of structural inequality, but achievable through individual and collective exercise of agency. From an extensive coding protocol, he develops a number of objective factors of dignity in the face of instrumentalism and abuse that are subsequently aggregated into the categories of *co-worker relations*, *resistance*, and *citizenship practices* (see Figure 3.2).

Relations are broadly defined as conforming to solidarity or conflict (within or between groups) in the organisation. Resistance refers to diminished effort, enthusiasm or sabotage whereas citizenship refers to pride, satisfaction, commitment and co-operation. Yet this remains a framework which derives its definition of 'dignity' by the focus upon its opposite; indignity. Furthermore, these seemingly universal criteria rely upon interpretation relative to the context and experience of the workers as well as the researcher when it comes to analysis.[2]

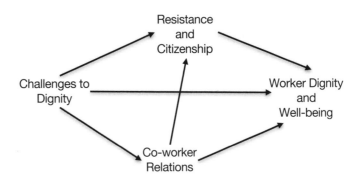

**Figure 3.2**
Hodson's factors of dignity and well-being at work (2001: 239)

What seems important here is to consider how such seemingly universal criteria might 'fit' the examples given at the start of the chapter. Bolton's dimensions highlight a distinction between the nature or content of the work and the form it might take in a particular organisation (see Bolton, 2006), while Hodson's (2001) framework recognises the influence of social relations between workers and with management. Yet the intrinsic and extrinsic rewards of work are understood to be universal, when they may well be experienced in specific ways by individuals. Taking the news excerpts as examples, the next section briefly discusses how each highlights a particular difficulty in frameworks such as those proposed by Hodson (2001) or Bolton (2007).

## 3.3    Dignity on the ground

> The White House pledged on Wednesday to help lower-income youth find summer jobs . . . 'There's no replacement for the dignity that comes with earning your first paycheck', said Secretary of Labor Hilda Solis. (Kuo, 2012)

> We believe staff can only deliver good quality care based on respect for people's dignity and wishes if they are themselves treated with dignity and respect. Increasing their skills and confidence should increase their ability to appropriately challenge the occasions when they are not treated with dignity and respect. (Rose, T., interviewed by the Joseph Rowntree Foundation in *The Guardian*, June 2013)

### 3.3.1    Little cogs in large wheels (Brooks, 2010)

The 'economic downturn' has had a consequent negative effect on working conditions for many people, or even whether they have paid work at all, as banks withdraw lines of credit and companies declare bankruptcy. The 'difficult times' are used to stall or reduce the wages of public sector workers and are equally identified by private companies as an independent circumstance necessitating reductions in pay, staffing levels (with consequent effects on job security for remaining employees), opportunities for advancement and consultation or voice. Not only are Bolton's (2007) 'at' dimensions in the form of working conditions drastically impoverished, but the increase in the intensification or hours of work queries the relationship between the worker and their dignity 'in' work. This more broadly engages with the question over work and consumption as a source of identity (Du Gay, 1996), as long hours of work and lower purchasing power leads to a diminished capacity to engage in conspicuous consumption and social relations outside of the workplace are adversely affected. Pride and citizenship, meaningful work and respect may be gained more significantly for employees from their lives outside of the workplace, yet employment for a wage may be a necessary condition to meaningfully engage in that life. Decline in the quality of the conditions of work may then leave individuals caught in a binding problem; meaningful work can be achieved neither through nor outside of employment.

### 3.3.2 Summer of work for the disenfranchised (Kuo, 2012)

Unemployment through a lack of opportunity is a situation sometimes described as a 'trap' for young people (see Oultram, Chapter 5 this volume). Without experience their employability is compromised, yet in a labour market awash with experienced unemployed people from downsized organisations they are unlikely to find work. Temporary or seasonal jobs may be offered as a solution, though there is no job security and rewards are likely to be low. Rather than offering dignity through decent conditions of work, the promise implicit for young workers seems to lie in the pride and respect from earning a wage, and a place (however transient) in the labour market. The 'first pay check' offers a rite of passage into the unreliable world of work, a route which the cash-strapped youth are given an opportunity to tread, but makes no guarantees as to the final destination. Young adults are thus transformed by such 'opportunities' into citizens, and are then individually responsible for making their own way in the economic world, dignified or otherwise. Once exposed to the workplace, they are also expected to have learned its discipline and rules of self-development and governance (see Rose, 1990). As an alternative to the skill and experience conferred by a more thorough system of training such as an apprenticeship, such opportunities place a lower expectation on the organisation to provide work in the future. So although the work experience may offer a chance at dignity conceptualised more broadly, it is uncertain that such treasure may be found in the workplace offered.

### 3.3.3 Sweatshop slavery (BBC, 2013)

The slave labour conditions of international manufacturing are oft-cited examples of a form of work lacking in dignity, reduced to case studies of poor corporate social responsibility in textbooks. The poor safety conditions of factories and long hours of work, combined with low pay, no union recognition and a lack of job security are emblematic of an absence of dignity at work. With such overwhelming evidence, inquiring into the meaning or autonomy experienced by workers seems a futile exercise, yet the content of the work may itself be rewarding, as is the provision of an income to support a family life. However, the unease which often accompanies such arguments in the field of international development lies not in the relationship between the worker and their work, but in the appreciation that relations of such employment conditions are perpetuated by a broader unequal political reality, and not only is the security of employees' position low, but the international supply chains may shift elsewhere and the industry as a whole teeters on precarious foundations. Nonetheless, the income provided from such work may be more secure than agricultural work, and the possibilities for improved conditions of life seductive.

### 3.3.4  No choice but the black market (Browning, 2013)

Counterfeit goods can be seen on every street corner in cities around the globe, yet selling a product illegally where it is regulated and taxed carries the stigma and potential repercussions of a criminal offence. Yet such social implications may be of little influence to particular individuals or communities, particularly where there is a distinct distance between community views and values and those held in the sphere of national politics. Furthermore, where individuals are highly educated and skilled, but unable to find work in alignment with such abilities, resorting to work where those skills might be useful, or where there are strong relations with other workers and a community offers a rare potential for dignity.

### 3.3.5  Caring about the carers (Rose, 2013)

Care work or working with the elderly and infirm to assist with basic daily needs is often featured in debates over patient dignity, but rarely considered in the context of worker dignity. The sector is often identified with extensive use of outsourcing, circumventing unionisation and employing low paid, low skilled workers. The Joseph Rowntree Foundation (JRF) argue for the increase in training and skill development in order to benefit the dignity of patients and workers, yet the aims of predominantly privatised care providers in training staff are not necessarily those of the employees. Credentials which are not widely recognised or which provide little real development offers employees little to improve their employability, and may undermine the meaning and pride they find in skills and techniques they have already learned. Enforced training may also be introduced to safeguard patients and attain quality kite marks, but without thought as to the implication of repetitive and demeaning training for employees.

## 3.4  Discussion

The examples above highlight the strengths of the existing dignity frameworks, as they identify key concerns that often arise as relevant to dignity.

However, they also expose the limitations of those frameworks in specific ways. One such limitation lies in the issue that work may be understood as related to employee dignity in a broader context. Although the content and form of a particular job may highlight particular opportunities or challenges to dignity, the broader social context including the cultural significance of the work and its relation to the access to other social activities play a significant role. Selling counterfeit or illegal goods may offer a route out of poverty, and in some cases even allow people access to supplies they need and would otherwise lack. It is likely such sellers think to themselves, as the Palestinian farmer does, that being enterprising in the face of difficult times brought about by government intervention is the responsible and dignified thing to do. Though worker solidarity or pride may have a significant effect on dignity and well-being at work, the solidarity of a community or family history may hold equal influence (see Ackroyd, 2007). Sayer (2007) stated that dignity needs to be understood in the context of dependency and trust, and this perhaps highlights what lies at the heart of the problem with the Kantian-inspired frameworks.

Kantian philosophy identifies rationality as a virtue, a normative mode of conduct to which all should aspire. However, such rationality, the basis of the need for autonomy, is not to be confused with industrial instrumentalism or the actual exercise of judgement by individuals. This Kantian view of dignity is based on dignity as something universal to *aspire* to. The basis of work as a danger to dignity, however, lies in dignity already being located within individuals in their capacity as worthy aspirants. Autonomy becomes a necessary precondition for the search for dignity by individuals. But there are two restrictions on the concept of autonomy in the above frameworks. The first, as already identified, lies in Hodson's (1996) definition of autonomy as freedom from control or abuse. Such a definition conceals the importance of understanding autonomy as *freedom to* engage in activity.

The summer jobs being facilitated by government programmes provide an example; once employed the youth are free from the stigma of inexperience and unemployment, but the work does not necessarily offer them freedom to pursue a career, start a family, or enjoy social solidarity. The second restriction of the concept of autonomy is that it and the rest of the frameworks are understood to apply only in the context of work and the workplace. Evident from the examples is the premise that work has a role in the opportunities for dignity outside of the 'factory gates', or even outside of formal employment. There is, therefore, a need to consider the influence of work and its benefits or challenges more broadly when considering dignity in the context of work. Employment may offer good co-worker relations or a source of pride, or it may offer an opportunity to gain skills and experience which then serve the individual in pursuit of another meaningful purpose.

Ciulla (2012) argues that profit-making organisations are not in a position to provide meaningful work, a factor Bolton (2006) identifies as key to dignity *in* work, though such work may well be worthwhile as contributing to the needs of wider society. Bolton's criteria of dignity in work focus on opportunities for learning and self-development, respect such as that described by the JRF as stemming from confidence in work, as well as job satisfaction and meaningful work. Ciulla (2012) argues, however, that organisations prioritise paternalist notions of development and what is 'good' for employees. These notions leave little room for conflict with the operation and activities of the organisation itself. Bolton's list of criteria for dignity *in* work are not simply a matter of the content of the work, perceived as meaningful by an independently reasoning worker, but also draw on broader normative understandings. Yet it seems that these understandings may differ for organisations and for employees.

Meaningful work and autonomy, for example, may be understood as not only subjective experiences of work, but connected to social and cultural norms around valued or stigmatised occupations (see Hamilton and McCabe, Chapter 7 this volume). Being able to enter into such occupations is not necessarily a choice many are free to make, when unemployment is high and the cost of a basic livelihood is ever rising. Ciulla's critique of organisational possibilities rests on a more sophisticated understanding of autonomy that recognises the distinction between freedom *from* constraint and freedom *to* pursue activities that seem worthwhile to the individual. As argued by Cooper and May (2007), illegal work may be stigmatised as criminal behaviour, but it nonetheless may offer a route to dignity otherwise impassable.

## 3.5    Conclusion

Though the contemporary view of dignity eliminates a view of worth based on relative position or rank, it is difficult to conceive of how dignity may lie wholly within universal and objective conditions applied to individuals rather than particular culturally specific or subject-specific understandings of worth that are social in nature. The tension between the universal and the relative understandings of individual worth, evident in the contrast of worth and price, has been debated in the context of other fields (see Leget et al., 2009), yet the fact that price is only one form of socially agreed 'currency' of worth is forgotten.

In the preceding analysis, Bolton (2007) and Hodson's (2001) dignity frameworks have been discussed as approaches to the problem of understanding dignity in employment with particular limitations. These limitations are specific to the ways in which the frameworks can be applied empirically to understand specific instances of work in current conditions, and focus significantly on autonomy. However, the underlying Kantian ideology of the frameworks which offers the promise of universalism is the most staggering concern. This ideology is used as grounding for promoting universal rights, but it does not follow that what individuals understand as good or meaningful, as *worthwhile*, is also universal, but is instead specific and plural.

This realisation, that less obvious attitudes towards the relative worth of particular circumstances or occupations are part of understanding how an individual may recognise what is 'right' or 'good' to them, transforms our understanding of dignity in organizational contexts. Such issues highlight further questions regarding whose criteria for worth are legitimate and acceptable and under what circumstances. Since normative views may conflict with the specific experiences of individuals, widely applicable definitions of dignity, even when applied to contexts of work in developed Western economic markets, are difficult to specify. Indeed the very notion of *dignity* as a conceptualisation of individual worth has also been argued as culturally specific notion (Bennoune, 2007; Berger et al., 1974; Bielefeldt, 2000; Brennan and Lo, 2007; Kim and Cohen, 2010; Riley, 2010; Shultziner, 2003; Whitman, 2004) Dignity, then, needs to be understood as a concept which is not neutral in its application to the context of work, but in line with the promotion of moral individualism rather than collective understandings of worth. The ideology promotes a utopian view of a good society with good work and good jobs; a simple answer to the evils of industrial capitalist society. Yet in order to study this concept empirically requires a more sophisticated and plural understanding of how individuals determine what is good or worthwhile than offered by the existing universalist frameworks. An alternative starting point is perhaps to suspend theory based on ideology; to undertake further qualitative empirical research drawing on more 'grass roots' approaches to understanding worth and value.

## 3.5.1 A radical alternative

A radical alternative to such frameworks might instead consider dignity as a matter of adherence to a particular set of criteria determined in the process of clarifying one's social identity. Hence returning to Hodson's (1996) focus on autonomy for determining one's own identity, freedom *to* pursue an unknown conception of worth through relations with others (in the workplace or outside of it) portends a restructured view of those criteria which *matter* to dignity. Yet this requires a broader study of people than one which stops at the office door, or at the limits of formal employment. To properly appreciate the relation between work and dignity perhaps requires a much broader conception of 'work' than paid employment, one that explores the relations between individual workers and *their* many different frameworks of dignity.

**NOTES**

1. The concept of meaningful work, for example, is debated as an appropriate one in the context of employment by Ciulla (2012), the relation between dignity and respect is contested and the definition of what might constitute a justifiable reward for specific types of work in a global marketplace is also debated (see Anker et al., 2003).

2. In the original work this would refer to the ethnographer, yet in Hodson's (2001) analysis this also relies upon the interpretation by the coder.

 **REFERENCES**

Ackroyd, S. (2007) 'Dirt, work and dignity', in Bolton, S.C. (ed.), *Dimensions of Dignity at Work*, London: Butterworth-Heinemann.

Anker, R., Chernyshev, I., Egger, P., et al. (2003) 'Measuring decent work with statistical indicators', *International Labour Review*, 142(2), 147–178.

BBC (2013) 'Bangladesh "slave labour" condemned by Pope' BBC News (online) 1 May. Accessed at: http://www.bbc.co.uk/news/world-asia-22370487 (retrieved 8 July 2013).

Bennoune, K. (2007) 'Secularism and human rights', *Columbia Journal of Transnational Law*, 45, 367–426.

Berg, P. and Frost, A.C. (2005) 'Dignity at work for low wage, low skill service workers', *Industrial Relations*, 60(4), 657–683.

Berger, P.L., Berger, B., and Kellner, H. (1974) *The Homeless Mind: Modernization and Consciousness*, Harmondsworth, Middlesex: Pelican Books.

Bielefeldt, H. (2000) '"Western" versus "Islamic" human rights conceptions?: A critique of cultural essentialism in the discussion on human rights', *Political Theory*, 28(1), 90–121.

Bolton, S.C. (2006) *ESRC End of Award Report Dignity in and at Work*. Accessed at: http://www.esrcsocietytoday.ac.uk/ (retrieved 15 April 2010)

Bolton, S.C. (2007) *Dimensions of Dignity at Work*, London: Butterworth-Heinemann.

Brennan, A. and Lo, Y.S. (2007) 'Two conceptions of dignity: Honour and self-determination', in Malpas, J. and Lickiss, N. (eds), *Perspectives on Human Dignity: A Conversation*, Dordrecht, Netherlands: Springer.

Brooks, L. (2010) 'The dignity of labour', *The Guardian* (online) 2 March. Accessed at: http://www.theguardian.com/commentisfree/2010/mar/02/dignity-of-manual-labour (retrieved 8 July 2013).

Browning, N. (2013) 'Palestinian tobacco faces threat from crackdown on black economy', Reuters [online] 20 June. Accessed at: http://uk.reuters.com/article/2013/06/20/us-palestinians-tobacco-idUKBRE95J06H20130620 (retrieved 8 July 2013).

Byars-Winston, A. (2011) 'Broadening sources of dignity and affirmation in work and relationships', *The Counseling Psychologist*, 40(2), 255–267.

Ciulla, J. B. (2012) 'Worthy work and Bowie's Kantian theory of meaningful work', in Arnold, D.G. and Harris, J.D. (eds), *Kantian Business Ethics: Critical Perspectives*, Cheltenham, UK and Northampton, MA, USA: Edward Elgar Publishing.

Cooper, N. and May, C. (2007) 'The informal economy and dignified work', in Bolton, S.C. (ed.), *Dimensions of Dignity at Work*, London: Butterworth-Heinemann.

Cotterrell, R. (2011) 'Justice, dignity, torture, headscarves: Can Durkheim's sociology clarify legal values?', *Social & Legal Studies*, 20(1), 3–20.

Doherty, E.M. (2010) 'Joking aside, insights to employee dignity in "Dilbert" cartoons: The value of comic art in understanding the employer–employee relationship', *Journal of Management Inquiry*, 20(3), 286–301.

Du Gay, P. (1996) *Consumption and Identity at Work*, London: Sage Publications.

Durkheim, E. (1893) *The Division of Labour in Society* (translated 1964), New York: Free Press.

Hill, R.J. (2009) 'Incorporating queers: Blowback, backlash, and other forms of resistance to workplace diversity initiatives that support sexual minorities', *Advances in Developing Human Resources*, 11(1), 37–53.

Hodson, R. (1996) 'Dignity in the workplace under participative management: "Alienation and Freedom" revisited', *American Sociological Review*, 61, 719–738.

Hodson, R. (2001) *Dignity at Work*, Cambridge: Cambridge University Press.

Horton, J. (1964) 'The dehumanization of anomie and alienation: A problem in the ideology of sociology', *The British Journal of Sociology*, 15(4), 283–300.

Ijzerman, H. and Cohen, D. (2011) 'Grounding cultural syndromes: Body comportment and values in honor and dignity cultures', *European Journal of Social Psychology*, 41(4), 456–467.

Kant, I. and Abbot, T.K. (1949) *Fundamental Principles of the Metaphysic of Morals*, New York: Liberal Arts Press.

Kim, Y. and Cohen, D. (2010) 'Information, perspective, and judgments about the self in face and dignity cultures', *Personality and Social Psychology Bulletin*, 36(4), 537–50.

Kuo, L. (2012) 'Obama promises 110,000 new summer jobs for youth' Reuters (online) 3 May. Accessed at: http://uk.reuters.com/article/2012/05/02/us-usa-obama-youth-jobs-idUK-BRE8411NT20120502 (retrieved 8 July 2013).

Lamont, M. (2000) *The Dignity of Working Men*, Cambridge, MA: Harvard University Press.

Leget, C., Borry, P. and De Vries, R. (2009) '"Nobody tosses a dwarf!" The relation between the empirical and the normative reexamined', *Bioethics*, 23(4), 226–235.

Lucas, K. (2011) 'Blue-collar discourses of workplace dignity: Using outgroup comparisons to construct positive identities', *Management Communication Quarterly*, 25(2), 353–374.

Lutgen-Sandvik, P. (2008) 'Intensive remedial identity work: Responses to workplace bullying trauma and stigmatization', *Organization*, 15(1), 97–119.

Lutz, M.A. (1995) 'Centering social economics on human dignity', *Review of Social Economy*, 53(2), 171–194.

Marx, K. (1844) 'Estranged labour', *Economic and Philosophical Manuscripts of 1844*. Accessed at: http://marxists.org/archive/marx/works/1844/manuscripts/labour.htm.

Peyton, P.R. (2003) *Dignity at Work: Eliminate Bullying and Create a Positive Working Environment*, New York: Routledge.

Pico della Mirandola, G. (1486) *Oration on the Dignity of Man*, University of Bologna and Brown University. Accessed at: http://www.brown.edu/Departments/Italian_Studies/pico/text/ov.html (retrieved 13 April 2010)

Pritchard, M.S. (1972) 'Human dignity and justice', *Ethics*, 82(4), 299–313.

Purser, G. (2009) 'The dignity of job-seeking men: Boundary work among immigrant day laborers', *Journal of Contemporary Ethnography*, 38(1), 117–139.

Rayman, P.M. (2001) *Beyond the Bottom Line: The Search for Dignity at Work*, New York: Palgrave.

Riley, S. (2010) 'Human dignity: Comparative and conceptual debates', *International Journal of Law in Context*, 6(2), 117–138.

Rose, N. (1990) *Governing the Soul: The Shaping of the Private Self*, London: Routledge.

Rose, T. (2013) 'Making sure care homes offer excellent service'. Interview by Joseph Rowntree Foundation, published in *The Guardian* (online) June. Accessed at: http://www.theguardian.com/partner-zone-ageing-population/excellent-care-homes (retrieved 8 July 2013).

Rosen, M. (2012) *Dignity: Its History and Meaning*, Cambridge, MA: Harvard University Press.

Sayer, A. (2007) 'Dignity at work: Broadening the agenda', *Organization*, 14(4), 565–581.

Sayer, A. (2011) *Why Things Matter to People: Social Science, Values and Ethical Life*, Cambridge: Cambridge University Press.

Scheff, T.J. (2006) *Goffman Unbound*, London: Paradigm.

Sensen, O. (2011) 'Human dignity in historical perspective: The contemporary and traditional paradigms', *European Journal of Political Theory*, 10(1), 71–91.

Shultziner, D. (2003) 'Human dignity – functions and meanings', *Global Jurist Topics*, 3(3).

United Nations (1948) *Universal Declaration of Human Rights*, New York: General Assembly of the United Nations. Accessed at: http://www.udhr.org/UDHR/default.htm. (retrieved 14 May 2010)

Westwood, A. (2006) *Is New Work Good Work?* London: The Work Foundation.

Whitman, J.Q. (2004) 'The two Western cultures of privacy: Dignity versus liberty', *Yale Law Journal*, 113(6), 1151–1221.

Wierenga, A. (2011) 'Transitions, local culture and human dignity: Rural young men in a changing world', *Journal of Sociology*, 47(4), 371–387.

Woolhead, G., Tadd, W., Boix-Ferrer, J.A., Krajcik, S., Schmid-Pfahler, B., Spjuth, B., Stratton, D., et al. (2006). '"Tu" or "Vous?" A European qualitative study of dignity and communication with older people in health and social care settings', *Patient Education and Counseling*, 61(3), 363–71.

# 4

# Is paternalism still relevant? Changing culture in a mutual UK insurance company

*Darren McCabe and David Knights*

## 4.1 Introduction

The word 'paternalism' is derived from the Latin term *pater*, meaning to act like a father, and in organisations is perhaps best defined as a style of management that seeks to exhibit care over worker interests. To that extent, it is possible to think of paternalism as a management approach that is no longer relevant in the 21st century workplace, as something belonging to 19th century Quaker businesses such as Rowntree's and Clarks. It may, however, return to significance once the current context of fear due to job insecurity subsides, particularly given its historical role in securing employee consent. This chapter draws on a qualitative case study from the UK insurance sector to explore paternalism as part of an emerging cultural context rather than a conscious or intentional strategy of management 'control'. It is argued that because paternalism is diverse and fluid, we cannot simply label it as positive or negative for employees. The case explores how shifting forms of paternalism can lead to an assumption of 'progress' because more obvious hierarchical, class and gender-based inequalities are less evident. To simply assume progress, however, would be to neglect the way in which contemporary ways of managing that echo the concerns of paternalism seek to fabricate consenting subjects: workers who do as they are told.

## 4.2 Perspectives on paternalism

One view of paternalism is that it is dangerous (Warren, 2000 quoted in Warren and Tweedale, 2002: 218) or anachronistic (Ogbonna and Harris, 2001; Phillips et al., 2008). In terms of the latter position, Ogbonna and

Harris (2001) argue that the mention of 'paternalism' in their respondents' 'quotations indicates an anachronistic use of language reminiscent of earlier dynasties' (p. 26). However, in a later article, they argue that there continues to be a paternalistic influence even when family owners 'cede control to' professional managers (Harris and Ogbonna, 2007: 22). By drawing on some data from a case study, our main objective in this chapter is to challenge simplistic assumptions about the 'progressive' or non-progressive nature of paternalism. We argue that insofar as the discourses and practices of paternalism are diverse and fluid, we cannot make universal claims for their positive or negative impact on employees.

In taking this approach, this chapter seeks to make a number of contributions. First, by locating the organisation historically, we argue that paternalism needs to be understood as part of an emerging cultural context rather than a conscious or intentional strategy of management control (Fleming, 2005; Padavic and Earnest, 1994; Wray, 1996). We consider how changing economic and political climates along with the dynamics of consent and resistance may condition but also be conditioned by paternalism. We explore paternalism in terms of its socio-historical and cultural evolution (see Ackers, 1998) and understand culture as something an organisation *is* rather than what an organisation *has* (Smircich, 1983). This follows in the anthropological tradition of culture as 'a process embedded in context' rather than 'an objectified tool of management control' (Wright, 1994: 4).

Second, if, as Anthony (1986) and Wray (1996) have argued, paternalism is not a single unified way of managing, then we need to consider the ways in which paternalism changes or remains constant. So, for example, Child and Smith (1987: 591) have identified how the transformation of a paternalistic employer such as Cadbury 'passed through several stages and did not exhibit a clear beginning or end' (ibid.). Likewise, Beech and Johnson (2005) have explored the tensions that emerge as organisations attempt to move away from paternalistic cultures such that the 'old' and 'new' oscillates back and forth. In our case management represented the organisation as becoming more 'caring'. Moreover, what we describe as paternalistic management was found to co-exist with other managerial practices, some of which could be seen to conflict with the ostensibly paternal approach. This highlights the tensions and ambiguities between competing management models that many 'mutual' organisations are currently facing (see He and Baruch, 2010: 57).

Our third contribution is to argue that paternalism is not necessarily the negative experience for employees that some have assumed, for example,

Fleming (2005a) has pointed to a worrying development where employers are creating a 'culture of fun' (p. 285) that 'resembles a happy family'
(p. 294). He reports that a number of employees expressed that they were
being 'treated like a child' (p. 295) because 'the school and kindergarten
environment gave management a rather patronising and mawkishly paternalistic flavour' (ibid.). By contrast, we explore a form of paternalism that
was moving away from treating employees in patronising ways; although, we
recognise that this can still be seen as a form of control. Consequently, we do
not argue that paternalism and management control are unconnected but
that we need to avoid viewing it as simply negative or positive for employees.

The chapter is organised as follows. The first section discusses the research
methods and in the second section we present our case study. In the final
section we draw out the implications of the case study before offering some
overall concluding comments.

## 4.3   The methods and methodology

Our concern in conducting this research was to generally immerse ourselves in the culture of the organisation, and we believe that this more
open approach towards research has the benefit of illuminating aspects of
paternalism that may not have been previously considered. In presenting
detailed qualitative material there has to be a degree of selectivity and so
the focus here is on supervisors and their interpretation of the organisation.
This is useful because as Ackers (2001) notes 'supervisors have often played
a central role in the reproduction of paternalism' (p. 378). The research
involved semi-structured, tape-recorded interviews, observational research
during service circle meetings and documentary investigation. Taking a vertical slice through the organisation, over 50 different grade staff, 8 deputy
supervisors, 10 supervisors, 4 assistant managers, 4 deputy managers, 2
departmental managers and the training, IT and personnel managers were
interviewed for at least 45 minutes each.

During the interviews, each participant was asked to reflect on the major
changes that they have observed, and what it was like to work at Sovereign
Insurance or hereafter SI (pseudonym). Copious notes were written during
the interviews so as to identify themes, issues, ideas, enigmas, patterns and
further questions to ask. Analysis began immediately and involved identifying key words, writing notes and expanded notes as ideas emerged and
connections were made. The focus was on 'meaning, not frequency' (Van
Maanen, 1979: 520) and so quotations have been selected in order to illustrate the complexity and ambiguity of paternalism.

## 4.4   The case study

There is a long history of paternalistic modes of management in UK financial services connected with owner management, mutual and co-operative forms of organisation (see Kerfoot and Knights, 1993; Morgan and Sturdy, 2000). Over the last 25 years, the financial sector has gone through a transformation and yet many mutuals survive where, as one manager put it, the word 'family comes to mind' (He and Baruch, 2010: 55). Sovereign Insurance has a 'no compulsory redundancies' agreement and provides other paternalistic policies that include a free staff and management restaurant, free coffee and drink machines, free parking, sports and recreation facilities. It recognises a trade union but, in common with paternalistic employers (see Greene et al., 2001: 215), historically there have been few disputes.

Consistent with maintaining the image of a 'respectable institution', managers have made 'a virtue of stability, security and moderation' (Morgan and Sturdy, 2000: 64), so that as Joan, a supervisor on the policy issues section remarked, SI is 'not one of life's forerunners'. She explained that SI portrays an image of being 'solid and dependable' but this does not mean that there has been an absence of change. Indeed, over the years, SI has embarked on various re-organisations and has reengineered business processes. A general program of modernisation has addressed some of the hierarchical, departmental, sectional, class and gender-based divisions.

The deregulation of UK Financial Services through the Financial Services Act in 1986 stimulated increased competition between the hitherto separate spheres of banking, mortgage provision and insurance. In this context, SI entered the market for pensions but avoided expanding into estate agencies. The widespread use of Direct Debit threatened its core business of selling insurance through the local collection of insurance premiums and these external changes brought with them a pressure for change. In particular, it was recognised that service quality needed to improve and IT facilities needed updating. In addition, the appointment of a new Administration General Manager paved the way for change, leading to the restructuring of administration into separate life and non-life insurance departments.

## 4.5 Moving to and from paternalism

### 4.5.1 Diminishing authoritarian paternalism

At the heart of paternalism is a contradiction between the trust and intimacy indicative of a community based on consensual family relations and the coercion, inequality and discipline that underpin corporate relations. This means that the 'caring' face of paternalism may not always be on show:

> **John (Underwriting Supervisor)**: You were actually sat, like you used to be in school, in regimental rows. I 'ad somebody directly in front of me, somebody behind and there was like an aisle in the middle. You go on a section it's not like that now.
> **Darren**: Was it like you couldn't talk to each other or . . .
> **John**: Definitely things like that. When I say you couldn't talk, course we used to have a laugh and everything. But I would say it's more stricter than it is now.
> **Darren**: And how did they treat you?
> **John**: My supervisor was OK, I've got no qualms about my first supervisor, Mr Pollard. Probably a bit old fashioned, you know, because of the age difference. He got one or two of the girls crying with his attitude. You know, telling them off about things.

These comments suggest that a paternal parent–child relationship once prevailed between supervisors and staff and this was evident in the physical layout of the office. It seems that women were on the receiving end of abrasive masculine supervisors:

> I remember, not long after I started, when erm, one of the girls who sat in the same row as me had just turned her chair around a little bit and she was just speaking to the girl behind her. I remember the supervisor bawling across the section: 'Julie, Julie, JULIE do you want me to turn your desk round to face the other bloody way?' And she spun round and head down you know? And you couldn't imagine that sort of thing happening now. It's a completely different atmosphere. (Jed, Fire and Accident Supervisor)

Both Jed and John drew on their memories of a more formal, hierarchical, class- and gender-divided culture to convey how things have changed:

> I can remember being asked by my manager because I was married. He actually asked me what was my intentions with regard to having children and I knew why he was asking me. You wouldn't do that today. Erm, because if I had said 'Well yes I

intend having some'. That would have been it for promotion at that time. I think they thought that you're there to do menial jobs not a career. (Carole, Domain Supervisor)

This extract is indicative of discrimination, however, it seems that legislative and office layout changes have contributed to a culture change. This has benefited women even though the senior management ranks continue to be dominated by men:

> **Joan (Policy Issues Supervisor):** My first supervisors meeting I was the only woman supervisor . . . now I would think it's 50–50.
> **Darren:** Is that different?
> **Joan:** That's certainly different, because when I first started here, you could have counted on your hand how many women supervisors there were. It's certainly been a big change from the fact that women are now allowed to move on. You were allowed to get up to a certain grade in here and then you were considered maybe not quite right. Because, you know, well the little woman has these problems at home and things.

The paternalistic culture was wedded to gender and hierarchical inequalities that were once the norm in UK financial services (see Kerfoot and Knights, 1993). This was not so much an intentional 'system of control' (Fox, 1985: 3; in Greene et al., 2001: 231) but a culture that the staff, supervisors and managers all contributed to and reproduced, albeit in different ways. According to Margaret, a Commercial Supervisor, the metaphor of a classroom encapsulated the earlier culture:

> To be honest, when I first started, it seemed to be like school. You didn't seem to have a proper job. You weren't given any responsibility erm you just sort of sit there. You never had any direction, you never had any proper training or anything structured like it is now and you never really got to speak to anybody like a supervisor or even an assistant. Yer just sort of shoved under the carpet sort of thing.

Margaret's comments confirm that the earlier paternalism regarded the staff as children, for 'in them days it seemed to be that you was sort of protected by everybody, you know, you couldn't sort of go an' speak to them type thing'. As Kerfoot and Knights (1993) found in their case study of a bank, the staff were treated as if they 'could not be trusted' and they were shielded from 'decision-making responsibility' (p. 668). Although it may appear to be the case that protecting the staff is 'caring', it is also coercive and 'patronising', as Fleming (2005a) contends. Indeed, Fleming's (2005a) research is worrying because the 'culture of fun' he describes appears to be going back to the type of regime that these supervisors first experienced when they began working for SI, which was an affront to their 'dignity and self-respect' (p. 299; see also Mitchell, Chapter 3 this volume). Jed reflected on the change of approach in a way that conveys how class and hierarchical divisions have begun to be challenged:

> After I had been here about 18 months, I got me first promotion . . . and the manager at the time called me in and said 'We're putting you up a grade' . . . and he leaned across the desk and he says 'You must remember now that you're not one of the boys anymore'. I think nowadays the emphasis is very much on the supervisors getting involved in things like the Christmas night out, and try and encourage a sort of team atmosphere, so the supervisors are much more approachable. When I first started, it was very much a case of you didn't speak to the supervisor unless you were spoken to and sort of the merest appearance of the manager walking through the Department was enough to get everybody er, 'What's going on? What's happening?' You know? 'Sit up straight' and it's just not like that at all nowadays. (Jed, Fire and Accident Supervisor)

As Jed's anecdote reveals, those who sought promotion within the 'older' culture were required to imbibe a hierarchical, middle-class, masculine identity that generated distance between supervisors and staff. This was part of the culture rather than an intentional strategy of management control. He explained that a working class identity of being 'one of the boys' or 'lads' (see Willis, 1977), had to be left behind by those with career aspirations.

Elaine, a Commercial Supervisor, felt that the emphasis on gaining qualifications has contributed to a new approach that can be associated with professionalisation. This had allowed younger people, rather than only those with long service, to climb the SI hierarchy. Explaining the identity shift that individuals once went through following promotion, she commented: 'They were one of the boys sort of on Friday and on Monday they came in as supervisors' and this hierarchical, gendered and class-based culture was passed from one generation to the next.

In contrast to many paternalistic employers (see Greene et al., 2001), managers were unknown, distant figures and many supervisors continued to refer to even departmental managers as Mr A or B, suggesting a subjectivity 'of obedience and deference' (Wager, 1987: 48; in Ackers and Black, 1991: 3). Nevertheless, Elaine underlined the sense in which managers have become more informal and visible:

> **Darren**: How do you think staff and management get on and got on?
> **Elaine (Commercial Supervisor)**: Got on? Erm, I don't think the staff were aware of the management before. They just knew that Mr B was their manager and they didn't really have anything to do with him. He was sort of sat on this piece of carpet on the floor, and if he was another grade up, he would have a screen round him and things like that. And he always went to the supervisor, and he didn't really, in my opinion, he didn't really pass any comments or anything like that with any particular members of staff, unless it was to reprimand them or tell them that they've done something wrong, and now I think that management are more involved and they're keeping us up to date, more approachable.

The sense that managers were becoming more informal, personal, communicative, visible, open and team-based, fits with a more caring, communal, family type culture, where individuals know one another. Yet it also fits with a more modern style of management. Sports and social clubs are often a feature of paternalistic organisations (see Joyce, 1980). They provide an opportunity for employees to interact outside of work and promote a sense of community. At SI, a Sports and Social club provides snooker tables and sunbed facilities. It was set up over 50 years ago when the Head Office (H.O.) was first built. Lee, a Quotations Supervisor, reminisced about these facilities in a way that suggests that some aspects of paternalism, at least for him, have diminished:

> **Lee**: We used to do a lot. They've got a dance hall on the fifth floor there.
> **Darren**: Have they?
> **Lee**: Yer, ballroom like, so we used to have discos and things there, regular, every week. A disco in the basement where there's the Sports and Social. The staff used to get together a lot more playing pool, snooker, downstairs. Now I feel like that side of it is not the same as it used to be. Whether it's me getting older? Perhaps the young one's still do that.

Lee pointed out that he was less involved with the social side of work due to his age and hierarchical position. We had already heard above that in becoming a supervisor, one has to give up being 'one of the boys' and this may help to explain Lee's distance. The works 'disco' that Lee remembers has long since fallen out of favour reflecting perhaps the shift towards a more individualised society. We can see that internal and external factors impact on paternalism and different individuals experience it in different ways.

Although a sense of community is promoted through paternalism via social events, it should not be romanticised, as being indicative of a golden era of collectivism. In-house football teams, for example, reflected and reinforced divisions between groups of staff:

> **Darren**: Were there tensions between the sections before?
>
> **Jed (Fire and Accident Supervisor)**: Oh yer, yer. You didn't speak [laughter]. Especially when I first started . . . there were a few lads on the fire sections . . . And you soon got the message that people on the other sections that you just didn't speak to. There was a great sort of rivalry. Played football against them, you know.
>
> **Darren**: Did that hinder work in any way, I mean is there an element of work overlap.
>
> **Jed**: Well yes the work does overlap . . . If you get something in your post that's for a section that's next to yer. Nowadays, I think people are more inclined to just walk over with it, whereas in the past, you just put it back in the post and readdressed it.

Jed's reflections highlight how the staff learned, or 'soon got the message', that they should not communicate with other sections. In this way boundaries between the staff were culturally rather than simply hierarchically established and reproduced. It appears that class-based antagonisms were diffused through intersectional rivalries especially between 'the lads' (see Willis, 1977), who displayed a masculine aggressiveness toward each other whilst playing football. As Wolfram-Cox (2001) puts it 'the lateralization of conflict among employee groups may overshadow vertical employer-employee conflict' (p. 181) and this applied to sectional as well as gendered conflicts. The earlier culture provided a training ground for discourses of macho masculinity and the staff weaved themselves and each other into this culture that took on and reproduced its own dynamics.

This section has explored some of the hierarchical, class, sectional and gender-based inequalities that characterised the earlier, more autocratic, form of paternalism. As we have seen, paternalism is an embedded part of the corporate culture and perpetuated numerous divisions. It is a contradictory regime because it 'partitioned' (Foucault, 1977) the workforce through creating numerous divisions and yet reproduced shared ways of understanding. Although paternalism protected the staff from decision-making and showed signs of 'caring' for them through a no-compulsory redundancy agreement and sports and recreation facilities, coercion often bubbled to the surface, when male supervisors disciplined or patronised women. Rather than simply a 'tool of management' (Wray, 1996: 701), this culture was learned and passed on by managers, supervisors and staff. We will now turn to the more recent 'caring' form of paternalism, arguing that it nonetheless retains coercive features.

## 4.6    A regime shift

> They are fair and understanding and it really is just like a family situation . . .
> as soon as the representatives of the Society know you've got a crisis they'll
> do anything that they can to help. They've got a medical section, a medical
> department, so if you're not feeling well, straight up to medical department and
> you know that they'll take care of you. (Elaine Weber, Commercial Supervisor)

In common with other mutual organisations (He and Baruch, 2010: 55),
Elaine described SI as a 'family' and she felt 'looked after' but expressed that
this sense of family was not evident when she first arrived due to the 'them
and us attitude with the management'. This contrasts with O'Leary's (2003)
case where there was an 'erosion of the family atmosphere . . . due to the
move towards a more profit-focused organization' (p. 689). Elaine's positive representation of the organisation also contrasts with Fleming's (2005a)
arguments which link the promotion of familial relations to a patronising
situation in which managers assume 'the role of a father figure' (p. 294).

As in many paternalistic companies, there are long-serving staff who met
their partner at SI or who have relatives in the company (see Greene et al.,
2001). In this way the company becomes a family or a community in more
ways than one and it facilitates the transmission of culture from one generation to the next (see Ackers and Black, 1991: 41):

> **Darren**: So your wife works here?
> **Lee (Quotations Supervisor)**: Wife works here yer.
> **Darren**: Did you meet her here?
> **Lee**: Yes, met here.
> **Darren**: Is that something that's common?
> **Lee**: Oh yer, very much so yer, if not girlfriends, you know people courting. It's
> er, yes quite a few have wives here, that work here and nowadays children coming.
> You know, there's whole families work here.

Joan, a Policy Issues Supervisor, asserted that appraisals and greater open-
ness, have contributed to a more caring approach: 'It's people having that
contact with you on a one to one basis which previously they never had . . .
there are quite a few people that have been helped in various ways . . . they
[management] can be very supportive'.

The management has introduced a free evening meal plus a night's hotel
accommodation for employees with 25 years of service. The event is held in
the ballroom at SI's H.O. with transport provided for the staff to and from

their hotel. Such public events are consistent with a concern to foster loyalty towards the company and the staff also have the choice of a gold watch or a canteen of cutlery as a reward for their 25 years of service. According to Jed, this is 'a concrete gesture' that SI 'care about the staff' (see also He and Baruch, 2010).

Irrespective of such endeavours, there are cracks in the new 'caring' narrative and hierarchical and class-based inequalities remain. An enduring symbol of which is the separate staff and management restaurant. The staff canteen is located in the basement of the H.O., whereas the heavily male-populated management restaurant is situated towards the top of the building. Supervisors are denied access to the management restaurant and Sue, an Endorsements Supervisor, considered this unnecessary:

> To be honest with you, I can't understand why we've got two restaurants, because there's nothing wrong with the restaurant that we've got downstairs. I think even if I was allowed to go upstairs, I wouldn't want to do it anyway. I am quite happy to go downstairs for my meals . . . We're all doing a job so why not treat us all the same?

Sue clearly resented this glaring symbol of inequality, which contradicts the more recent caring discourse of free meals, long-service awards and support. The remnants of a 'master–servant' relationship is evident in these 'Upstairs' and 'Downstairs' restaurants that punches through any pretence of equality and so, in contrast to other studies, it cannot be said in this instance that 'adopting a paternal role helps legitimise managerial prerogative' (Kerfoot and Knights, 1993: 665).

We visited the management restaurant on a number of occasions during the fieldwork when we were treated to a free lunch by senior male managers. The grandeur and elitism of hierarchy was on display during these visits. Along with waiter service, diners enjoy panoramic views of the surrounding city. All the rituals of an upmarket eating establishment are apparent and it is literally possible to look down on the mortals below. It feels as if one has entered an old-fashioned 'Gentleman's Club' and this conveys a very different sense of being 'one of the boys'.

Both restaurants provide free meals and, according to those interviewed, this can be traced back to the Income Policies of Harold Wilson and James Callaghan's Labour Governments (1974–1979). Thus, following the call for wage restraint, free meals were provided instead of a pay increase. We can observe therefore that 'structures of and behaviour in present organisations reflect culture-specific historical developments' (Kieser, 1994: 609). Various paternalistic policies have developed for different reasons but history is being re-written so as to convey an apparently new approach. For example, information packs are sent out to job applicants informing them of certain practices in a way that seeks to procure employee loyalty whilst rubbing out their history:

> The Personnel Department now send them [new recruits] a package out explaining all about SI and that, so you're not taking a lot of the interview time up. In this package it tells them about yer get free meals, car park, tea, coffee, flexitime and that. So that when they get here they want to come and work for this firm because they feel that SI looks after the staff. And they do really. (Sue, Endorsements Supervisor)

The policy of free drinks, like the free meals, did not begin as managerial largesse but reflected the specific circumstances of Edward Heath's Conservative government (1970–1973), when strikes by miners led to a 'three-day week':

> SI kept going 5 days a week but they were on reduced power, reduced lighting and no heating and they moved all the desks on every floor as near to the window as they could. And it was bloody freezing in the building and they made the vending machines all free just as a gesture. They knew that people were cold and a hot drink would keep them going and they left it free after that. (Jed, Fire and Accident Supervisor)

Like the free meals, the free drinks reflect external and internal antagonisms, rather than a more caring management approach. It also reflects operational priorities in that management wanted to ensure that the staff continued to work. Yet management represents these policies as examples of a caring approach to current and prospective employees, which obscures their origin and presents an intention that was not evident when they first were instigated:

> **Jed (Fire and Accident Supervisor)**: Nowadays I think most people appreciate that, well most people gain the impression that SI cares a lot more about its employees, than it used to. This is what we're told constantly.
> **Darren**: What that we care more?
> **Jed**: Oh yes. I mean they tell you this. . . . We've been to seminars and workshops. I admit it's mostly the supervisors that go and it's passed on, but one thing that you're constantly told now is that the staff are important.

Jed explained that a caring approach is promoted during management-only seminars. The socialisation of new and current staff aims to re-write the past and reconstitute staff subjectivity. Nevertheless, irrespective of their origin, Lee felt that the staff welcome these policies and hence they communicate them to friends and relatives in a positive way:

> In interview, 9 times out of 10 you'll say 'Why did you think of coming to work for SI?' Oh me friend works, or me auntie works here and she's told us how good the meals are and what a nice place to work for. (Lee, Quotations Supervisor)

In Greene et al.'s (2001: 225) case 'the existence of family networks and long service' was regarded by management as 'incestuous' and a 'force for stasis' (ibid.) but, at SI, it represented a positive feature of the company. Another example of paternalism is the free car parking facilities, which, in an expensive city centre, provides a considerable financial saving. Privilege is intertwined with this policy because only managers are guaranteed a place in the car park that is nearest to the Head Office. Moreover, hierarchical inequalities are reproduced through the waiting list for as Sue explained:

> Certain people at different levels, if they come in they'll jump the queue, which again I don't think is right. If you've worked here 10 years and you are number two on that list . . . because he's an official [manager], he gets your space, I think that's a little bit naughty. (Endorsements Supervisor)

Although paternalism may seek 'to generate a relation of trust through the pretence of equality' (Kerfoot and Knights, 1993: 670), the inequity of these policies contradicts this pretence. This ostensibly caring form of paternalism endeavours to promote consensus and yet whilst earlier inequalities are breaking down, others endure and are reproduced. Some of the more patronising aspects of the earlier paternalism appear to be fading even as others surface. The 'school or family situation' (Fleming, 2005: 1478), where 'employees are cast as naïve children and supervisors as paternal figures who know what is right for workers' (p. 1479) is being challenged but only in part:

> They're not so heavy handed as they used to be. It used to be a case of you will do as I say. They're now open to the fact of saying 'Well let's see things that are coming up from the other end'. Instead of it always being down, everything went down, now things are being fed up. (Joan Evans, Policy Issues Supervisor)

## 4.7    Discussion and conclusion

According to Joyce (1980), 'It was the personal embodiment in the family or the family head that gave paternalism its cutting edge' (p. 136). Warren (1999) makes a similar point that 'the company board are the parents and the employees are the children' (p. 54). In SI, by contrast, paternalism is not embodied in a single person or family but much more in the institution and culture. Paternalism has been shaped by policies authorised by senior management but the relationship between employees–supervisors–departmental managers plays a significant role in shaping the culture on the office floor. The culture has changed in-line with a shift towards a more caring form of paternalism at least according to these supervisors. These insights endorse the view that paternalism is not necessarily incompatible with contemporary ways of managing (Black and Ackers, 1988).

In this chapter, we have argued that the literature which represents paternalism as an intentional strategy of management control, or as wholly negative in its effects, is problematic. To understand paternalism in such deterministic fashion neglects the cultural context in which it is located and this is often precarious, shifting and unstable. In our case study, we observed paternalism mutating but this was often a function of serendipity rather than planned change. Padavic and Earnest (1994) view paternalism as 'a regulatory discourse that dampens and contains dissonant experiences, not an absolute one that prevents them from being registered as experience at all' (p. 7). Similarly, Fleming (2005) highlights instances of resistance and in so doing, modifies the degree of determinism within his thesis but he does not go so far as to explore how paternalism itself may change in and through its embeddedness in corporate cultures, as we have attempted here.

Paternalism, for us, is not simply done to others by a benevolent or patronising corporate owner/manager but is part of a culture that is learned, shared, contested, maintained and reproduced at every level of the organisation. Padavic and Earnest (1994) are sensitive to such possibilities for they explore how employees, once helped by a paternalistic employer 'seemed to feel obligated to demonstrate a sense of gratitude' (p. 7). In such instances, employees exercise power in ways that help to reproduce extant inequalities. Nevertheless, this also indicates that paternalism is not simply control from above and it can be traced, at least in part, to conditions that reflect external and internal struggles. The paternalistic approach at SI is, therefore, at least partly an unintended consequence of these conditions.

We have considered how supervisors were expected to absorb and secrete a paternalistic culture as they gained promotion. This is not a static or a top-down process but fluid and shifting. It is bound up with gender and class-based inequalities that are changing even as inequalities are reproduced. Yet individuals are not passive vessels of culture such that management can fill them with compliant ways of thinking. The supervisors in this case were aware of gender and hierarchical inequalities, which they resented. If we think in terms of everyone acting in ways that produce and change culture, rather than in terms of top management controlling culture, then it becomes possible to envisage culture changing in ways that are not simply directed from above. This is a more unsettling way of understanding culture that allows for greater possibilities of change. It does not rely on identifying instances of resistance against an otherwise immutable culture, but seeks to understand culture as a product of everyone's actions and subjectivity that can, therefore, be otherwise. It is to understand individuals as 'embedded in, rather than enveloped or determined by, these social contexts' (Morgan and Sturdy, 2000: 257).

It has to be recognised that even the more 'caring' form of paternalism that has been identified here is bound up with control. Aspects of inequality went underground in the sense of its more obvious signposts but through ameliorating the more blatant disparities between managers and workers, extant inequalities were reproduced. To adapt the arguments of Paulo Freire (1970), paternalism embodies a 'false generosity' that 'makes of the oppressed the objects of its humanitarianism' (p. 36). Although less coercive than the crack of the whip, paternalism, therefore, helps to maintain the status quo. It calls for gratitude 'towards the "generous gestures" of the dominant class' (p. 41). This 'generosity is nourished by an unjust order, which must be maintained in order to justify that generosity' (p. 42). Nevertheless, in this study, we can observe the form of oppression changing and if it can change then it can continue to do so.

Although paternalism reinforces extant power relations and inequalities, we have argued that it is a mistake to simply dismiss it as patronising, not least because paternalism takes different forms (see Ackers and Black, 1991; Wray, 1996). We have observed the corporate approach moving from what Gabriel (1999) describes as the space occupied by 'the terrifying primal father' to that of the 'omnibenevolent primal mother' (p. 190). It would be erroneous, however, to regard these two faces of paternalism as polarised because they can coexist within the same organisation. They also may shift in relation to different socio-economic and cultural climates and in terms of their relative impact on the organisation and its members.

To conclude, a number of writers have theorised paternalism as a singular and negative means to control employees. By contrast, we believe that paternalism is not necessarily an end product but part of an unfolding culture that is forged through contested and consensual relations. We have observed how paternalism can take different forms that are not equally negative for employees. Consent can be generated through different types of paternalistic regime but this does not mean that resistance is displaced or that control/coercion is absent. Our argument is that paternalism should not simply be welcomed because it is bound up with sustaining and reproducing unequal relations, albeit not necessarily in an entirely intentional or negative way. However, neither should it be summarily dismissed since the fluid dynamics of its operation mean that its impact on employees can change. An important question for future research is whether the remnants of a 'caring' paternalism can survive in an age of austerity and whether employers can afford to abandon it entirely given the loss of consent that this might engender.

 **REFERENCES**

Ackers, P. (1998) 'Review essay: On paternalism: Seven observations on the uses and abuses of the concept in industrial relations, past and present', *Historical Studies in Industrial Relations*, 5, 173–193.

Ackers, P. (2001) 'Paternalism, participation and partnership: Rethinking the employment relationship', *Human Relations*, 54(3), 373–384.

Ackers, P. and Black, J. (1991) 'Paternalist capitalism: An organization culture in transition' in Cross, M. and Payne, G. (eds), *Work and the Enterprise Culture*, London: Falmer Press.

Anthony, P.D. (1986) *The Foundation of Management*, London: Tavistock.

Beech, N. and Johnson, P. (2005) 'Discourses of disrupted identities in the practice of strategic change: The mayor, the street-fighter and the insider-out', *Journal of Organizational Change Management*, 18(1), 31–47.

Black, J. and Ackers, P. (1988) 'The Japanization of British industry? A case study of quality circles in the carpet industry', *Employee Relations*, 10, 9–16.

Child, J. and Smith, C. (1987) 'The context and process of organizational transformation – Cadbury Limited in its sector', *Journal of Management Studies*, 24(6), 565–593.

Fleming, P. (2005) '"Kindergarten cop": Paternalism and resistance in a high-commitment workplace', *Journal of Management Studies*, 42(7), 1469–1489.

Fleming, P. (2005a) 'Workers' playtime? Boundaries and cynicism in a "Culture of Fun" program', *The Journal of Applied Behavioural Science*, 41(3), 285–303.

Foucault, M. (1977) *Discipline and Punish*, Harmondsworth: Penguin.

Fox, A. (1985) *History and Heritage: The Social Origins of the British Industrial Relations System*, London: Allen and Unwin.

Freire, P. (1970/1996) *Pedagogy of the Oppressed*, London: Penguin Books

Gabriel, Y. (1999) 'Beyond happy families: a critical reevaluation of the control–resistance–identity triangle', *Human Relations*, 52(2), 179–203.

Greene, A., Ackers, P. and Black, J. (2001) 'Lost narratives? From paternalism to team-working in a lock manufacturing firm', *Economic and Industrial Democracy*, 22, 211–237.

Harris, L.C. and Ogbonna, E. (2007) 'Ownership and control in closely-held family-owned firms: An exploration of strategic and operational control', *British Journal of Management*, 18, 5–26.

He, H. and Baruch, Y. (2010) 'Organizational identity and legitimacy under major environmental changes: Tales of two UK building societies', *British Journal of Management*, 21, 44–62.

Joyce, P. (1980) *Work, Society and Politics: The Culture of the Factory in Late Victorian England*, Brighton: Harvester.

Kerfoot, D. and Knights, D. (1993) 'Management, masculinity and manipulation: From paternalism to corporate strategy in Britain', *Journal of Management Studies*, 30(4), 659–678.

Kieser, A. (1994) 'Why organization theory needs historical analysis – and how this should be performed', *Organization Science*, 5(4), 608–620.

Morgan, G. and Sturdy, A. (2000) *Beyond Organizational Change*, London: Macmillan.

Ogbonna, E. and Harris, L.C. (2001) 'The founder's legacy: Hangover or inheritance?', *British Journal of Management*, 12, 13–31.

O'Leary, M. (2003) 'From paternalism to cynicism: Narratives of a newspaper company', *Human Relations*, 56(6), 685–704.

Padavic, I. and Earnest, W.R. (1994) 'Paternalism as a component of managerial strategy', *The Social Science Journal*, 31(4), 389–405.

Phillips, N., Sewell, G. and Jaynes, S. (2008) 'Applying critical discourse analysis in strategic management research', *Organizational Research Methods*, 11(4), 770–789.

Smircich, L. (1983) 'Concepts of culture and organizational analysis', *Administrative Science Quarterly*, 28(3), 339–358.

Van Maanen, J. (1979) 'Reclaiming qualitative methods for organizational research: A preface', *Administrative Science Quarterly*, 24, 520–526.

Warren, R.C. (1999) 'Against paternalism in Human Resource Management', *Business Ethics: A European Review*, 8(1), 50–59.

Warren, R.C. (2000) *Corporate Governance and Accountability*, Liverpool: Liverpool Academic Press.

Warren R. and Tweedale, G. (2002) 'Business ethics and business history: Neglected dimensions in management education', *British Journal of Management*, 13, 209–219.

Willis, P. (1977) *Learning to Labour*, London: Saxon House.

Wolfram-Cox, J. (2001) 'Remembrance of things past? Change, development and paternalism', *Journal of Organizational Change Management*, 14(2), 168–189.

Wray, D. (1996) 'Paternalism and its discontents: A case study', *Work, Employment and Society*, 10(4), 701–715.

Wright, S. (1994) 'Introduction', in Wright, S. (ed.), *Anthropology of Organizations*, London: Routledge.

# 5

# Youth employment, masculinity and policy

*Teresa Oultram*

## 5.1  Introduction

The ways in which young people make the transition from school or college to work are important not least because decisions made at this time often have long-term implications through the person's life-course. According to Mills and Blossfield (2005) this transition is made more difficult due to increased uncertainty within contemporary society. They claim that globalisation and technical change have led to increased complexity and the generation of unprecedented levels of uncertainty for societies, which impacts on how organisations operate and, thus, impacts on individuals within the labour market. For young people, this uncertainty is even more challenging as they tend to lack experience and social networks, which help to smooth transitions within the labour market.

In response to the unpredictable future, government policy for education and training in England places great emphasis on ensuring that employees (and future employees) not only have the skills for employment for the short-term but also have the capability to be 'effective workers' long-term. There is an assumption that workers will change jobs, and possibly vocations, multiple times during their working life. This has led to a focus on more generic, transferable skills which are understood to help employees to be flexible in terms of the types of occupations they can enter, enabling workers to move from one job or industry to another as demand for work changes.

In this chapter, I will examine how the apprenticeship, a traditional form of initial workplace learning, has been appropriated by the UK government to socialise young people into adopting particular desirable behaviours which promote worker flexibility as normal and desirable. Building on ideas by Foucault (1983; 1984; 1986; 1991) and Rose (1996; 1999a; 1999b), I claim that the apprenticeship is not just a training scheme to learn the skills of the job, but a mechanism to socialise young people into becoming enterprising workers and citizens.

The chapter will begin with a discussion of 'enterprising' and flexible workers and examine how this discourse fits with the wider aims of neo-liberal government policy. These ideas will then be explored through the example of youth transition from school to work, focusing on apprenticeship schemes. Finally, using a case study of young male apprentices, I will challenge the idea that enterprise discourse is totalising by considering alternative notions of being a worker.

## 5.2 Enterprising and flexible workers: A lifelong commitment to the capitalist agenda

In Britain, along with many other Western cultures, the late 20th century saw a move towards neo-liberalism, or advanced liberalism (Miller and Rose, 2008) whereby government began to change its relation to the state, with a reduction in the emphasis of the welfare state. In its place, free market competition was to be encouraged in all aspects of life, including previously state controlled functions, such as education and health. This has been portrayed as providing choice and power to citizens, allowing the individual more freedom about the decisions affecting his or her life. But along with choice comes responsibility, as emphasis is now placed on the individual (Burchell, 1996) who is 'compelled to assume market-based values in *all* of their judgements and practices' (Hamann, 2009: 38). According to Foucault (1984), this puts the onus of responsibility for societal issues onto the individual and positions the individual into having to behave in particular ways, thus 'everything would be controlled to the point of self-sustenance, without the need for intervention' (Foucault, 1984: 241).

Foucault believed that under the right conditions, and with support, individuals could be persuaded to act in desired ways, not through laws and formal powers but through activation of their desires. Thus, working through 'the promotion of subjectivities, the construction of pleasures and ambitions, and the activation of guilt, anxiety, envy and disappointment' (Rose, 1999a: 213), the individual as homo œconomicus ('an entrepreneur of himself', Foucault, 1991: 225) will work on him/herself to achieve personal fulfilment, whilst minimising the cost to the state (Tuschling and Angemann, 2006). Within capitalist society, success, prestige and status are typically associated with our productive ability, namely, 'by how much we earn' (Nesbit, 2005: 6). Thus, being a 'good citizen' now appears to translate into being an enterprising-self, who is aspirational, self-developing, self-motivating and self-regulating (Garrick and Usher, 2000) in pursuit of the capitalist agenda.

Fundamental to ensuring that individuals adopt the principles of an enterprising self is that it seems 'natural' (Keat, 1991), the foundation of being an autonomous and free citizen (Gallagher, 2008). Yet the notion of an enterprising self, rather than being a natural concept, is an ideological political discourse which provides norms for thoughts and actions, influencing how we understand ourselves and therefore ultimately how we behave and act (Rose, 1996; Garsten and Jacobsson, 2004). The freedom being offered is not a natural state of human beings, but is linked to self-governing behaviour (Simons and Masschelein, 2006). These discourses of enterprise and the free citizen are artificially arranged, requiring certain technologies and mechanisms to maintain and embed them as *natural* practices (Burchell, 1996). For example, normalising discourses render certain behaviours (being entrepreneurial, autonomous, risk aware, prudential, responsible) as desirable, whilst casting others (being unemployed, failing to improve oneself, engaging in risky activities) as problematic (Fenwick, 2002a).

We learn to become socialised into accepting and maintaining these discourses, internalising them as 'truths', within institutions such as the school, the workplace, the training facility and the prison (Foucault, 1983). Such spaces carefully socialise the individual (Lambier, 2005), attempting to construct representations of 'reality' which guide an individual on how to behave and respond appropriately (Rose, 1999a). As ideas become normalised, they become taken-for-granted and internalised as the only acceptable way of behaving (Dean, 1999; Garsten and Jacobsson, 2004). Thus, the danger of this pressure for individuals to focus on purely capitalist agendas leaves very little space for alternative ways of living (Rose, 1999a; Taylor, 1989; see also Mangan, Chapter 12 this volume).

Within enterprising discourse, responsibility is increasingly being placed on the individual to engage proactively with lifelong learning. Originally lifelong learning was portrayed as an emancipatory discourse (Garsten and Jacobsson, 2004), but according to a number of writers (Coffield, 1999; Garrick and Usher, 2000; Rose, 1999b) it has been appropriated as a mechanism of social control aimed at making workers more flexible and employable. From this perspective, individuals are expected not only to be productive workers but also to ensure that they develop themselves in anticipation of the changing demands of the workplace (Coffield, 1999). The enterprising self and lifelong learning discourses are eternally optimistic, always offering the potential to keep on developing, keep on improving, with individuals 'required to engage in a ceaseless work of training and retraining, skilling and re-skilling, enhancement of credentials' (Rose, 1999b: 161), to remain desirable in an uncertain capitalist system. Therefore, there can be no ultimate success and as there will always be more learning and development required until the end of life, the enterprising worker/citizen can be understood as something that is always in the making rather than as something to be achieved. Or as Ulrich and Verne (1976, as cited in Coffield, 1999: 489) argue, it is 'a guarantee of our permanent inadequacy'.

The individual, throughout life, is therefore expected to adapt and upgrade his or her skills and abilities in anticipation of market needs and in an attempt to remain wanted (Zemblyas, 2006). Within these discourses it becomes the individual who is expected to take responsibility for his/her education, training and employment. What were previously seen as societal risks, such as unemployment and poverty, become the responsibility of the individual (Lemke, 2000). This has a number of implications. First, social problems and inequalities are rendered invisible, as it is the individual who becomes judged as having made unwise choices and investments within life (Hamann, 2009; Fenwick, 2002b) rather than he/she being the victim, a circumstance of the structural disparity of society. Second, all aspects of life become geared towards competition, which, according to Rose (1999a: xxiv) removes a sense of community and solidarity:

> There is the pervasive sense that, whatever might be gained by stressing the autonomy and rights to self-actualization of each and every one of us, something is lost: the ways of relating to ourselves and others that were encompassed in such terms as dependency, mutuality, fraternity, self-sacrifice, commitment to others.

In particular, enterprising discourses, with the focus on the individual and on competition, attempt to weaken 'intermediary institutions' (Keat, 1991: 7) such as unions which may offer alternative, less individualistic, understandings of being a worker.

Finally, life becomes aligned with organisationally desirable attributes such as increased productivity, flexibility and maximisation of outputs (Edwards et al., 2004), which according to Keat (1991: 8) leads to individual motives such as 'greed, opportunism and the like' becoming 'dignified and sanitized by the rhetoric of enterprise'. Whilst extolling the discourse of enterprising selves, neo-liberal governments endeavour to moderate the excesses and potential dangers of the enterprising selves through other discourses such as 'active citizen' (Keat, 1991: 72) and 'moral individual' (Lemke, 2000: 12). Here, there is an attempt to bring community back into the discourse whereby individuals, in addition to pursuing self-enterprise and development, should also find time to 'serve their local community . . . be more engaged in social action to tackle problems in their own community' (Cameron, 2010: 2). Note that, whilst calling for solidarity and community, there is still the expectation that it is the individual, rather than the state, who is supposed to improve the situation.

Before illustrating how the enterprising discourse operates in practice, it is worth noting that according to Foucault (1983), power can only operate when it is addressed to individuals who have the capacity to act. Rather than acting purely in government-sanctioned ways, however, this also provides individuals with the capacity to act in alternate ways, a point that I will come back to at the end of the chapter.

## 5.3 Young people learning to become enterprising workers

### 5.3.1 Youth transitions into employment and the problem of youth unemployment

Today full-time education until 18 years of age in OECD countries is the norm (Wolf, 2011). In England, the figure is around 68 per cent (Department for Education, 2013). Those not in full-time education may choose to study part-time, perhaps in conjunction with part-time work. Others will find work, either full or part-time, with everyone else being classed as economically inactive (unemployed).

For those that choose to leave education before 18, the prospects are often poor, with youth unemployment consistently above the average unemployment figures for other age groups, usually around 10 per cent higher (ONS, 2012). Young people not in education, employment or training (NEET) are often demonised by society, the media and politicians as failures. The politician John Hayes (2007), writing in *The Guardian*, claimed that NEETs undermine 'social cohesion, damaging the economy and putting a strain on the exchequer'. Being long-term NEET is problematic as it can have many detrimental effects on the young person's life course (UKCES, 2012; Hasluck, 2012; Gracey and Kelly, 2010; Bynner and Parsons, 2002). For example, Gregg and Tominey (2005) found that a young male who has been unemployed during his youth is likely to face a wage scar of 13–21 per cent by the time he is 42. But the concern is not just about economic well-being, but also social well-being, with a review by the House of Lords (2008: 1) concluding that:

> Young people who are not in education, employment and training post-16 are
> more likely to be involved in anti-social behaviour and crime, more likely to be
> teenage parents and more likely to be misusing drugs or alcohol.

As can be seen from this quote, the stance from the UK government is that young people need to be within some form of constructive learning or work environment. Within such an environment, young people can be disciplined and socialised into learning how to act responsibly and to serve the well-being of the state (Burchell, 1996; Doherty, 2008) as productive citizens (Rose, 1996). Alternative discourses of being a young person are problematised as dangerous and a cost to society. Yet criticism of NEETs tends not to be about the system, nor about inequalities within society, but about the individual (Fenwick, 2002b); there appears to be an assumption that young people have made a choice to be NEET. Jones (2012) believes that NEETs have conveniently become demonised and stereotyped into a particular caricature, namely the 'chav', focusing on negative traits such as 'violence, laziness, teenage pregnancies, racism, drunkenness and the rest' (Jones, 2012: 8). This opens up an attitude of 'they get what they deserve' because they have 'chosen' a negative lifestyle which does not fit with the enterprising responsible citizen. This allows people to disassociate from the actual plight and hardship of being unemployed and removes the need to ask difficult questions of society, such as why inequality and deprivation are still features of 21st century society. For example, there is no questioning as to whether there are suitable employment opportunities for young people from disadvantaged backgrounds, living in deprived areas, or why young people would attend college courses if there is no prospect of a secure job when completing the course.

Gaining employment for young people can be difficult as, given a choice, many employers select older, more experienced workers over young workers. This is particularly exasperated in times of economic downturn or in deprived geographical locations where there is surplus labour to jobs. Partly, this is because young people often require a longer period of training and much more support than those who already have work experience. The problem is compounded by UK government guidance that frames 16–18 year olds as minors who need additional protection, over and above normal employee protections. Thus, there are stricter regulations on things like hours worked, supervision, and health and safety, which may make it less desirable for an employer to recruit a young person. This can lead to a catch-22 situation whereby young people need to gain work experience to increase their attractiveness to employers, but are unable to achieve this if employers are not willing to employ them (UKCES, 2012).

To counter the risk of young people becoming NEETs, and as a means to increase the skills level of young people, legislation was passed in the UK which raises the participation age of young people to 18 (Education and Skills Act, 2008). This means that from 2015, it becomes compulsory for everyone to the age of 18 to either continue with full-time education, participate in a combination of part-time training and part-time work, or undertake work-based learning (such as an apprenticeship). During this time, the young person will be closely monitored to ensure that he or she is actively engaged in learning, with a penalty system criminalising any young person who does not participate.

Whilst increasing the school leaving age is portrayed by the UK government as crucial for long-term skill development and employability, some commentators challenge whether the changes will be beneficial to all young people (Wolf, 2008). There is concern that college and training courses are not a viable alternative to work experience (Oultram, 2012). Similarly, many of the jobs without training which are currently available for young people will not translate into jobs with training. For many young people, their entry into the workplace is through casual or temporary positions, typically within the service sector (in retail and hospitality, for example). During their teens, they may move between jobs regularly, picking up skills and learning what it means to be a worker. This type of employment may indeed suit many young people as there is little long-term commitment. Whilst this is not formalised and accredited learning as desired by the UK government, it still provides the young person with learning opportunities. For example, Sissons and Jones (2012) claim that such roles develop soft skills such as communication, time management and self-motivation. Despite the benefits of such work to young people, it is questionable whether these types of jobs will transfer successfully to the government's new learning requirements. It appears that government has now begun to determine what it considers to be suitable arrangements for socialising young people into becoming enterprising workers. Alternative arrangements, such as casualised working as outlined above, appear to be deemed as unsuitable and as such are to be removed as options for young people.

## 5.3.2 Apprentices as enterprising workers

One approach to fulfil the requirements of UK government legislation for training, at the same time as enabling the young person to be in employment, is through an apprenticeship. Apprenticeships in England have a long history with examples dating back to medieval times. Traditionally apprenticeships have been associated with crafts and trades, whereby an apprentice would work alongside a master of the trade to gradually learn the practices and skills of the job. Today, apprenticeship schemes are more formalised and are partially funded by the government. An apprentice is required to complete both on-the-job and off-the-job training. The off-the-job training, which is typically taught through a third party training provider or further education college, includes qualifications in both practical and technical aspects of the job, along with academic qualifications in English, Mathematics and Information Technology. Young people are also expected to take modules that develop wider skills for employability; learning to learn and being a good citizen.

The UK government claims that there is a clear apprenticeship brand which is central to their training and development agenda, with Prime Minister, David Cameron (2013) declaring, 'I want it to be the new norm for young people to either go to university or into an apprenticeship'. Yet there is often confusion surrounding apprenticeships as they appear to be offered to diverse groups of people. In one respect, apprenticeships are seen as a mechanism to reduce the number of NEETs and to re-engage young people who have become disengaged. A number of large organisations like Barclays Bank and Pret A Manger offer apprenticeships to young people who are classed as long-term unemployed. The organisations will often accept these young people without any academic qualifications or work experience (Wheldon, 2012). In this way, the organisations can be seen to be acting in a socially responsible way in order to help with societal problems. At the other end of the spectrum, there are some apprenticeships which are seen as very elite and prestigious. For example, apprenticeships offered by companies such Rolls Royce, British Telecom, and Bentley are heavily oversubscribed, enabling the companies to select young people with outstanding academic qualifications. Whilst both schemes are classed as apprenticeships, there are likely to be very different learning opportunities between these different schemes.

There are different levels of apprenticeships, starting with intermediate, which provides basic skills and is equivalent to GCSEs, and continuing to advanced, which develops higher levels of competence and in some cases is the requirement to practice the trade (for example electricians). Apprentices can then take their learning to a foundation degree level with a higher apprenticeship. From 2013 onwards, there will be further progression of apprenticeship to graduate and post-graduate level in certain occupations. Nowadays, apprenticeships are offered in most industries, with frameworks available in the traditional sectors such as construction, engineering, hairdressing, in professions such as business administration, law and management, in new industries such as information and communication technology, creative media, and in service sector roles such as retail, hospitality and care industries (cf. NAS Website, 2013). Modern apprenticeships tend to be much shorter than the traditional apprenticeships which could take up to seven years to complete, with many lasting only for a year. Some apprenticeships that require specialised training last for at least two years. There has been criticism that training which requires limited skills levels, which can be developed over a relatively short period of time (such as in retail), are not comparable with what are often termed 'traditional' forms of apprenticeship which require prolonged learning to gain the skills and should not be labelled as apprenticeships (Richard, 2012). The diverse range of apprenticeships is currently under government review to determine what should be classed as an apprenticeship.

Apprenticeships are promoted under slogans such as 'opening doors to a better future' (NAS Website, 2010), 'the sky's the limit' (NAS Website, 2013), 'don't dream it, do it' (NAS Website, 2013), 'Great Employers, Great Opportunities, Great Prospects – Apprenticeships Deliver' (NAS Website, 2013), 'Improve yourself, Improve your prospects' (NAS Website, 2013). The apprenticeship frameworks are structured and operated to ensure that the young person achieves:

> *The acquisition of skills that enhance employability, effectiveness at work and personal prosperity . . . The development of skills that contribute to the social and economic well-being of the learner and extend their opportunities for active citizenship . . . improve the behaviour of learners . . . promote good attendance . . . help learners to adopt safe practices and a healthy lifestyle.* (BIS, 2010: 34)

Here we can see the discourse of enterprise clearly, with calls for the learner to take responsibility for his/her self, not only to pursue progression and development but also to take care of the self (Foucault, 1986). According to these discourses, opportunity is there for the taking, it just requires the individual to take responsibility and action. At present, practice does not meet the UK governmental rhetoric, with young people experiencing problems such as lack of available apprenticeship places, limited opportunities for progression after the apprenticeship and very basic apprenticeships offering little chance of becoming a skilled worker (Kennedy and Mehta, 2012; Jofre, 2012; James, 2010; Loveys, 2012; Richard, 2012).

As explained earlier, these discourses require the individual to be active, to accept and engage with the discourses and to internalise them as 'truths'. To explore this further, we can examine how a group of young male apprentices explained what being a 'good worker' meant to them. The material is drawn from a study undertaken between 2008 and 2009 of 16 apprentices in construction, motor vehicles maintenance and engineering (Oultram, 2010).

Most of the apprentices did have aspirations, wanting to be successful and to make 'lots of money', but their understanding of success was defined as becoming a skilled worker in their trade. Only two of the apprentices considered the job that they were training for to be a stepping stone to other things, with the rest stating that they perceived the job to be a life-long career. The apprentices were realistic and understood that they would probably need to change jobs throughout their career, but they only saw it in terms of doing the same job with a different employer rather than progression or changing career. For many, the vocation was inter-generational, with fathers and grandfathers also having been in that particular trade. Thus, they had very limited exploration of other careers. As an apprentice electrician stated:

> I thought about other jobs but I wasn't really serious about them. My family have always done this type of work. My granddad was an electrician for the council and my dad's an electrician in a factory. I thought about being a fireman or something like that but decided this is what I really want to do.

In this example, an apprenticeship allowed the young person to train in an occupation which was considered appropriate for his perceived familial social status. There appears to have been little broadening of his horizons, in contrast to what is promoted in the apprenticeship enterprise discourses.

The apprentices portrayed certain enterprising traits and were calculative, in some respects, understanding the value of qualifications as currency within the world of work. Qualifications were perceived as a necessity for 'getting on in life' (apprentice) as they were unlikely to remain with the same organisation indefinitely and would need some form of qualification to prove their ability when applying for jobs in other companies:

> NVQs [a form of qualification] are a proof you know how to do something properly. I think it's more for the employer side of things – they want to see qualifications. You can say you can do something but the qualification actually proves it. (Apprentice mechanic)

Whilst the apprentices believed that the ability to actually perform the job came from practical knowledge and experience, they realised that they needed to have this certified in the form of qualifications for it to matter. Willis (1977: 56–57) argues that practical knowledge is valued more by the working class, with qualifications and theoretical knowledge associated with middle class values:

> Practical ability always comes first and a condition of other kinds of knowledge. . . . The working class view would be the rational one were it not located in class society, i.e. that theory is only useful insofar as it really does help to do things, to accomplish practical tasks and change nature. Theory is asked to be in a close dialectic with the material world. For the middle class, more aware of its position in a class society, however, theory is seen partly in its social guise of qualifications to move up the social scale. In this sense theory is well worth having even if it is never applied to nature.

Again this fits with an enterprising discourse, because qualifications act as a potential enabler to progression at work and within society. Interestingly, the apprentices had changed their understanding of the value of qualifications since starting their apprenticeships. Many of them had been unsuccessful in achieving academic qualifications from their schooling, with some of them claiming that they had failed, whilst at school, to understand the importance of gaining qualifications.

The apprenticeships were for fixed periods and the trainees were clear that on successful completion they would become accepted as skilled workers. They were also aware that this would not be the end of their learning; they would be expected to undertake training and development throughout their working lives. They did not see this as necessarily for progression to higher jobs, but merely to remain secure within their own chosen occupations:

> I think I'll be learning for years yet – there are so many things that you can learn. I don't think I'll ever stop learning. (Apprentice electrician)

> [E]ven those who have been doing the job for years have to keep going on training courses, it's just part of the job. You have to keep your skills up-to-date. (Apprentice engineer)

Working hard and striving towards a career, or profession, and being seen as a skilled worker was very important for the apprentices. They were quick to challenge the idea that they were learners or trainees, instead promoting themselves as qualified workers, who work hard and contribute to the success of the company. The apprentices identified working productively and efficiently through terms such as 'working hard', 'help each other out' and 'do as I'm told' and were keen to stress that they made a full contribution to the team's work effort. The apprentices feared that if they did not work hard and were not perceived as 'good workers' that there would be hardships in terms of becoming unemployed. One of the apprentice builders outlined what having a job meant to him:

> Doing an apprenticeship is worthwhile because it's a job. You don't want to be not having a job. Having a job means you get your money and you can buy the stuff you want. . . . If you haven't got a job then there is a risk that you'll get in with the wrong crowd and get into trouble and stuff. So yeah I'm dead glad I'm working.

For this apprentice, work is associated with positive benefits such as having consumer power and not having a job is portrayed as the path to criminality and destruction of the self.

As can be seen from this short case study, the apprentices are internalising some of the enterprising-self discourse. There is an understanding that the apprentices need to work on developing themselves and fitting in with the requirements of the organisation to remain wanted. Yet as will be seen later in the chapter, for the apprentices, work means much more than being productive enterprising workers.

## 5.4 Ambiguity, agency and space for alternate understandings of being a worker

Within the workplace individuals become socialised with certain discourses surrounding what it is like to be a worker. We have already seen one of these discourses at play in the promoting of the enterprising worker. For the rest of the chapter, I will discuss alternate forms of being a worker in contemporary society.

Alongside the formal practices expected of the worker, there are also informal understandings of being a worker within a particular workplace. New entrants to work not only have to learn the formal practices and expected behaviour as outlined by the employer, but also the informal behaviour which is expected of an employee by other employees. Failure to understand the social codes and norms, can lead to a failure to be accepted as part of the informal working community.

Lave and Wenger (1991) introduced the idea of community of practice (COP) as a group of people who sustain a relationship over time in pursuit of achieving a purpose, typically to get the job done, working together and forming social bonds. According to Lave and Wenger, these COPs develop over time and through continued practice, with people who work closely together establishing routines and particular ways of working, leading to communal memory and an understanding of 'how things are done around here' (Hughes, 2007: 36). This communal memory and shared belonging creates an exclusivity of understanding to accepted participants and can help to form boundaries around the COP which exclude those not accepted into the COP. Whilst formal organisational structures can set up team membership, Boud and Middleton (2003) claim that COPs are different and are not necessarily bound by organisational choice. They argue that whilst employers and managers can create the environment which encourages team work and communities to develop, COPs develop naturally through practice. Similarly, whilst an employer can choose to introduce a new member to the team in the workplace, it should not necessarily be assumed that the newcomer will be allowed access to the COP. Outsiders, who do not appear to conform to the perceived norms of the group, may find it difficult to gain acceptance, and thus access, to the COP's resources.

According to Lave and Wenger (1991: 29), entry to the COP is through what they term 'legitimate peripheral participation', in which newcomers become socialised into the practices of the COP through learning:

> [S]hared ways of engaging in doing things together; local lore, shared stories, inside jokes, knowing laughter; specific tools, representations and other artefacts. (Wenger, 1998: 125)

Gradually the peripheral participants learn the norms and practices of the COP and begin to gain acceptance and increased responsibility from others in the group. Whilst COPs have histories and often shared rarefied practices, they are not fixed and static, nor should COPs necessarily be understood as warm, democratic, apolitical or inclusive social groups (Edwards et al., 2004). The relationships within the COP are continually re-negotiated with actors forming different alliances seeking to achieve their own objectives, which may be in conflict with other alliances and objectives (Jewson, 2007). COPs are therefore sites where people who are in a position to dominate the network are able to 'develop mythologies, narratives and stories that characterise and justify their actions' (Jewson, 2007: 77).

According to McDowell (2003), COPs can be gendered, with masculinity being actively defined and maintained through the practices of the COP. There is an enactment of practices which has traditionally been associated with 'working class masculine shop floor' jobs:

*[A] whirlpool of workplace dynamics commonly comprising; a strict male chauvinism, a 'breadwinner'/manual production mentality, and a coarse sexist humour manufactured around practical jokes, gestures and racist/homophobic connotations.* (Parker, 2006: 695)

For an individual to gain acceptance into masculine dominated COPs, he has to be able to demonstrate that he is 'fully masculine' (Paechter, 2003: 74) by demonstrating these particular characteristics and behaviours. Those not conforming sufficiently to the local understanding of 'what it is to be a man' face rejection by the COP. This exclusion and socialisation of particular behaviours as acceptable within the COP helps to continue to reproduce the norms of masculine behaviour in these workplaces.

Returning to the case study of the male apprentices, we can explore these alternative understandings of being a worker. For all the apprentices in the study, the social aspects of the job were important and they all felt that they belonged, and had been accepted, into a particular COP. For example one of the apprentice mechanics described his work group:

> We're all like a close knit family. There is a mix of age groups, with a couple of us under 18, a few mid-20s, a manager in his 30s and then the oldies.

The apprentices described how they needed to be able to get on with the people they worked with and had learnt how to behave appropriately to enable them to be accepted by their work colleagues. One apprentice was moved from his original team as he was struggling to fit in, but had luckily found a different team which seemed to accept him. The apprentices all described how they had been introduced into their teams and described the point at which they felt that they belonged:

> At the start your workmates are a bit wary of you and therefore they test you out with various pranks. (Apprentice builder)

> Once they sent me to the stores for stripy paint and a long weight. After a few weeks you become wise and start to think about what they say but to start with I just went and did everything I was told. Eventually you become wise to them messing about – and then they stop. There is always banter . . . there is a lot of winding up but everyone tends to be involved – we don't pick on people. (Apprentice mechanic)

These pranks appear to be a ceremonial 'rite of passage' for the apprentice and a way of the team ensuring that the young person will 'fit in' socially.

Here the definition of being a good worker is not about the job but about being collegial and able to 'have a laugh':

> I gave it [banter] back straight away. I think that is why I became one of the lads straight away, more quicker because I gave it back straight away – that was important as it showed that I could take it but also able to give it. You just seem to settle in quicker if you are willing to give it back. (Apprentice mechanic)

The banter, which is often sexist and victimising, is celebrated in these particular work cultures and having a laugh is, according to many of the apprentices, the 'best bit of the job':

> Without the banter and messing about, the job would be quite boring. (Apprentice builder)

Within these workplaces there seems to be a form of masculinity being played out. The young males appear to have chosen these traditional occupations as they associated the roles as 'masculine work'. The apprentices appeared to invest a lot of effort into ensuring that they fitted in with their work colleagues. There were a number of references to 'being one of the lads' and references to masculine behaviour. That is not to say that the apprentices and workers in the study did not work hard: the apprentices believed that, like their work mates, they worked hard and liked to get the job done. There was a sense of pride in completing tasks to a high standard and ahead of schedule, ensuring that the job got done, but in reward for this there was an understanding that the work teams were left alone and had freedom to 'have a laugh' and behave in ways that are potentially perceived as unacceptable in many modern workplaces. Thus, the masculine behaviour, to some extent, allows the workers to keep some control over their working day, ensuring that there is space for alternate understandings of being a worker, rather than just the performative discourse of enterprising worker.

## 5.5   Summary

This chapter has explored some of the challenges facing young people as they make the transition from school to work. UK government policy focuses on development of skills and learning through this period. Increasingly, young people are being monitored and controlled during this time, with new legislation ensuring that young people are contained within the education system as long as possible. As discussed in this chapter, the intended development of the young person is not just about learning the skills to perform a particular job, but about learning to be 'enterprising' and productive workers and citizens.

Whilst young people can be encouraged to adopt certain practices and behaviours, it is not inevitable that they will choose to accept other peoples' understandings of being a worker. Once the young person enters the workplace, there are alternate understandings of being a worker which may not align to official discourses. There is unlikely to be one fixed notion of being a 'good' worker, with priorities and understandings changing and adapting within different contexts and times. Hence, at the micro level there is always space for localised understandings and interpretation of the official discourses.

 **REFERENCES**

BIS (2010) *Raising Standards*. Accessed at: http://www.dcsf.gov.uk/readwriteplus/raisingstandards/embeddedlearning/achieve/achieve/trends/ (retrieved 2 December 2010).

Boud, D. and Middleton, H. (2003) 'Learning from others at work: Communities of practice and informal learning', *Journal of Workplace Learning*, 15(5): 194–202.

Burchell, G. (1996) 'Liberal government and techniques of the self' in Barry, A., Osborne, T. and N. Rose (eds), *Foucault and Political Reason: Liberalism, Neo-liberalism and Rationalities of Government*, Chicago, IL: University of Chicago Press.

Bynner, J. and Parsons, S. (2002) 'Social exclusion and the transition from school to work: The case of Young People Not in Education, Employment, or Training (NEET)', *Journal of Vocational Behavior*, 60(2), 289–309.

Cameron, D. (2010) 'Queen's speech revealed: David Cameron's 500 day programme to change Britain', *Daily Telegraph*, 22 May 2010.

Cameron, D. (2013) Speech at the opening of National Apprenticeship Week, 11 March 2013.

Coffield, F. (1999) 'Introduction: Past failures, present differences and possible futures for research, policy and practice' in Coffield, F. (ed.), *Speaking Truth to Power – Research and Policy on Lifelong Learning*, Bristol: ESRC, The Policy Press.

Dean, M. (1999) *Governmentality – Power and Rule in Modern Society*, London: Sage Publications.

Department for Education (2013) *Statistical First Release: Participation in education, training and employment by 16–18 year olds in England (revised end 2001 to end 2011)*, Department for Education.

Doherty, R. (2008) 'Critically framing education policy: Foucault, discourse and governmentality' in Peters, M.A. and Besley, T. (eds), *Why Foucault? New Directions in Educational Research*, New York: Peter Lang.

Education and Skills Act (2008) Chapter 25: Duty to participate in education or training.

Edwards, R., Nicoll, K., Solomon, N. and Usher, R. (2004) *Rhetoric and Educational Discourse – Persuasive Texts?*, London: Routledge Falmer.

Fenwick, T. (2002a) 'Tides of change: New themes enterprising selves in the new capitalism', *New Directions for Adult and Continuing Education*, 92, 3–18.

Fenwick, T. (2002b) 'Transgressive desires: New enterprising selves in the new capitalism', *Work, Employment and Society*, 16(4), 703–723.

Foucault, M. (1983) 'The subject and power' in Dreyfus, H. and Rabinow, P. (eds), *Beyond Structuralism and Hermeneutics*, Chicago, IL: University of Chicago Press.

Foucault, M. (1984) *The Foucault Reader*, Rabinow P. (ed.), New York : Pantheon.

Foucault, M. (1986) *The History of Sexuality: Volume Three – The Care of the Self*, New York: Pantheon.

Foucault, M. (1991) 'Governmentality: Lecture given at College de France Feb 1978' in Burchell,

G., Gordon, C. and Miller, P. (eds), *The Foucault Effect – Studies in Governmentality – with Two Lectures by and an Interview with Michel Foucault*, Chicago: Chicago University.

Gallagher, M. (2008) 'Foucault, power and participation', *International Journal of Children's Rights*, 16, 395–406.

Garrick, J. and Usher, G. (2000) 'Flexible learning, contemporary work and enterprising selves', *Electronic Journal of Sociology*, 5(1).

Garsten, C. and Jacobsson, K. (eds) (2004) *Learning to be Employable: New Agendas on Work, Employability and Learning in a Globalizing World*, Basingstoke: Palgrave Macmillan.

Gracey, S. and Kelly, S. (2010), *Changing the NEET Mindset: Achieving More Effective Transitions Between Education and Work*, London: LSN Centre for Innovation in Learning.

Gregg, P. and Tominey, E. (2005) 'The wage scar from male youth unemployment', *Labour Economics*, 12(4), 487–509.

Hamann, T. (2009) 'Neo-liberalism, governmentality, and ethics', *Foucault Studies*, 6, 37–59.

Hasluck, C. (2012) *Why businesses should recruit young people*, UK Commission for Employment and Skills.

Hayes, J. (2007) 'The shameful growth of a generation of "neets"', *The Guardian*, 24 April 2007. Accessed at: http://www.theguardian.com/education/2007/apr/24/furthereducation.educationguardian2 (retrieved September 2013).

House of Lords (2008) *Short Guide to Education and Skills Bill*.

Hughes, J. (2007) 'Lost in translation. Communities of practice: The journey from academic model to practitioner tool', in Hughes, J., Jewson, N. and Unwin. L. (eds), *Communities of Practice Critical Perspectives*, London: Routledge.

James, S. (2010) 'What is apprenticeship?', Oxford: Skope.

Jewson, N. (2007) 'Cultivating network analysis: Rethinking the concept of 'community' within "communities of practice"', in Hughes, J., Jewson, N. and Unwin, L. (eds), *Communities of Practice Critical Perspectives*, London: Routledge.

Jofre, S. (2012) 'Panorama: The great apprentice scandal', BBC, first aired Monday 2 April 2012.

Jones, O. (2012) *Chavs: The Demonization of the Working Class*, London: Verso.

Keat, R. (1991) 'Introduction: Starship Britain or universal enterprise?' in Keat, R. and Abercrombie, N. (eds), *Enterprise Culture*, London: Routledge.

Kennedy, D. and Mehta, K. (2012) 'Apprentices learn bed-making and vajazzling', *The Times*, London.

Lambier, B. (2005) 'Education as liberation: The politics and techniques of lifelong learning', *Educational Philosophy and Theory*, 37(3), 349–355.

Lave, J. and Wenger, E. (1991) *Situated Learning – Legitimate Peripheral Participation*, Cambridge: Cambridge University Press.

Lemke, T. (2000) 'Foucault, governmentality, and critique', *Rethinking Marxism Conference*, United States: University of Amherst.

Loveys, K. (2012) 'Public pays for McJob training', *Sunday Times*, London.

McDowell L. (2003) *Redundant Masculinities? Employment Change and White Working Class Youth*, Oxford: Blackwell Publishing.

Miller, P and Rose, N. (2008) *Governing the Present*, Cambridge: Polity Press.

Mills, M. and Blossfield, H. (2005) 'Globalization, uncertainty and the early life course a theoretical framework', in Blossfield, H., Kiljzing, E., Mills, M. and Kurz, K. (eds), *Globalization, Uncertainty And Youth In Society*, London: Routledge Chapman & Hall.

NAS (2013) National Apprenticeship Service Website, http://www.apprenticeships.org.uk/Types-of-Apprenticeships.aspx (retrieved 26 April 2013).

NAS (2010) National Apprenticeship Service Website, http://www.apprenticeships.org.uk/ (retrieved 15 March 2010).

Nesbit, T. (2005) 'Social class and adult education', *New Directions for Adult and Continuing Education*, 106, 5–14.

ONS (2012), *Labour Market Statistics, April 2012*, http://www.ons.gov.uk/ons/dcp171778_260957.pdf (retrieved 22 April 2013).

Oultram, T. (2010) *Exploring the identities of the young male worker: A case study of English Apprenticeship schemes*, PhD, Keele University, Staffordshire.

Oultram, T. (2012) 'Simulated work environments: Facilitating learning within the pre-apprenticeship program', *International Journal of Organizational Analysis*, 20(2), 238–250.

Paechter, C. (2003) 'Masculinities and femininities as communities of practice', *Women's Studies International Forum*, 26(1), 69–77.

Parker, A. (2006) 'Lifelong learning to labour: Apprenticeship, masculinity and community of practice', *British Educational Research Journal*, 32(5), 687–701.

Richard, D. (2012) *The Richard Review of Apprenticeships*, UK Government sponsored report.

Rose, N. (1996) 'Governing "advanced" liberal democracies' in Barry, A., Osborne, T. and Rose, N. (eds), *Foucault and Political Reason: Liberalism, Neo-liberalism and Rationalities of Government*, Chicago, IL: University of Chicago Press.

Rose, N. (1999a) *Governing the Soul: The Shaping of the Private Self*, London: Free Association Books.

Rose, N. (1999b) *Powers of Freedom: Reframing Political Thought*, Cambridge: Cambridge University Press.

Simons, M. and Maaschelein, J. (2006) 'The learning society and governmentality: An introduction', *Educational Philosophy and Theory*, 38(4), 417–430.

Sissons, P. & Jones, K. (2012) 'Lost in transition? The changing labour market and young people not in employment, education or training', Lancaster: The Work Foundation, Lancaster University.

Taylor, C. (1989) *Sources of the Self: The Making of Modern Identity*, Cambridge, MA: Harvard University Press.

Tuschling, A. and Angemann, C. (2006) 'From education to lifelong learning: The emerging regime of learning in the European Union', *Educational Philosophy and Theory*, 38(4), 451–469.

UKCES (2012) *The Youth Employment Challenge*, Wath-upon-Dearne: UKCES.

Wenger, E. (1998) *Communities of Practice: Learning, Meaning and Identity*, Cambridge: Cambridge University Press.

Wheldon, D. (2012) 'Why are young people everyone's business?', *The Guardian*, http://www.guardian.co.uk/sustainable-business/barclays-unicef-youth-unemployment?INTCMP=SRCH (retrieved 26 April 2013).

Willis, P. (1977), *Learning to Labour – How Working Class Kids get Working Class Jobs*, Farnborough: Saxon House.

Wolf, A. (2008) *Diminished Returns How Raising the Leaving Age to 18 Will Harm Young People and the Economy*, London: Policy Exchange.

Wolf, A. (2011) *Review of Vocational Education – The Wolf Report*.

Zemblyas, M. (2006) 'Work-based learning, power and subjectivity: Creating space for a Foucauldian research ethic', *Journal of Education and Work*, 19(3), 291–303.

# 6

# Hard work, productivity and the management of the farmed environment in anthropological perspective

*Steven B. Emery*

## 6.1   Introduction

Studies in organisational management have predominantly focused on urban workplaces, with very little attention given to rural businesses, or to agriculture in particular. And whilst the concept of the 'organisation' might seem somewhat removed from 'the farm', the vicissitudes of agriculture and the many internal and external variables that must be responded to necessitate continuous management and adaptation of the farming business. Moreover, the concept of work and its relationship to identification processes is acutely evident amongst farming communities and studies of agriculture thus offer important insights into the role of work as a virtue that shapes (and is shaped by) approaches to management in a broader range of organisational settings.

This chapter sets out to understand how farm work and a cultural value in the work ethic influences farmers' responses to new political and societal incentives to adopt environmental behaviours. I draw on ethnographic fieldwork with farmers in the North York Moors (UK) which was conducted within the context of changing expectations of the role and function of farming. In particular, new agri-environmental policies offer financial incentives to farmers to act as 'land managers' or 'environmental stewards' in order to protect, maintain and enhance the environmental quality of agricultural landscapes. The North York Moors is characterised by livestock farming with enclosed pasture at lower altitudes and open common moorland on higher ground. It is designated a National Park and the moorland is protected for its conservation value. The grazing of sheep on the moorland is integral to its favourable conservation management, and a considerable focus of agri-environment schemes during my fieldwork, therefore, was to encourage farmers to keep grazing their sheep on the moor, and to do so in an environmentally sensitive way. My fieldwork was informed by participant observation on three farms and forty semi-structured interviews with farmers in an area defined by the catchment of the River Esk (for full details and an extended presentation of the argument made here see Emery, 2010).

This chapter demonstrates how environmental schemes lay challenge to farmers' personhoods,[1] since they seek to alter both the practices (the types of work undertaken) and the means of expression (the physical appearance of the farm) through which farmers uphold their virtue in the work ethic. I show that the work ethic has often been associated with ideals of productivism and economic benefits but ask and seek to explain, therefore, why it is that farmers continue to farm, and to value the work ethic when their financial returns continue to fall. During fieldwork I also found that the work ethic was often expressed in multiple, complex and counter-intuitive ways. I seek to explain this through recourse to rhetoric culture theory from anthropology, and to consider its implications for our understanding of the relationship between cultural values and workplace practices. In other words, I ask what can be learnt about workplace behaviours when the values that influence behaviour are seen as multiple and changing rather than singular and fixed.

## 6.2 Theorising work and the work ethic

To foreground the ethnographic material that follows, this section explores the relationship between (1) farm work; (2) a virtue in the work ethic, or being hard-working; (3) farmers' processes of identification or personhood, and (4) the physical appearance of the farm. These relationships are then reflected upon in terms of religious and capitalist ideology and consideration is given to how they come to bear on farmers' responses to environmental initiatives that alter the type of work they are expected to do and the physical appearance of the farm.

The anthropological literature has demonstrated the cultural rather than purely utilitarian economic value associated with work. Wallman (1979: 7) defined work as 'the production, management or the conversion of the resources necessary to livelihood', and in doing so recognised that 'the task of meeting obligations, securing identity, status and structure, are as fundamental to livelihood as bread and shelter'. In this sense work can be considered not only as an economic investment, but as an 'identity investment', and broadens the concept of work to include the 'processes through which cultural and ideological values are achieved and maintained' (Cohen, 1979: 264). Equally, cultural geographers have demonstrated the cultural significance of places for identification and personhood (e.g., Penrose, 1993). For farmers, however, there is a particularly strong and intimate relationship between their daily practices (work) and place; the place is the medium on and through which the work is performed (Wallman, 1979: 12). Consequently, personhood is extended to the landscape (Ravetz, 2001) as family biography and farm-as-place become intertwined (Gray, 1998); and the materiality of the farm comes to serve as 'an evolving testimony to the life's work of those who have left their mark on [it]' (Ingold, 1984: 116).

It is not only work but a particular *type* of work that has been shown to be important for farmers' personhoods and collective identities; *hard work*. The work ethic is something so commonly associated with farming that its significance often passes by unnoticed. Yet a relationship between agriculture and *hard work* as a virtue can be found as far back as classical Greece and Rome (Duckworth, 1959; Rosivach, 2001; Schwimmer, 1979; Wolf, 1987) and as existing in various contemporary forms from Europe (Abrahams, 1991; Newby, 1977), the United States (Osthaus, 2004; Walter, 1995), Africa (Davidson, 2009; Long, 1984) and the Philippines (Borchgrevink, 2002). The importance of *hard work* for gaining moral respect within British farming communities has been demonstrated by Rapport (1993) and Cohen (1979). Cohen shows, however, that rather than something that is measured quantitatively with moral worth ascribed in equal measure, the hard-working referent 'expresses the proximity to a symbolic ideal rather than an actual record of effort' (1979: 250). The symbolism and virtuosity of the work ethic means that it is central to cultural conceptions of 'the good farmer' (Burton, 2004; Silvasti, 2003) and it finds expression in the landscape. Since it is symbolic, however, it does not necessarily follow that the symbol must represent the quantity of work done, but instead somehow represents proximity to the community ideal of the good farmer. Hard work is thus often symbolised by a neat and tidy farm, the absence of weeds and the uniform and well-ordered appearance of boundaries and other physical features (Burton, 2004; Egoz et al., 2001; McEachern, 1992; Silvasti, 2003).[2] As something symbolic, I will go on to argue that the work ethic and its means of expression are open to interpretation and changes in meaning.

It is impossible to discuss the work ethic and religion without mention of Max Weber. To put it simply, Weber's thesis in *The Protestant Ethic and the Spirit of Capitalism* (1930) is that the strong work ethic associated with puritanical Protestantism was instrumental in the development of capitalism. In this guise hard work is valued as a means to creating wealth. This idea has been extended to agriculture by Paul Thompson (1995). Thompson argued that farmers were particularly suited to this work ethic and a belief in its religious foundation because, unlike wage labourers, they were not alienated from the product of their labour and industriousness was a very public virtue. For Thompson, 'good farming is associated with the production of more and larger', and 'the linking of work and reward characterizes a work ethic that converts production into a sign of the farmer's moral worth' (1995: 68).

Such an interpretation clearly links the value of work to its productive outputs. Burton (2004) has also made the link between the good farmer and production. However, since it might not always be straightforward to demonstrate the quantity of produce, good farming is instead symbolised by a farm that it is representative of the principles of productivism: in terms of its tidiness and uniformity and the carrying out of farm activities in pursuit of productivist ideals (such as hedgerow removal and farm expansion). This literature, and that that has demonstrated the work ethic as expressed through the physical appearance and tidiness of the farm have thus presented organic farming, or new forms of agri-environmental management, as an interference with the symbolic acts (the type of farm work) and the aesthetics (the visual expression through the appearance of the farm) associated with the ideal of the good, hard-working farmer (Egoz et al., 2001; Silvasti, 2003). This interpretation is used to suggest that a fundamental reason that farmers do not want to engage in organic farming or agri-environmental schemes is because it contradicts their cultural ideal of the good farmer and lays challenge to their personhoods.

However, if the association between the work ethic and agriculture pre-dates both Christianity and capitalism, and if (as the anthropological literature has shown) work is valued for more than economic reasons, then can it be the case that the work ethic and farmers' responses to their new role as environmental land managers proceed only on the basis of productivist interpretations of the work ethic? Why is it that hill farmers continue to farm despite falling financial returns? In the ethnographic material that follows I hope to show that there are a variety of different interpretations of the work ethic, in terms of what it means and how it is to be expressed, that are evident amongst a community of hill farmers in the UK. In order to analyse and explain this variety I draw on an approach which recognises that cultural components (such as a value in the work ethic) are versatile and that alternative interpretations arise as groups and individuals deploy those components persuasively to pursue or defend a range of different interests (Carrithers, 2005; Strecker and Tyler, 2009).

## 6.3 Work, hard work and their rhetorical deployment

### 6.3.1 Personhood and the virtue of work

I begin my presentation of ethnographic material with two very small, subtle, but nevertheless telling examples of the virtue of the work ethic to farmers; its centrality to farming personhoods, and its rhetorical potential as a persuasive device. In short, the importance of 'work' in both self-definition and how it gets deployed in argumentative strategies. Both examples present the responses of two elderly farmers whose work ethic was accidentally challenged by the naïve questions of the anthropologist.

Fred Atliss[3] is 72 and although his neighbour told me he was too old to be farming, Fred values the unremitting toil of hill farming which he stresses can only be sustained by treating it as a 365-days a year job and as a lifetime's work. In light of his age, I asked Fred whether he was starting to 'wind down' and he was quick to correct me; 'slowing down, not winding down . . . slowing down's the word, you get slow'. Reflecting on this, I realised that Fred took this as an affront to his work ethic since 'winding down' could be associated with relaxation, leisure, and freeing up time for the 'good life'. It might also be taken to mean 'scaling down', which would also cast judgement upon his farming achievement, or as having a more terminal outcome than simply slowing down which is an uncontrollable – and hence forgivable – consequence of the ageing process.

In a similarly succinct but evocative example, I was struck by the response of Ernest Mullaney, 81, when I asked him at the end of an interview if he felt that he'd had a good life. In response to my question Ernest looked at me, contemplated for a moment and replied 'well, I've had a hard life'. He offered no more direct clues as to what he meant by this. Instead of beginning his response with 'well' he could have used either 'no' or 'yes'. However, to say 'no' would imply that he hadn't enjoyed his life, which, through his nostalgic recollections, he had already let me know that he had. On the other hand, if he had replied 'yes' to my question this could have implied that he'd had an easy life. And in line with Fred's thinking, an easy life would not be considered virtuous. By using 'well' Ernest was able to imply synonymy between a good life and a hard life *without* implying that it had been easy.

Because the work ethic is considered virtuous and is tied to farmers' conceptions of themselves – to their personhoods – laying challenge to that work ethic can be seen to bring about a response and demonstrates its rhetorical potential. I will later explore further examples of the work ethic's rhetorical potential in terms of farmers' responses to new environmental initiatives. First there is something else to draw out from the examples of Fred and Ernest, and that is that hard work and the suffering with which it is associated appear to be valued in their own right.

In my discussions with farmers I was offered many examples of what seemed to be a genuine relationship between a hard life and a satisfying life. Arthur Livingstone for instance, recalled an anecdote of a particularly strenuous day's work in the 1950s and concluded his story by reminding me that 'they were good days'. As what might be an extension of what Carro-Ripalda (n.d.) has referred to as 'making oneself through suffering', hard work is so integral to farming personhoods that it is presented as inseparable from happiness and its recollections are drenched in nostalgia. Cockcroft, writing about the Esk Valley in North Yorkshire in the 1970s illustrates this value in contrast with those who moved away from farming:

> Certainly the Sunleys, the Welfords and their kind, those whose forbears did not flee the land for the loom, do not have their emotions mauled every fine weekend. They know a serenity which is special to those who stayed and suffered with the land. And a few fortunate people have reaped such a reward from this loyalty and their happiness is so complete, that it hurts the soul. (Cockcroft, 1974: 121)

## 6.3.2  Good farming, the land and management for the environment

Time and time again in my discussions with farmers, labelling someone as hard-working was used to endorse their credentials as a good farmer. The following extract – from Tom and Lynn Richie – is a typical example and demonstrates that hard work's reward is not always financial, that profit alone does not serve as a symbolic referent and that hard work finds expression in the land:

> **TR**: The Burmans are good farmers
> **SE**: What do you mean by good farmers?
> **TR**: Puts the farm before everything else . . . will stay home and look after the land before going out for dinner
> **LR**: Real hard workers
> **TR**: The best farms aren't always the most profitable, we don't do ourselves any favours if we don't look after the land.

Here, the appearance and condition of the land, above all else, symbolises the synonymic good and hard-working farmer. Alternative approaches to farming, or environmental schemes that alter the appearance of the land, are thus presented as unable to uphold the aesthetic ideal of the good hard-working farmer. Ernest Mullaney indicted hobby farmers[4] on such grounds, stating that they were unable to keep their farms tidy because farming is a lifetime's work. Similarly the Spencers (three brothers in their twenties) indicted conservation management with an example from an article they had read in the *Farmers Weekly*. The story told of a farmer creating a new wetland on his farm for the purpose of habitat creation:

> There was a bloke in t' *Farmers Weekly* once and he was digging all these stone drains out to make his field a marshland and he said his forefathers 'd be turning in their graves, they'd be stood in a hole, digging all these drains in by hand, and he's there with a big digger ripping them all out to make it a bog, just so he can make more money by not doing anything, by having a mess.

In this example again, the aesthetic critique (making a 'mess') is tied to the work ethic ('by not doing anything') and is framed in opposition to its economic benefits ('just so he can make more money'). In addition, it is set apart from the honourable work of the ancestors who had industriously and enduringly dug the original drains by hand, only to have them ripped out in a matter of minutes by a mechanical excavator. This demonstrates that for work to be valued, and for it to achieve the moral approval of being 'hard work', it must also be part of a long-term process of engagement with the land; it must be tied to a process of betterment that is seen as long-term and steady, as part of a 'lifetime's work' with a central objective of passing on the farm to the next generation 'in better fettle' than when it was found (Emery, 2010).

These examples show that hard work is considered virtuous, that it is commonly upheld through recourse to the land but that it is often disassociated with any financial connotations. It may not be so straightforward to suggest that good farming and the work ethic is merely an expression of productivity (Thompson, 1995). Instead, there is an associated value in a type of work that is enduring and persistent. As a symbolic ideal, it also holds true that hard work can be interpreted differently by different people and in different situations.

### 6.3.3 Alternative interpretations and uses of the work ethic

In spite of the above examples, it would be incorrect to suggest that earning a living is not important, or to suggest that being able to earn a living is not considered constitutive of the good farmer. Indeed, as Fred Atliss put it, there is a dual imperative on the farmer to keep the farm 'in good heart' and to produce a product that meets the requirements of the market. Clive Fisk demonstrated that this can cause something of a dilemma in terms of how one spends one's time. Symbolically important work such as tidying and attending to the appearance of one's stock, Clive told me, has to be balanced with work that is aimed at achieving efficiency and hence the profitability of the farming operation. For, as he told me, 'you don't get paid for tidying the farm do you?' Again, there is evidence that work considered an 'identity investment' does not correlate to productive economic output. In fact, it might well stand in direct opposition to it. This distinction might be not so straightforward however, because the reputation of being a good farmer achieved through symbolic work on the appearance of the farm can lead to a greater price being achieved at market. This would be particularly the case when one is selling livestock to another farmer, but where livestock is being sold for slaughter its quality is more likely to be judged on its own merits such as size or leanness (see Gray 1999).

We saw in the previous section that the appearance of the farm and the work ethic can be used to indict alternative systems of farming (especially environmental approaches). However, I want to elaborate an example between two sets of neighbours – the Spuhlers and the Colleys – that demonstrates the versatility of the work ethic as a value, and how it can be alternatively interpreted and expressed. Whereas the Colleys were one of the few farms that I visited that had not joined any of the agri-environmental schemes on offer, their neighbours the Spuhlers had joined the highest tier agri-environment scheme and were also farming organically. In spite of this, both used the work ethic and symbols expressing it to cast aspersions against one another. This was only possible on account of the utility of the work ethic to be interpreted differently.

The Colleys criticise the appearance of the Spuhlers' farm by referring to what they do as 'growing a field full of thistle' (or 'a jungle' as another neighbour put it). Furthermore, they link this criticism to the work ethic (or lack thereof) by complaining that the Spuhlers probably earn more than they do 'for doing nothing'; for leaving the fields to grow wild and taking payments from the agri-environment scheme. The Spuhlers, on the other hand, do not buy into the association between work and suffering. Mr Spuhler, a recent 'incomer', said that he could not understand why the local farmers trudge about in the wet and the cold to earn just a few thousand pounds a year. He said the other farmers probably 'think we play at it [farming]' but because they don't have all the specialist equipment 'we probably work a lot harder than they do'. He was not particularly interested in farming, but had bought the place for his wife, and was investing his time and money on renovating the farmhouse into four luxury holiday apartments. He had no long-term plans to stay on the farm, but planned to sell it on for a large profit, to buy another house in a 'nice part of the country' and a yacht to sail around the world on. Aesthetically, he preferred the appearance of buttercups and hay-fields as opposed to the blue-green fields of his neighbours.[5] And he cast aspersions against the success of his neighbours not in terms of the visual appearance of the land, but on account of their decrepit machinery; describing their farm as 'a wreck'.

Although Mr Spuhler might not be casting aspersions on whether the Colleys are good or bad farmers, his pointing to the appearance of the machinery as opposed to the appearance of the land suggests that he judges success in terms of wealth, rather than the keeping of the land in good condition. So, the Colleys think that Mr Spuhler cannot be working hard because it is not expressed in the appearance of the land; he's getting paid for doing nothing, for growing a 'jungle'. Alan Spuhler, on the other hand, suggests that he works a lot harder than other farmers (though he doesn't directly point to his neighbours) and is able to demonstrate this by the amount of money he is likely to make on the sale of the farm once the renovations have been completed. Capital assets (such as property, machines, yachts), then are the signs of *work's reward*, of wealth, whereas the land is just the sign of work. For one party capital assets are demonstrative of the *outcome* of work, while for the other party the land is demonstrative of the *process* of work.

This example shows that the work ethic is used by both parties to indict one another, which represents its rhetorical utility in trying to convince their audience (on these occasions the anthropologist posing the questions) that their approach was best. I now want to briefly present three additional examples of how farmers employ the work ethic rhetorically in varied and, at first glance, counter-intuitive or contradictory ways. The reason for the different deployments, I suggest, is because rhetoric needs to be tailored to its situation, the audience at which it is targeted and the particular argument being pursued at any one moment in time (Emery, 2010; Emery et al., 2013). The work ethic nevertheless remains effective on account of its virtuous associations.

## 6.4  Using hard work negatively

Given that hard work is upheld as virtuous it is quite rare amongst farmers for it to be referred to with negative connotations. It would be quite unexpected, for instance, for a farmer to say 'I'm not doing that, it's too much like hard work'. This is because if hard work is virtuous, then this is precisely the sort of activity that they should want to engage in. Re-instating flocks of sheep on the open moorland[6] was one activity in which the farmers did refer to the work associated with it in a negative light. Re-instating grazing sheep on the moors was being encouraged by conservation bodies and the government, since the grazing by sheep is essential to maintaining the protected wildlife habitat on the moors. Tom Hasling had previously kept sheep on the moor but said that the conservation bodies would have to pay him a lot of money to re-instate them. Similarly his neighbour Graham Wilson stated that it's a major operation to take on and he does not want to 'tramp about on the moor' as he gets older.

I would suggest that the reason for these farmers deploying the work ethic negatively is because their audience has changed: they are not demonstrating the value of their work to other farmers, who judge them on the appearance of their farm, but to policy-makers with the financial means available to increase the support available for upland farms. Because this different audience with the power to affect the farmers' situation does not uphold the same moral value (or does not uphold it through the same means of expression) the farmer must translate his own moral value in work into an economic one. In such a guise it is acceptable to talk of work negatively, because work's only reward is monetary and not moral. Or, it could be that monetary success and reward is deemed to be morally endorsed but it is endorsed through the symbols of wealth, rather than the symbols of the landscape.

## 6.5 Environmental payments as 'money for old rope'

When I asked farmers about the payments they received as part of agri-environment schemes, I was quite surprised that many of them said it did not require them to do anything differently from what they had already been doing, and that it was 'money for old rope'. I wondered why they did not take the opportunity to uphold the value of the work they did as part of these schemes (I certainly knew that many of them didn't think that the payments amounted to much). Surely they would want to demonstrate to the UK or European taxpayer (the ultimate source of the subsidy payments) that their money was being well-spent. Instead of downplaying the value of their work, however, I suggest this strategy is aimed at upholding it. Farmers used this opportunity to uphold the value of their work symbolically, as the creator of all that is good in the first place; it is their work that created the valued landscape which the policy-makers want to protect and they don't need to justify their work in terms of monetary reward in this instance (in contrast to the example above). The situation and the strategy has changed. In this instance, the farmers want to take the opportunity to make an indictment on the policy itself, to demonstrate that the policy is ineffectual and to make one of the commonest arguments of all: that farmers are in the best position to look after the environment as demonstrated by the results of their previous (unpaid) landscape management.

## 6.6    Hard work and environmental benefits go hand in glove

In contrast to the arguments made between different farmers about the relative merits of 'conventional' vis-à-vis 'organic' or environmental approaches to farming, there was one arena where environmental aesthetics were presented as a sign of hard work, rather than as a sign of laziness. This was in the use of the work ethic in the marketing of farm produce. During my fieldwork a campaign was launched to market locally reared lamb from the moors. This marketing was based on the environmental benefits to the landscape that the purchaser would be supporting, and also deployed the work ethic to uphold the value of the farmer in maintaining the valued moorland environment.

> The argument is that losing the animals means losing much more. Without grazing of the hills, walkers and hunters would be fighting through bramble, blackthorn and bracken. It has already happened on some Lakeland fells.
> Without the need to keep livestock from wandering, there would be no incentive to keep up the stone barns and walls which complete the pattern on the picture postcards.
> *The whole of our 'traditional' landscape, we are reminded, has been created over the past 900 years, since Cistercian monks demonstrated what could be achieved with organised hard work.* (Benfield, 2007: *Yorkshire Post*)

The initiative has been given strong support by the *Yorkshire Post* through its *Save Our Uplands* campaign. Interestingly, the campaign ties environmental and landscape values together with motifs of hardship and suffering for particular rhetorical effect. Articles under headings such as 'Beauty and hardship go hand in hand up on the moors' and 'Hidden hardships of heartbeat country's farmers' (Hickling, 2008a; 2008b) infer an inherent value amongst the readership of the *Yorkshire Post* in both environmental protection and the hard work and struggles of the upland farmer. There are two implications of this. The first is that work, in this instance, seems to be valued and expressed in relation to the landscape. The second implication is that this suggests that the *work ethic* is still valued as important to a broader general public compared to a more economic value in work that is directed towards the policy-makers. The reason is that the audience has changed again. So, whilst the environmental and landscape values of farmers' work are aimed at the public, arguments made using the economic value of farmers' work are directed at the policy-makers: at those with the direct ability to control farm support. This suggests that the work ethic is of wider societal appeal (one only has to listen to a politician talking about the need to deliver policies that help 'hard-working families'), and that farming and farmed landscapes remain associative with those values (for another example see Hinrichs, 1996).

## 6.7    Discussion and conclusion

This chapter has demonstrated the importance of the work ethic for farmers' personhoods and how that work ethic is upheld through particular practices and farmland aesthetics. A Weberian interpretation of this work ethic has been linked to outputs that provide income; it links the value in hard work squarely to productive capacity (Thompson, 1995). This interpretation has been used to argue that organic farming, or new agri-environmental schemes, challenge the work ethic of the farmer because they affect the practices (the type of work undertaken) and their means of expression (the physical appearance of the farm) that are demonstrative of a productivist conception of the work ethic (Burton, 2004; Egoz et al., 2001; Silvasti, 2003). In this chapter I have agreed that farming personhoods are challenged by alternative approaches to farming that alter both the practices and the farmland aesthetics that farmers subscribe to. The ethnographic material presented, however, has demonstrated that hard work is valued not only in terms of its economic and productive symbolism but is interpreted and expressed in a plurality of ways. Such alternatives, moreover, are often expressed in opposition to, rather than in support of, a financially motivated conception of the work ethic. Hence, it was shown that making the most money was not necessarily demonstrative of the good, hard-working farmer, and that those farmers who follow the environmental route are not castigated because they are shunning productivist ideals but because, on the contrary, they are driven by financial motives. There is certainly an aesthetic associated with the work ethic, often expressed through the notion of the 'tidy farm'. However, it is important to point out that this is not a fixed interpretation and that it is as much about demonstrating the *process* of work as the *outputs* of work that is important. Thus, a dynamic and changing landscape is illustrative of the work ethic (Emery, 2010; Silvasti, 2003) and the emphasis is placed on being engaged in the activities that seek to better the farm over the long-term and leave it to the next generation in improved condition (Emery, 2010).

Those that have equated the work ethic to productivism have suggested that environmental schemes that are equally productive (focused on the production of environmental outputs and accordingly weighted payments) may appeal more to farmers and lead to more effectual behaviour change (Burton et al., 2008). This is a sensible suggestion since farmers often complain that 'you can't see the benefits' of agri-environment schemes (Emery and Franks, 2012). However, if we accept that the work ethic and farmers' cultural values more broadly are influenced by more than productivism (see also Davidson, 2009), then we need to consider how a more complex set of values interacts with policy incentives and does or does not influence changes in behaviour. If work is valued as a process rather than in terms of its outputs, for instance, concentrating on types of activities required, rather than on how their success is monitored might increase the acceptability of agri-environment schemes. This interpretation adds support to the need for caution in extending the use of results-based approaches to the management of the farmed environment (Burton and Schwarz, 2013) and to the use of target-based incentives in wider organisational settings.

The survival of a plurality of interpretations of the work ethic, despite the ingress of capitalist ideology, has been explained through recourse to rhetoric culture theory; whereby the variety of interpretations represents (1) their continued salience to the interests and argumentative strategies of groups and individuals as they seek to persuade others through social interaction, and (2) the need to tailor those argumentative strategies to the changing situations in which interaction occurs (Emery, 2010; Emery et al., 2013). This helps us to understand the sometimes counter-intuitive and contradictory ways that values can get used in different argumentative strategies, but also the practices through which values are adapted to shifting external conditions. This chapter has emphasised that work is not just a process creating value, but is itself a valued process. Examining how and why it is valued, its diversity, and the means by which it is expressed, can help us to understand workplace behaviours and how, why and whether they change as a consequence of shifting social, economic, political and environmental conditions.

### NOTES

1. Personhood(s) is used broadly here to refer to a sense of self and worth that is not fixed but relatively and subjectively mediated through interaction in changing sociocultural settings.
2. For livestock farmers it may also find expression in the appearance and quality of the stock (see Gray, 1999).
3. All names are pseudonyms.
4. Hobby farmers are those that farm as a lifestyle choice and do not farm for a living. They are typically considered to be wealthy incomers to the area.
5. Heavily fertilised pasture is often said to take on a bluish hue.
6. Many were lost to the culls of the foot and mouth outbreak in 2001 and never re-instated.

 **REFERENCES**

Abrahams, R.G. (1991) *A Place of Their Own: Family Farming in Eastern Finland*, Cambridge: Cambridge University Press.

Benfield, C. (2007) 'Standing up tall for the hill farmer', *Yorkshire Post*, 31 August 2007, http://www.yorkshirepost.co.uk/news/features/standing-up-tall-for-the-hill-farmer-1-2469443 (retrieved September 2013).

Borchgrevink, A. (2002) 'Clean and green: Indigenous knowledge and cultural models in a Philippine community', *Ethnos*, 67(2), 223–244.

Burton, R.J.F. (2004) 'Seeing through the "good farmer's" eyes: Towards developing an understanding of the social symbolic value of "productivist" behaviour', *Sociologia Ruralis*, 44(2), 195–215.

Burton, R.J. and Schwarz, G. (2013) 'Result-oriented agri-environmental schemes in Europe and their potential for promoting behavioural change', *Land Use Policy*, 30(1), 628–641.

Burton, R., Kuczera, C. and Schwarz, G. (2008) 'Exploring farmers' cultural resistance to voluntary agri-environmental schemes', *Sociologia Ruralis*, 48(1), 16–37.

Carrithers, M.B. (2005) 'Why anthropologists should study rhetoric', *Journal of the Royal Anthropological Institute*, 11(3), 577–583.

Carro-Ripalda, S. (n.d.) 'Making oneself through suffering', *Rhetoric of Personhood Workshop*, Durham University, 25–27 March.

Cockcroft, B. (1974) *Sunley's Daughter: The Ways of a Yorkshire Dale*, London: Dent.

Cohen, A.P. (1979) 'The Whalsay croft: Traditional work and customary identity in modern times', in Wallman, S. (ed.), *Social Anthropology of Work*, London: Academic Press.

Davidson, J. (2009) '"We work hard": Customary imperatives of the Diola work regime in the context of environmental and economic change', *African Studies Review*, 52(2), 119–141.

Duckworth, G.E. (1959) 'Vergil's Georgics and the Laudes Galli', *The American Journal of Philology*, 80(3), 225–237.

Egoz, S., Bowring, J. and Perkins, H. (2001) 'Tastes in tension: Form, function and meaning in New Zealand's farmed landscapes', *Landscape and Urban Planning*, 57(3), 177–196.

Emery, S.B. (2010) *In Better Fettle: Improvement, Work and Rhetoric in the Transition to Environmental Farming in the North York Moors, Doctoral Thesis, Department of Anthropology*. Durham: Durham University. Accessed at: http://etheses.dur.ac.uk/379/ (retrieved 27 September 2013).

Emery, S.B. and Franks, J. R. (2012) 'The potential for collaborative agri-environment schemes in England: Can a well-designed collaborative approach address farmers' concerns with current schemes?', *Journal of Rural Studies*, 28(3), 218–231.

Emery, S.B., Perks, M.T. and Bracken, L.J. (2013) 'Negotiating river restoration: The role of divergent reframing in environmental decision-making', *Geoforum*, 47, 167–177.

Gray, J. (1998) 'Family farms in the Scottish Borders: A practical definition by hill farmers', *Journal of Rural Studies*, 14(3), 241–356.

Gray, J. (1999) 'Open spaces and dwelling places: Being at home on hill farms in the Scottish Borders', *American Ethnologist*, 26(2), 440–460.

Hickling, M. (2008a) 'Beauty and hardship go hand in hand up on the Moors', *Yorkshire Post – Country Week*, 28 July, 10–11.

Hickling, M. (2008b) 'Hidden hardships of heartbeat country's farmers', *Yorkshire Post – Country Week*, 22 March, 10.

Hinrichs, C.C. (1996) 'Consuming images: Making and marketing Vermont as distinctive rural place', in Dupuis, E.M. and Vandergeest, P. (eds), *Creating the Countryside: The Politics of Rural and Environmental Discourse*, Philadelphia: Temple University Press.

Ingold, T. (1984) 'The estimation of work in a Northern Finnish farming community', in Long,

N. (ed.), *Family and Work in Rural Societies: Perspectives on Non-wage Labour*, London: Tavistock.

Long, N. (ed.) (1984) *Family and Work in Rural Societies: Perspectives on Non-wage Labour*, London: Tavistock.

McEachern, C. (1992) 'Farmers and conservation: Conflict and accommodation in farming policies', *Journal of Rural Studies*, 8(2), 159–171.

Newby, H. (1977) *The Deferential Worker: A Study of Farm Workers in East Anglia*, London: Penguin.

Osthaus, C.R. (2004) 'The work ethic of the plain folk: Labor and religion in the Old South', *The Journal of Southern History*, 70(4), 745–782.

Penrose, J. (1993) 'Reification in the name of change: The impact of nationalism on social constructions of nation, people and place in Scotland and United Kingdom', in Jackson, P. and Penrose, J. (eds), *Constructions of Race, Place and Nation*, London: UCL.

Rapport, N. (1993), *Diverse World Views in an English Village*, Edinburgh: Edinburgh University Press.

Ravetz, A. (2001) *Vision, Knowledge and the Invention of Place in an English Town*, Unpublished PhD Thesis, Faculty of Economic and Social Studies, University of Manchester.

Rosivach, V.J. (2001) 'Class matters in the "Dyskolos" of Menander', *The Classical Quarterly*, 51(1), 127–134.

Schwimmer, E. (1979) 'The self and the product: Concepts of work in comparative perspective', in Wallman, S. (ed.), *Social Anthropology of Work*, London: Academic Press.

Silvasti, T. (2003) 'The cultural model of the "good farmer" and the environmental question in Finland', *Agriculture and Human Values*, 20(2), 143–150.

Strecker, I. and Tyler, S. (eds) (2009) *Culture and Rhetoric*, Oxford: Berghahn Books.

Thompson, P. (1995) *The Spirit of the Soil: Agriculture and Environmental Ethics*, London: Routledge.

Wallman, S. (ed.) (1979) *The Social Anthropology of Work*, London: Academic Press.

Walter, G. (1995) 'A "curious blend": The successful farmer in American farm magazines, 1984–1991', *Agriculture and Human Values*, 12(3), 55–68.

Weber, M. (1930) *The Protestant Ethic and the Spirit of Capitalism*, London and New York: Routledge.

Wolf, A. (1987) 'Saving the small farm: Agriculture in Roman literature', *Agriculture and Human Values*, 4(2–3), 65–75.

# 7

# Disjointed, degraded and divided? A tale of dirty work at the chicken factory

*Lindsay Hamilton and Darren McCabe*

## 7.1    Introduction

In 1990, organisational scholars Steve Ackroyd and Philip Crowdy published a research paper on slaughterhouse workers which posed the question, 'can culture be managed?' The article questioned whether a core objective of human resource management (to manage organisational culture) was possible in any meaningful sense. Drawing on research of a group of slaughterhouse workers in a British abattoir, Ackroyd and Crowdy argued that the dominant values of society at large were implicated in 'the spontaneous formation and character of occupational cultures' (Ackroyd and Crowdy, 1990: 4) even within small groups such as the one they studied. In other words, workplace culture was said to exist in tandem with influences from outside the factory – status, class, race and gender – which impacted upon the expectations and behaviours of the workforce at the factory-floor level.

Their article showed how the slaughter workers reproduced these forces as they collected together to form a tight-knit work group. One of the ways in which the slaughtermen displayed membership of this group was through exhibiting indifference towards the blood, mess and smells of the factory – they worked hard and did their 'fair share' of the heavy manual work involved. Ackroyd and Crowdy argued that the factory management allowed the slaughtermen to work as an autonomous group to 'make life easier' for themselves. Hence the men self-regulated and watched each other, thereby ensuring that the work was done quickly and well. There was then little need for managerial interference. The aim of this chapter is to re-think and reflect upon some of the significant aspects of Ackroyd and Crowdy's (1990) influential study within a contemporary chicken factory. We draw out some of the comparisons and the contrasts between their case study and our own by considering our first-hand observations of life in the contemporary slaughterhouse.

## 7.2    Contemporary meat work

Today's meat industry looks very different from that observed by Ackroyd and Crowdy in 1990. The contemporary meat industry is highly special-ised between slaughterhouses which supply 'red meat' (beef and lamb for example) and poultry processing plants (known in the industry as 'white meat'). Small, family run slaughterhouses are increasingly rare and in their place are extensive and highly mechanised plants that respond to the rising demand for meat (Buller and Roe, 2013). Chicken is now a major part of that demand and in the UK alone, some 800 million birds are butchered each year and 50 billion chickens are killed globally (Cudworth, 2008). The meat industry as a whole is extremely profitable and has become more industrial-ised, reliant upon high-tech solutions and complex supply chains. The labour force has also changed. Whereas Ackroyd and Crowdy were able to sub-title their (1990) paper, 'the case of the English slaughtermen' the workforce in today's meat industry includes large numbers of economic migrants travel-ling to live and work in the UK. Employed on temporary contracts through agencies, many rely upon the high demand for chicken meat production to secure their employment.

In seeking to consider some of these issues in greater depth we have selected a chicken slaughter and packing plant as our main research site – anonymised as 'Farmstock'. Farmstock is a large food processors and it supplies chicken to food retailers and foodservice distributors in Britain and other parts of Europe. Farmstock employs over 7,000 managers, technologists and opera-tives across the UK and Ireland; approximately 1,000 are employed at the factory discussed in this chapter. In 2012, the holding company that owns Farmstock made a pre-tax profit of £24m which presented a £20m increase from 2011's figures, largely because of increased sales to supermarkets (BBC, 13 August 2013). Clearly, our case study focused on a much larger busi-ness than the case study that Ackroyd and Crowdy investigated and, with a focus on chickens rather than large animals, it was processing 'products' that had rather different qualities than those handled by Ackroyd and Crowdy's slaughtermen. However, we found that there was still a useful basis for com-parisons which could be drawn from these different case studies.

The way that we attempt to reflect upon this is by attending to one particu-lar analytic point; the concept of 'dirty work' in the meat industry. Our key research question, then, is whether or not a strong team culture existed or emerged at Farmstock to help workers to cope with the potential 'dirty work' of slaughtering. In excavating some potential answers to this, we start with a review of the literature on slaughtering and 'dirty work' before elaborating upon our research. We then provide a detailed description of the production process at Farmstock and discuss some of our interactions with the factory's workers. The chapter then concludes with a discussion of our findings and (some) conclusions about the contemporary world of meat work.

## 7.3 What is 'dirty work'?

From cleaning, domestic and care work (Noon and Blyton, 2007; Vachhani and Pullen, 2011) to prostitution and exotic dancing (Grandy and Mavin, 2012), the perception of certain occupations as 'dirty' often serves to stigmatise those involved (Kreiner et al., 2006: 621; Sayer, 2007). Such occupations are often perceived as disgusting or degrading such that 'dirty workers' are tarnished by a variety of 'pollutants', both tangible and symbolic (Ashforth and Kreiner, 1999; Baran et al., 2012; Dick, 2005; Tyler, 2011). The slaughterhouse is a particularly fine example of a space where 'dirty work' is carried out because it has both symbolic and tangible 'dirt'; the ubiquitous presence of death, the regimented and routine practicalities of killing and an array of biological by-products and 'mess' like blood, bones and flesh.

At first sight, then, slaughterhouses appear to be straightforwardly 'dirty' workplaces. Organised, mass-killing combined with blood, odours and body parts lend both physical and symbolic 'taint' to the job of meat production (Ackroyd and Crowdy, 1990; Inkson, 1977; Stull and Broadway, 2004). The secretive nature of the slaughterhouse is something which has, for a long time, contributed to this perceived stigma (Vialles, 1994; Wilkie, 2010); something which has been exacerbated by recent food controversies such as the UK horse-meat scandal. The suggestion of physical and ethical 'contamination' has created heightened suspicion regarding meat plants and their 'shadowy' operatives and added to this, the idea that such spaces pose unacceptable harm to animals via organised 'violence' (Pachirat, 2011) and cruelty has taken hold in the public consciousness.

In Ackroyd and Crowdy's (1990) study, they argued that the work was strongly team-based and that such teams had developed 'a high degree of autonomy from close supervision' (p. 5). A large factor in this team culture was gender; in fact Ackroyd and Crowdy argued that the abattoir was a highly 'masculine' environment involving heavy, physical work and toughness (p. 8; see also Meara, 1974). This gave workers a degree of pride on account of such 'toughness and self-sacrifice' (p. 414), a view subsequently endorsed by Ashforth and Kreiner (1999) who argue that 'the stigma of dirtiness often fosters relatively "strong" occupational and workgroup cultures' (p. 414). The behaviour that Ackroyd and Crowdy (1990) observed was argued 'to have little to do with technological factors' (p. 10) and managerial control was considered to be relatively unproblematic due to the strong team culture and the absence of division and resistance. In our research at Farmstock, however, we found there to be some clear contrasts between these findings and our own.

Farmstock had a highly mechanised production line and, unlike the red meat factory, processed thousands of chickens each day. The repetitive and mundane nature of the work sometimes led to boredom; a problem that resulted in moments of tension and resistance. On account of the relative size of the animals involved, the workers – a mixture of males and females – required little physical strength to do the work. They also required fewer butchery skills such that the work was highly repetitive. The tedium of factory life was echoed by the ways that workers behaved on the production line; they rarely spoke to each other and appeared to be highly focused upon the regimented tasks in hand (sorting offal, for example). Even during their time in the staff canteen, there was little evidence of joking or interaction that studies of other factory workers have pointed to as an essential strategy for coping with 'dirty' or boring work (Roy, 1960).

At Farmstock the number of employees was far higher than in Ackroyd and Crowdy's study and these were split (broadly speaking) into 'high prestige' (directors, managers, meat inspectors, vets) and 'low prestige' (production line operator, slaughterer) jobs. It is worth noting that the majority of those working on the production line were agency employed and had travelled from abroad to work in the UK. In keeping with UK legislation, Farmstock must also utilise the services of Food Standards Agency meat inspectors. The inspectors were not employed by Farmstock because they are government workers, contracted out to different slaughterhouses to do quality checks, but they had a key role in ensuring the hygiene and quality of the meat produced and sold from the plant. Vets also worked at Farmstock to ensure the health and welfare of the chickens as they came into the factory and progressed to the 'killing floor'. At least a third of the meat inspectors and almost all the factory vets were also economic migrants and on temporary agency contracts.

The (apparently) higher status, higher paid workers tended to view the production process through managerial eyes and considered themselves to be professionals. Perhaps because of the highly regulated and technocratic environment, there were, however, relatively few hands-on managers which meant that much of the day-to-day supervision was carried out informally by the 'high status' vets and meat inspectors. Yet these individuals were not 'managers' in the strictest sense as they did not have line-management responsibilities for those on the production line. The status of the meat inspectors and vets was sometimes vague and, since they frequently switched jobs between Farmstock and a number of other plants, it was hard for them to form group attachments within the factory.

A sizeable proportion of these 'professional' workers were qualified vet-erinarians from outside the UK and were legally prohibited from finding employment in the clinical treatment of animals. Employed by agencies to fulfil the meat inspection and animal welfare requirements at a number of abattoirs, we noted that these migrant professional workers seemed to accept inferior terms and conditions of employment, often with full aware-ness that UK qualified vets enjoyed a significantly better quality of employ-ment. In common with many of those employed on the production line, then, their 'strong economic attachment to work' (Inkson, 1977: 6) coupled with the insecurity of short-term agency contracts shaped how these workers engaged with or resisted work (Nichols et al., 2004: 667). These factors chal-lenged our initial view of the meat inspectors as higher status or 'managerial' workers in the factory and presented yet a further contrast between Ackroyd and Crowdy's research findings and ours. Hence it was not only the lack of a clear masculine identity or group culture in our research findings that pointed towards different findings but also the importation of different eth-nicities (Ram, 1991) and different expectations of the wage-effort bargain (Baldamus, 1967).

Our initial observations broadly support the general principle that 'the nature and efficacy of managerial controls cannot be understood outside wider structures such as the social wage and the nature of contracts in the labour market' (Thompson and van den Broek, 2010: 8; Ackroyd and Crowdy, 1990; Cooke, 2006) but they also suggest that it is misguided to regard all of those who work in the meat industry (and indeed within our chicken factory) as 'dirty workers' in exactly the same way. Unfortunately, within organisation studies, the 'dirty work' label covers a wide diversity of occupa-tions from those which have more explicit connotations of social disapproval such as those who work in the sex industry (Thompson and Harred, 1992; Tyler, 2011; Grandy and Mavin, 2012; Selmi, 2012) and investment bankers (Stanley and Mackenzie Davey, 2012) to those who deal with 'pollutants' in a more physical way: construction workers (Riemer, 1979); cleaners (Noon and Blyton, 2007); janitors (Gold, 1964); funeral directors (Thompson, 1991) and gravediggers (Petrillo, 1989, 1990). Within much of this research, there appears to be a limited understanding of how workers can be *differently dirty*, even within the same factory and one of our concerns in this chapter is to highlight how this is the case.

## 7.4    Different 'dirty workers'?

As Hughes (1958) asserts, while 'dirty jobs' are often done by those at the lower end of the wage scale, it is also the case that higher status jobs sometimes attract the label of 'dirty work' by association with stigmatised others – the police (Dick, 2005) and social workers, for example (Anderson, 2000). This broad range of roles substantiates Hughes's early (1958) definition of dirty work as 'physically, socially or morally' tainted tasks (p. 122). According to Ashforth and Kreiner (1999) 'the boundaries between the physical, social and moral dimensions are inherently fuzzy, and many occupations appear to be tainted on multiple dimensions' (p. 415); an argument that applies to the meat inspectors, vets and production line workers at Farmstock. All these workers were 'physically' and 'morally' tainted on some level because their work was associated with death and, in the case of those working on the line, it involved not only the killing but also the routine dismemberment of dead animals.

Meat inspectors and vets were one step removed from such manual labour but were 'socially' tainted by regular contact with individuals that are 'stigmatised' (Ashforth and Kreiner, 1999). One could argue that meat inspectors and production line operators shared a similar 'breadth' of 'dirtiness', in the sense that both spent almost all of their time in the meat trade (Kreiner et al., 2006). But the 'depth' of their association with 'taint' was different because meat inspectors and vets were employed to ensure that the killing was carried out to the required standards (indirect involvement) whereas operators were fully implicated in the doing of killing (direct involvement). Adding more complexity still, the different stages within the production process carried different levels of 'dirtiness'. So, for example, those packing (trussing) chickens had particularly low status among line workers; it was a part of the factory that nobody appeared to want to work in. All of the factory's jobs can be said to have a degree of 'stigma' (Kreiner et al., 2006), but they differed in the degree of 'involvement' and the 'intensity' (ibid.) of their association with the 'dirty work' of killing. Finding out how and why such forms of 'pollution' operated inside the factory was a key part of our research.

Our research took an ethnographic approach (Van Maanen, 1979; 1988). We carried out observational research as well as interviews with 18 meat inspectors, 6 slaughter-workers and 11 factory vets during 2011. The aim was to gather first-hand information about social processes without heavy reliance upon structured interviews. To that end, some interviews were conducted at participants' homes or by telephone. The rest were conducted during time spent in the factory. At times data gathering in the factory was hindered by the need to wear ear protectors; it was a noisy environment that – coupled with the language barriers that were routinely encountered – made it difficult to talk. Nonetheless, we attempted to immerse ourselves in the everyday culture of the organisation, joining in the routines and the conversations. In the next section of the chapter, we reflect on the experience of life at Farmstock, drawing out some of our observations from our time in the field.

## 7.5 Life (and death) in the chicken factory

Farmstock is a large industrial unit on an out-of-town trading estate. Arriving at dawn for the change of the shifts, the researcher (in this case LH) observed hundreds of production line workers streaming to and from the bus stop. Most were heading to and from a changing room which (from the street doorway) looked dirty with a wet and muddy tiled floor and peeling paint on the walls. Nobody stopped to use the anti-bacterial hand gel dispenser mounted on the wall. Walking towards the glass-fronted reception area, set well back from the staff entrance, there was little clue as to the scale or indeed the nature of the work going on behind the scenes.

After signing into the visitor's log, the researcher was directed up two flights of steel and glass stairs to a plush, blue-carpeted corridor with cream walls where the management offices were located. At the end of this corridor was an unmarked white door and this was where the meat inspectors and the factory veterinarians were based. In this office, there were files, clothes and other office paraphernalia everywhere. There was only one desk and one computer and six workers used the rest of the floor-space to change into their protective clothes. The lack of clear marking (and office space) seemed to suggest that these 'professional' workers were held in low esteem by the management at Farmstock.

### 7.5.1 The dirty side

The researcher followed one of the meat inspectors, Bobby, to work on the factory floor, a process which began in what was described as the 'dirty side'. Here, articulated lorries reversed into the warehouse (lairage) and unloaded plastic crates of identically small, white birds. Operatives in this space stacked the crates onto a conveyor belt which was heading for the gas chamber. Tracking the conveyor belt, it was possible to see the crates as they emerged from the gas chamber. The birds had been gassed with a lethal cocktail of Argon and Nitrogen so potent that they were dead within seconds. In the next zone, a group known as the 'hangers on' worked silently and robotically in their red aprons and white wellingtons to shackle or 'hang on' the lifeless chickens onto the moving production line. It was a fast and silent process. The apparent tedium with which the dead birds were pegged out was notable and no emotions were displayed.

The production line transports the birds from the 'dirty side' of the factory to the 'clean' post-mortem zone where not only the 'meat' but the feathers, feet, head and innards are removed, sorted and packaged for sale. The production process involves relatively little meat handling, cutting or butchery work and instead relies upon a series of machines to carry out much of the preparation work. The first of these machines is the 'neck cutter'; a sharp automated blade that removes the heads from the chickens. When this machine is not working, a slaughter-worker is on hand to perform the task manually; this is the only individual in the plant that has the job title of 'slaughterman'.

> **Factory slaughterman**: You don't want the birds coming towards the neck cutter alive, but sometimes things go wrong and . . . on occasion . . . it happens. We call them [the live birds] 'red necks' [laughs]. That's why I have to be here.

The importance of the factory slaughterman to safeguard against such 'system errors' is described here in ways that downplay the occasionally gruesome processes at work. This was further illustrated by one of the meat inspectors in a subsequent interview:

> **Simon**: it should be gas (killing) all the time but they've got backup electrical stun in case. They've had a few problems with the gas, it has to be an exact mix of argon – 5% – and nitrogen – 95% – and when the mix changes it automatically stops the line. So then they'll have to go on to electric stun for a bit while they sort that out. They can run at the same speed whichever. But, for the hangers on, it's a lot easier to do gas kill because the things aren't moving.

If the chickens were killed by gas then their limp bodies were easy to handle and the 'hangers on' could easily hook the birds to the line, for as Simon stated: 'the things aren't moving'. But if the gas was not working then this made the task much harder. It meant that the birds had to be put into shackles alive and this was a far more difficult process.

## 7.5.2 The clean side

Progressing through the factory, the (now headless and bloodless) birds began to look far less like animals and more like meat. Entering the 'scald tank', the birds had their feathers removed and so they were first submerged in hot water (52 degrees) to open the pores. Passing into the 'plumpers', the birds were then de-feathered by rotating rubber 'fingers'. The feathers were collected in a hopper; just one of several by-products that can be sold separately. The de-feathered birds passed into the next room where they were inspected by the Food Standards Agency officials for colour, quality and any other obvious defects.

The birds that passed the inspection were conveyed into the 'evisceration room'. This comprised a series of machines that systematically removed and gathered together the internal organs. The chicken and its (separate) intestines, lungs and heart had to be viewed together by the next group of meat inspectors, located in an adjacent room. More birds were removed from the production line at this inspection point. Strict time limits governed the entire inspection process. Following this inspection, the internal organs were picked off the line by a team of approximately twenty workers. Gizzards, hearts, feet and livers were hand trimmed and sorted into large steel bins. In the offal sorting room, the fluorescent lighting was dazzling and despite this being a separate zone, the operatives worked at steel tables in clinical silence. This was one of the few places where a small amount of chicken blood and other body parts were observable on the floor.

When the steel sorting bins were full, they were wheeled into the packing department. The eviscerated birds were inspected again before passing through to the trussing station. Here a female group of workers 'dressed' the birds ready for packaging. This work involved tucking the wings of the birds under their body and tying the legs together with elastic and inserting them into plastic trays. The trussers were the last group in the production process and, at this point, the birds were graded and weighed. The finished packages were wrapped and labelled and passed through a final inspection before being made ready for despatch.

## 7.5.3 A clean kill

Overall, our observations of this process suggested that slaughtering in a contemporary chicken factory is a surprisingly sanitised affair with few signs or celebration of blood as Ackroyd and Crowdy (1990) found. It appears that killing on an industrial scale is designed to wash away the 'taint' of such work.

Perhaps the industrialised nature of the process enables those employed in this industry to disassociate or distance themselves from the horror and the 'stigma' of what they are doing (Pachirat, 2011). Yet, in listening to those that we spoke to in the factory, we noted that the 'dirty' work of slaughtering went deeper than the physical contact with dead animal bodies.

In fact, the production process itself became a source of 'taint'. The speed of the production line, for example, put pressure on all of those employed here. Hangers on didn't speak for fear of losing momentum, just as meat inspectors viewed thousands of birds each day (at a rate which they estimated to be three per second). The speed of the line produced an intensity of work that the inspectors felt could only be maintained by taking regular breaks; a freedom not extended to production workers. These divergent experiences underline the status gap between these workers just as the lack of butchery and other applied skills devalued the line work of the operatives even further, reinforcing the tedium and repetition of the factory floor.

Within the factory, continual reference was made to the distinction between the 'dirty end' of the factory where the birds were killed and the 'clean end' where they were processed and inspected. Yet despite their association with the 'clean side', with quality assurance and professional knowledge, the inspectors experienced a sense of taint from the work which they sometimes expressed through financial allusions. In the following excerpt, for example, one inspector suggests that – like the birds whose carcasses he is paid to inspect – he is also a cost of production:

> **Simon**: To the meat plant we're just a cost. I mean legally they've got to have us because we're stopping anything bad going into the food chain. . . . There are no showers either for us. We haven't got proper changing facilities either . . . cost cutting.

Simon referred to 'stopping anything bad' and in this way referred to the valuable job that he was doing both for the factory and society thus reframing and representing the work with 'positive value' (Ashforth et al., 2007: 157). This may have been an 'identity-enhancing' technique (Baran et al., 2012: 598) to compensate for the negative view that others even within the factory seemed to hold of them, as Bobby suggests:

> Sorry the office is such a mess . . . it's just that we are sort of like the poor relative here.

As we noted at the outset, the stark contrasts between the luxurious offices of management and the basic facilities provided for the inspection team (and the even less salubrious changing space for the production line workers) denoted clear demarcations between these 'dirty workers'.

## 7.6   Close-knit culture versus individualisation and resistance

Ackroyd and Crowdy (1990) identified a lack of resistance in the slaughterhouse they researched. A different set of dynamics was observable at Farmstock, where the production line was far more individualising. Moreover, it seemed that working lives were dominated by pecuniary as opposed to group concerns and this, at least partly, reflects the itinerant nature of the workforce. The lack of group cohesion may help to explain the instances of conflict and resistance that we will explore in this our final empirical section.

> **Simon:** They are processing at least 7,000 birds a day so it goes very quickly on the line . . . sometimes when they finish earlier than that, they have to go through to trussing but they don't like doing that. The hangers on sort of hang one on, miss one, hang one on, miss one.
> **Alan:** Well that drags the job out I suppose.
> **Simon:** Yes that's the point because they know they'll have to go into trussing if they get finished before time. So if they slow it down a bit they will finish at their normal time. Whereas if the management say they don't have to go into trussing then you don't get any gaps on the line, it's amazing. Crazy.

The above conversation between two meat inspectors, illustrates the type of resistance we observed on the shop floor at Farmstock. Despite the boring nature of the work, there are some jobs that the workers disliked more than others and Kreiner et al. (2006: 633) have posited that research into such 'colloquial notions of dirty work' needs to be investigated. Trussing appears to be particularly detested so the workers created ways of adjusting the rhythm of their work to avoid being moved onto that section. An informal 'pecking order of tasks' (Kreiner et al., 2006: 633) prevailed and, as a feminine task, trussing appeared to be tainted by association with gendered work. It is curious that the production line workers created their own version of 'dirty work', serving to further highlight diversity within 'dirty work' even within single occupations.

Trussing, a task which was disassociated from blood or killing and was located in the 'clean' end of the factory, was feminised and, therefore, appeared to be experienced as a threat to the 'personal dignity' of those working in the 'dirty side' (Sayer, 2007). As Hughes (1970) argued, some tasks 'are gladly delegated to those' that are considered a 'lesser breed, such as women' (p. 149) and so there are gendered as well as functional 'differences' between these 'dirty workers'. Simon described the workers avoiding trussing as 'crazy' but, while it may seem irrational from his perspective, it is entirely rational from the point of view of the employees, who wanted to avoid what Roy (1960) described as the 'beast of boredom'.

In Roy's (1960) account, workers found ways to reduce boredom by playing tricks on each other and, in Meara's (1974) research, they told jokes whereas, in this case, the employees simply reduced their work effort to avoid the more boring jobs. Engaging in 'go slow' tactics to avoid trussing was something that (arguably) relied less upon language than other, more embodied modes of resistance. This observation is supported by considering other examples of *sub rosa* rule breaking in the factory.

The company policy is that 'hangers on' should wear full ventilation masks and suits to protect themselves against dust and feathers and to preserve hygiene. Yet, during several of our observation days, it was apparent that they flouted this rule. It is intriguing that even as the meat inspectors talked about these dress codes, within eyesight they were broken, which the inspectors ignored.

The ability of workers to disrupt the work process surfaced during a conversation between the Head Vet (Trevor) and Bobby, the Head Meat Inspector:

> **Trevor**: I feel it is important to keep production staff happy in the lairage. I need to look into why the duty vet didn't report in on time this morning and, of course, why the staff had to wait for a replacement . . .
> **Bobby**: [Turning to one of us] You have to keep the staff motivated down there . . . it can be very important . . . they don't like breakdowns or waits. Because if you don't keep them busy they use that to fight you all the time.
> **Trevor**: I agree, they must be kept busy because the work is very mundane and if they are not occupied at all times, then their minds start thinking.

In the above extract, Trevor and Bobby are talking about a situation that arose during one of the research visits. The duty vet did not arrive in time for the start of the shift, which meant that, according to legal regulations, the work should not have proceeded. In practice, however, this rule was broken and production commenced. This can be regarded as a 'fiddle' (Mars, 1982) sanctioned by management (see Bensman and Gerver, 1963) in order to maintain output. Bobby and Trevor discussed the importance of keeping the staff motivated by keeping them active and this reflects the boring nature of the work. It would seem that there is one thing worse than being engaged in boring work and that is being kept waiting for it to begin.

Although the production line work is 'very mundane' and can be regarded as low-skilled, it is evident that the workers are still able to exercise considerable power over the production process; hence Bobby's concern that 'if you don't keep them busy they use that to fight you all the time'. The staff are able to resist in numerous ways and Trevor did not want this to be exacerbated. He asserted that once their 'minds start thinking' problems can emerge.

Despite this potential for resistance, workplace relations were largely characterised by consent. This supports Ackroyd and Crowdy's (1990) findings but here the consent was not linked to collective bonds forged through the cultural community or to masculine identities as such. Instead, it appeared to reflect, at least in part, the international composition of the workforce, which gave rise to different economic expectations of the 'effort bargain' (Baldamus, 1967):

> **Bobby**: There are lots of workers there, many Kurdish and Iraqis but also a lot of Polish. There's been a large influx in Polish people coming over and they get signed on by the agencies who supply to these plants. But the Polish are good workers. You get people saying emigrants are taking British jobs but a lot of English . . . young people . . . they don't want the jobs. Like fruit picking, even though it pays about £9 an hour, they won't do it. Yet the Polish guy thinks it's Christmas. He'd work and he'd enjoy it you know? The British don't want it.
> **Author**: Is it easy to get a job here?
> **Bobby**: Yes I suppose it is. It's quite good pay though you know? I was speaking to a few of the production staff the other day and . . . for some reason they think we know everything . . . everything about their tax and things. They are on £16K a year and I know it is a manual kind of job but when you think that people in offices, some of those will be on less than that . . .

The majority of the production line employees were from outside the UK and despite the boring work, maintaining consent on a daily basis was not a major problem for management because they appeared to be motivated by the relatively higher pay. These economic factors appear to be important to this 'dirty work' just as they are to the meat inspectors, which leads us to question Kreiner et al.'s (2006) argument 'that strong occupational stigma will tend to result either in exiting the occupation (or not joining it in the first place)' (p. 624) because such arguments neglect the economic imperative that dominates people's lives.

## 7.7 Conclusion

This chapter has taken a closer look at the operation of a chicken factory to shed light on the contemporary nature of 'dirty work'. There are some contrasts to be drawn between our study and Ackroyd and Crowdy's earlier investigation (1990), not least of which is the fragmentation of the labour force which produces very different experiences of work throughout the factory. Kreiner et al. (2006) refer to 'slaughterhouses' as 'dirty work' (p. 621) and yet, as we have shown in this chapter, this type of work varies considerably depending on the scale and type of production and the nature of the 'products' being slaughtered. The small scale of red meat production in comparison to the extensive, heavily engineered production line of the chicken factory produces a very different work experience for those involved, something which differentiates our study from more recent accounts (Pachirat, 2011). Such work also varies significantly between different groups of workers within this factory (e.g., inspectors versus production line workers).

Clearly, our observations and interview findings suggest that not all 'dirty work' is synonymous with 'a strong occupational or workgroup culture' (Ashforth and Kreiner, 1999: 413). At Farmstock, such cohesion is disrupted by the language barriers, the strict zones of the factory floor and the regimented and routine nature of the production process itself. In this context, we also attribute the lack of strong team culture to the mixture of genders and the absence of a masculine 'work ethic'. It was apparent that management remained dependent on employee 'consent' (Burawoy, 1979) for the factory to be productive and employees occasionally resisted work that they regarded as boring or low status. We also noted that such moments of resistance were diluted by the nature of the workforce; non-unionised, migrant, agency workers who had limited interaction at work and whose *relatively* high pay compensated for their endeavours (see also Inkson, 1977). These findings suggest that 'dirty' workers may not be preoccupied with the 'stigma' (Kreiner et al., 2006: 626) attached to their work when they feel financially recompensed for what they do. Although for a number of workers, particularly the higher status groups such as vets, the exchange is sometimes a tense one; infused by frustration and disappointment.

Despite such tensions, we feel that our findings question generalised assertions such as 'those who do dirty work' are 'highly stressed and dissatisfied workers' (Baran et al., 2012: 621). These broad claims are problematic even within single occupations (Tyler, 2011: 1492). They are also questionable when comparing our case of slaughtering with that of Ackroyd and Crowdy (1990). In fact, our research has pointed out the complexity of 'dirty work' even within single groups such as production line workers and within single factories where differently qualified workers come into contact with each other. As we have shown, the work that carried the greatest stigma among the factory workers at Farmstock was 'trussing' and this was at the 'clean' end of the factory. At Farmstock, it is not simply that the physical environment of the factory created different work experiences that demarcated between 'dirty' and 'clean' zones; indeed, we found that distinctions and partitions were discernible even within the same zones where workers spoke different languages and were engaged in different tasks.

To conclude, these different work conditions inhibited the type of strong occupational or workgroup culture that Ackroyd and Crowdy (1990) identified as important to those engaged in large-animal slaughter work. In our case, economics appeared to be more significant in terms of establishing 'positive self-definitions' (Ashforth and Kreiner, 1999: 419) than the work group or, indeed, masculinity, despite 'trussing' being demeaned by its association with 'women'. Although the work was largely characterised by consent there were still instances of resistance and so, overall, this highlights that there are considerable differences in terms of the experience, subjectivity and cultures of slaughtering as a form of 'dirty work'.

 **REFERENCES**

Ackroyd, S. and Crowdy, P.A. (1990) 'Can culture be managed? Working with "raw" material: The case of the English slaughtermen', *Personnel Review*, 19(5), 3–13.

Anderson, B. (2000) *Doing the Dirty Work? The Global Politics of Domestic Labour*, London: Zed Books.

Ashforth, B.E. and Kreiner, G.E. (1999) '"How can you do it?": Dirty work and the challenge of constructing a positive identity', *Academy of Management Review*, 24(3), 413–434.

Ashforth, B.E., Kreiner, G.E., Clark, M.A. and Fugate, M. (2007) 'Normalizing dirty work: Managerial tactics for countering occupational taint', *Academy of Management Journal*, 50(1), 149–174.

Baldamus, W. (1967) *Efficiency and Effort: An Analysis of Industrial Administration*, London: Tavistock.

Baran, B., Rogelberg, S.G., Lopina, E.C., Allen, J.A, Spitzmueller, C. and Bergman, M. (2012) 'Shouldering the burden: The toll of dirty tasks', *Human Relations*, 65(5), 597–626.

Bensman, J. and Gerver, I. (1963) 'Crime and punishment in the factory: The function of deviancy in maintaining the social system', *American Sociological Review*, 28(4), 588–598.

Buller, H. and Roe, E. J. (2013) 'Modifying and commodifying animal welfare: The economisation of the laying chicken', *Journal of Rural Studies*, 1–9.

Burawoy, M. (1979) *The Manufacture of Consent*, Chicago, IL: University of Chicago Press.

Cooke, H. (2006) 'Seagull management and the control of nursing work', *Work, Employment and Society*, 20(2), 223–243.

Cudworth, E. (2008) 'Most farmers prefer blondes: The dynamics of anthroparchy in animals becoming meat', *Journal for Critical Animal Studies*, 6(1), 32–45.

Dick, P. (2005) 'Dirty work destinations: How police officers account for their use of coercive force', *Human Relations*, 58(11), 1363–1390.

Gold, R.L. (1964) 'In the basement – the apartment-building janitor', in Berger, P.L. (ed.), *The Human Shape of Work: Studies in the Sociology of Occupations*, New York: Macmillan.

Grandy, G. and Mavin, S. (2012) 'Doing gender in dirty work: Exotic dancers' construction of self-enhancing identities' in Simpson, R., Slutskaya, N., Lewis, P. and Hopfl, H. (eds), *Dirty Work: Concepts and Identities*, London: Palgrave Macmillan.

Hughes, E.C. (1958) *Men and their Work*, Glencoe, IL: Free Press.

Hughes, E.C. (1970) 'The humble and the proud: The comparative study of occupations', *Sociological Quarterly*, 11(2), 147–156.

Inkson, J.H.K. (1977) 'The man on the dis-assembly line: New Zealand freezing workers', *Australian and New Zealand Journal of Sociology*, 13(1), 2–11.

Kreiner, G.E., Ashforth, B.E. and Sluss, D.M. (2006) 'Identity dynamics in occupational dirty work: Integrating social identity and system justification perspectives', *Organization Science*, 17(5), 619–636.

Mars, G. (1982) *Cheats at Work*, London: Counterpoint, Unwin Books.

Meara, H. (1974) 'Honor in dirty work: The case of American meat cutters and Turkish butchers', *Sociology of Work and Occupations*, 1(3), 259–283.

Nichols, T., Cam, S., Chou, W.G., Chun, S., Zhao, W. and Tongqing, F. (2004) 'Factory regimes and the dismantling of established labour in Asia', *Work, Employment and Society*, 18(4), 663–685.

Noon, M. and Blyton, P. (2007) *The Realities of Work, 3rd Edition*, Basingstoke: Palgrave Macmillan.

Pachirat, T. (2011) *Every Twelve Seconds: Industrialized Slaughter and the Politics of Sight*, Yale: Yale University Press.

Petrillo, G. (1989/1990) 'The distant mourner: An examination of the American gravedigger', *Omega*, 20, 139–148.

Ram, M. (1991) 'Control and autonomy in small firms: The case of the West Midlands clothing industry', *Work, Employment and Society*, 5(4), 601–619.

Riemer, J.W. (1979) *Hard Hats: The Work World of Construction Workers*, Beverly Hills, CA: Sage Publications.

Roy, D. (1960) 'Banana time: Job satisfaction and informal interaction', *Human Organization*, 18(2), 156–168.

Sayer, A. (2007) 'Dignity at work: Broadening the agenda', *Organization*, 14(4), 565–581.

Selmi, G. (2012) 'Dirty talks and gender cleanliness: An account of identity management practices in phone sex work' in Simpson, R., Slutskaya, N., Lewis, P. and Hopfl, H. (eds), *Dirty Work: Concepts and Identities*, London: Palgrave Macmillan.

Stanley, E. and Mackenzie-Davey, K. (2012) 'From high-flyer to crook: How can we understand the stigmatization of investment bankers during the financial crisis?' in Simpson, R., Slutskaya, N., Lewis, P. and Hopfl, H. (eds), *Dirty Work: Concepts and Identities*, London: Palgrave Macmillan.

Stull, D. and Broadway, M.J. (2004) *Slaughterhouse Blues: The Meat and Poultry Industry in North America*, California: Thomson, Wadsworth.

Thompson, P. and van den Broek, D. (2010) 'Managerial control and workplace regimes: An introduction', *Work, Employment and Society*, 24(3), 1–12.

Thompson, W.E. (1991) 'Handling the stigma of handling the dead: Morticians and funeral directors', *Deviant Behavior*, 13(4), 403–429.

Thompson, W.E. and Harred, J.L. (1992) 'Topless dancers: Managing stigma in a deviant occupation', *Deviant Behaviour*, 13(3), 291–311.

Tyler, M. (2011) 'Tainted love: From dirty work to abject labour', *Human Relations*, 61(11), 1477–1500.

Vachhani, S. and Pullen, A. (2011) 'Home is where the heart is? Organizing women's work and domesticity at Christmas', *Organization*, 18(6), 807–821.

Van Maanen, J. (1979) 'Reclaiming qualitative methods for organizational research: A preface', *Administrative Science Quarterly*, 24(2), 520–526.

Van Maanen, J. (1988) *Tales of the Field: On Writing Ethnography*, London: University of Chicago Press.

Vialles, N. (1994) *Animal to Edible*, Cambridge: Cambridge University Press.

Wilkie, R. (2010) *Livestock/Deadstock: Working with Farm Animals from Birth to Slaughter*, Philadelphia: Temple University Press.

# 8

# Migration into the United Kingdom: Employers and the *function* of migrant labour

*Steve French*

## 8.1 Introduction

On 1 January 2014, the transitional measures which the United Kingdom government has in place to limit the citizens of Romania and Bulgaria entering the country to work were lifted, under the requirements of European Union law, to enable the free movement of people between 27 member states.[1] Estimates about the impact of the ending of transitional measures upon the UK labour market range from 20,000 and 300,000 new arrivals from these two states (*The Observer*, 2013), based upon different interpretations of the respective influences of: the economic situation in Romania and Bulgaria; the range of alternative migration destinations to the UK; linguistic and cultural barriers to entry; and, significantly, the UK labour market and the strategies of British employers in relation to recruitment and retention of workers.

The uncertainty surrounding the number of new arrivals to the UK creates problems for social policy formulation, including assessing the capacity of the housing market and the provision of public services such as health, social welfare and policing. However, it should be noted that problems in providing reliable estimates on migration to the UK are not new. In 2004, when workers from eight central and east European states that had acceded to the EU (A8[2]) were provided access to the UK labour markets, initial government estimates placed the number likely to arrive at 13,000 per year, while the actual numbers of registered A8 migrant workers had reached 427,000 by August 2006 (bringing with them an additional 36,000 dependents), with estimates of the numbers of non-registered self-employed workers, bringing the total closer to 600,000 (BBC News, 2006). Such divergent expected figures is not novel, but evidence of the difficulty of making such predictions. Böhning (1972: 1), writing shortly before the UK entered the European Economic Community (EEC, the predecessor of the EU), observed that:

> Very little is known in this country about the continental countries' concept and experience of labour immigration. Even less is known about what the Treaty of Rome terms 'freedom of movement for workers'. . . . When one reads through the various stages of the Immigration Bill 1971, in which the possible repercussions of entry into the EEC are mentioned, one is astounded by the lack of information and the amount of wrong information.

It is not difficult to see how this lack of reliable knowledge about migration numbers as an ongoing issue creates problems for the state in the management of migration and can foster more than practical problems with state infrastructure, but fuel a wider political reaction. Notably, such rejections by the public appear with the periodic rise of far-right parties such as the National Front and British National Party in periods of immigration and economic recession and, in the contemporary context of freedom of movement within the EU, the success of the UK Independence Party (UKIP).

The aim of this chapter is to place migration to the UK in an academic context that provides a (small) degree of clarity in explaining migration patterns, particularly in terms of the key role of employers and the management of labour. To do this the chapter needs to address three central issues; migration theory, historical comparison and employer strategies in relation to migrant workers.

In the first substantive section of the chapter, the weaknesses of the traditional economic model of 'push–pull' migration and the importance of historical and political factors are considered, examining some of the complexities of explaining migration patterns. The second section then provides an overview of a key period of earlier migration to the UK, from the 1950s to the early 1970s, drawing upon the arguments developed by Castles and Kosack (1973) in their seminal work on migration and class structure in Western Europe. Their work which locates migration within wider political economy debates and provides important empirical evidence of migrant workers and their employment, provides a foundation for analysing contemporary migration patterns in the third section, specifically considering the migration of A8 workers to the UK since 2004. Drawing upon this analysis the final section of the chapter seeks to explain the main themes to emerge from this research, arguing that the consistent use of migrant workers in specific sectors facing (periodic) labour shortages raises important questions about the function of migrant workers especially in the contemporary context under the EU's freedom of movement provisions.

The empirical evidence presented here suggests that migration, at least within selected migrant dense sectors, provides employers with ample scope to secure more productive labour, based upon reliability, flexibility and holding down pay and conditions. Using migrant workers to secure short-term improvement, in turn, sustains the low-wage and low skilled trajectory of the UK economy and has wider implications for longer term employment patterns and investment, as well as state policies in relation to industrial development, welfare, labour market regulation and education.

## 8.2    Theorising migration: Complexity and limitations

Salt and Clout (1976) argue that, before exploring international migration patterns involving the movement of workers, there needs to be careful consideration of internal migration patterns within countries, particularly as they pass through different periods of industrialisation (and deindustrialisation). Similarly, there are long and important histories of migrations caused through political events; notably during and in the aftermath of war; through periods of colonisation and de-colonisation; and by those seeking refuge from persecution. These are important developments in their own right, but have also helped to shape migration to the UK.

For example, the result of deindustrialisation and internal migration in the UK has led to a concentration of economic activity in London and the South East, creating important labour shortages in sectors such as hospitality (Lucas and Mansfield, 2008), for which migrant workers have been recruited from overseas. Further, rural to urban migration has created a demand for migrant workers in British agriculture and food processing to address labour shortages and the higher labour costs of employing local workers in tight labour markets (Scott, 2008). The colonial history of the UK is also important in considering historical patterns of international migration too, with settled Irish and black and minority ethnic communities a testament to immigration from former dominions of the British Empire. Similarly, a number of communities in the UK can be traced back to the sanctuary offered (often begrudgingly) to refugees; notably those fleeing fascism, those seeking to escape Communist rule, those displaced during decolonisation as well as those fleeing more recent conflicts in Iraq, Afghanistan, Eritrea and Rwanda.

Even this extremely limited oversight of internal and politically framed migration patterns begins to unveil the complexity of migration. It also indicates the problem of theorising migration more narrowly in economic terms where the emphasis is placed upon migrant workers, as 'persons with a different nationality or place of birth than the country in which they are working' (Galgóczi et al., 2012: 38).[3] However, the standard theoretical explanation of economic migration is located within neoclassical economics, focusing upon push–pull theories, with migrant workers driven (pushed) to leave their country or origin (or, more broadly, current work location) by low living standards, a lack of opportunities, and political or environmental considerations and oriented (pulled) to certain countries by a demand for labour and economic opportunities, and better political and environmental conditions. As Castles and Miller (2003: 22–23) observe, this model emphasises the individual decisions to migrate, where informed rational decision making evaluates the relative costs and benefits of remaining in a specific location or migrating. It is predicated on a version of human capital theory (Sjaastad, 1962), whereby people invest in migration, as they would education, to raise their human capital and gain an improved rate of return (higher earnings).

Like most economic models, this approach is based upon a number of assumptions, notably perfect information to facilitate the cost–benefit analysis made by persons considering migration, and has to deal with many issues, notably government policies on migration, as 'distortions' of the operation of free markets. Castles and Miller highlight how challenges to this economic approach have arisen from a number of other disciplines in terms of: wider historical experiences; the reality of segmented labour markets and imperfect information; evaluating decision-making focused upon families and communities rather than individuals; and the significant role of states in influencing and controlling migratory processes. This leads them to argue that:

> The idea of individual migrants who make free choices which not only 'maximise their well-being' but also lead to an 'equilibrium in the marketplace' (Borjas, 1989: 482) is so far from historical reality that it has little explanatory value. It seems better, as Zolberg suggests, to analyse labour migration 'as a movement of workers propelled by the dynamics of transnational capitalist economy, which simultaneously determines both the "push" and the "pull"' (Zolberg et al., 1989: 407). (Castles and Miller, 2003: 25)

This discussion of the complexity of migration flows and the critique of the traditional economic theory does help to explain the difficulties of predicting future migration patterns. Two important issues also emerge from this brief exploration of migration theory. First, the discussion highlights the need to carefully consider historical experiences when seeking to understand migration processes. Second, there is a need to analyse migration not simply in terms of labour demand, but also in relation to the policies of employers and the state in supporting and controlling migration. These two issues, therefore, provide the focus for the following sections of the chapter.

## 8.3 Migration to the UK and Western Europe: An historical comparison

In order to provide some historical analysis of migration into the UK, it is useful to examine the large-scale migrations that took place in the 1950s and 1960s into the most developed west European economies. These migrations occurred in response to significant increases in the demand for labour created by the sustained period of economic boom, the so-called 'Golden Age of Capitalism' (Toniolo, 1998) and the scale of the migrations are useful in providing a point of comparison with contemporary developments.

In examining the reasons for this period of migration into Western Europe, Salt (1976) identifies a number of classic push and pull economic factors: the low birth rates in industrial economies of Europe leading to limited growth of the industrial workforce, which could no longer be complemented by internal migration from agriculture to industry or from (refugee) resettlements that took place in the aftermath of the war; uneven patterns of labour supply within industrial nations that could not be adjusted by internal migration; higher birth rates in countries surrounding the north-west of Europe (primarily Mediterranean Europe, north and west Africa) with high levels of unemployment and low levels of economic growth. However, before examining the key characteristics of this period of migration, it is important to provide a more detailed overview of the migration patterns during this period, highlighting the need to move beyond an explanation focused exclusively upon push and pull factors.

First, it is important to highlight the political and historical factors that influenced migration. As noted above, the migrations into industrial nations were mediated by historical factors and 'cultural' ties. The first major 'market distortion' was the effective end of migration from Central and Eastern Europe through the political division of Europe and the beginning of the Cold War.[4] Furthermore, while the majority of sending countries could be said to fall within the geographical orbit of north-west Europe, it is important to highlight the continuing colonial ties that influenced migration into France (Algeria, Morocco and Tunisia), the Netherlands (Indonesia and Surinam) and the UK (new Commonwealth countries). This partly reflects a desire for workers from countries where political ties made entry into the workforce easier, for example, a related language and a shared understanding of legal and administrative structures. In this respect it should be noted that migration into Sweden focused primarily upon Finland because of shared linguistic patterns and cultural norms (Korkiasaari and Söderling, 2003: 5).

Second, there were important national variations in recruitment policies pursued. While in much of north-west Europe 'recruitment of foreign workers became a central plank for continued growth and prosperity' (Salt, 1976: 84), permanent settlement was actively discouraged in some states, notably Germany and Switzerland, with workers recruited under time-limited, and renewable, labour contracts (as guest workers or *Gastarbeiter*). These included workers from Turkey, Yugoslavia, Greece, Spain and Portugal. The aim of such a policy was to provide 'a buffer against the vagaries of the unemployment cycle for the indigenous labour force. In times of unemployment it was assumed that nationals of the host country could be protected by the release from employment of aliens' (ibid.: 84), but it was also intended to prevent social problems arising from migration and integration (or assimilation). By contrast, in some cases the recruitment of workers from former colonies was (initially) associated with rights of citizenship, for example in the UK, France and the Netherlands.

Finally, a third group of workers fell outside both of these categories, namely those with freedom of movement under the EEC Treaty of Rome. While membership of the EEC was limited to six member states during the period in question, migration under the terms of the treaty was significant from Italy into Germany and, to a lesser extent, France.

It is important to note that while migration into north-west Europe continued in this period due to persistent demand for labour, patterns between countries and sources changed over time. While migration from Italy occurred at the beginning of the boom period, by the mid-1960s Italian economic growth and wage increases led to a downturn in emigration (Salt, 1976: 89). Similarly, while France received migrant workers from its former African colonies, these migrants had relatively low activity rates and the economy also relied upon migrant workers primarily from Spain and Portugal, but also Yugoslavia and Turkey. It was also after Algerian independence in 1962 that the flow of migrants from this country into France increased, though this included refugees from among the population that had supported France in the civil war (Böhning, 1972: 31).

In this respect, the distinctive patterns of migration into the UK are significant. After initial migration from Europe under the Volunteer Workers scheme, relatively little migration into the UK came from Europe other than continuing migration from Ireland. Rather, the UK relied substantially upon migrants from the new Commonwealth to meet additional demands for labour; focusing initially on the Caribbean and later on, in terms of numbers, the Indian sub-continent (Phizacklea and Miles, 1980). However, these migrant workers, because they came from former British colonies, were accorded, at least until the passing of the 1962 and 1968 Commonwealth Immigrants Acts, the status of British subjects and had legal settlement rights and no restrictions on occupation. Thus, while Castles and Kosack (1973: 4) claim that by 1970 the UK had the third highest level of immigration in Western Europe, behind Germany and France (with 2.6 million or 5.0 per cent or the population), Salt (1974: 82) does not list the UK amongst the top eight west European economies in terms of the employment of 'foreign' workers.

While this section has outlined the factors contributing to, and shaping, migration in the period of the Western European economic boom, as Castles and Miller (2003, above) suggest, there needs to be a more analytical approach to the study of migrant workers within transnational capitalism. For this reason the remainder of this section examines key characteristics of this period of migration, both in terms of the labour market and wider economy, by drawing on the work of Castles and Kosack (1973).

Castles and Kosack located their work within a Marxist political economy framework which emphasised the 'function of migrant workers' within international capitalism. In this approach, the use of migration is seen as a mechanism to create a 'reserve army of labour' which helps reduce demand for labour and thus the employer's labour costs. Castles and Kosack (1973: 377) argued that in practice this did not occur during the economic boom period due to policies of governments and unions that prevented wage-cutting and the fact the labour quality of migrant workers did not facilitate a direct substitution of 'indigenous' workers. Nevertheless, they observed that the availability of migrant labour influenced employers' strategies, maintaining lower-skilled work rather than further rationalising production processes and permitting increases in production without new investment, for example, through using shift work. While they noted in their discussion of wider issues of immigration on economic productivity, inflation and balance of payments that the arguments were 'controversial and not measurable' (ibid.: 408), they do posit an argument subsequently pursued by Temin (2002) that the expansion of west European economies in the post-war boom period, reflected the completion of the Industrial Revolution for many of these states, so that the use of migrant labour as part of an expanding labour supply was essential to meet the demands of economies that were shifting from agriculture to manufacturing.[5]

It is against this background that Castles and Kosack (1973: 57–115) analysed the labour markets of France, Germany, the UK and Switzerland, exploring a number of key characteristics of migrant workers and the nature of the work they undertook. First, in relation to the characteristics of migrant workers, they observed that they were predominantly young and male and had higher rates of economic activity than the overall population. However, where data were available, it was also the case that differences in activity rates between different groups of migrants existed; with a pattern emerging that suggested the longer migrants stayed in the country the closer their activity rates came to that of the indigenous population, reflecting in part the increase of dependents. Second, the majority of migrants arriving in these four countries came from rural areas in their country of origin and had limited education, industrial experience and vocational training, as well as being unable to speak the language in the host country. While this position is more complex for the UK, particularly in relation to the contested arguments around the skills of West Indian migrants and (inadequate) English language skills, the overall argument around lack of skill was argued to be valid for most Irish and new Commonwealth migrants.

In relation to the labour market, it is argued that although migrants only constituted between 6.3 and 7.0 per cent of the labour force in France, Germany and Britain,[6] their relative importance to these economies lay in the occupational structure of migrant work. The pattern of employment of migrant workers in France, Germany and Switzerland indicated concentrations in certain sectors. For men these were construction, engineering and other manufacturing activities, hospitality and, for France, agriculture. For women these were domestic service, textiles and clothing, hospitality, with high concentrations in manufacturing in Germany. While there were variations between different groups of migrants in terms of sectoral distribution of work in these three countries, the picture was more complex for the UK for men, with certain sectors employing different migrant groups. There was a concentration of Irish migrants in construction, West Indians in metal manufacturing and transport, Indian men in metal manufacturing, engineering, transport and textiles and Pakistanis in textiles and metal manufacturing. By contrast, most women were concentrated in professional and scientific services (especially health) and private services.

Notwithstanding these distinctions, Castles and Kosack (1973) highlight that the work undertaken within these sectors was usually unskilled and in the lowest segments of the labour market, representing jobs that many indigenous workers had left. Further, the opportunities for migrants to enter higher qualified jobs, with more security and improved terms and conditions, were severely restricted. Even where there was greater variation in the sectors where migrants were employed in the UK, further analysis highlighted that the type of jobs where new Commonwealth migrants were highly represented 'were generally unskilled and relatively low status ones' (ibid.: 79) where earnings were low. Consequently, and in line with the (initial) intention of migrant workers to return home and to maximise their income in order to improve their material situation at home (i.e. through remittances), this meant that migrant workers had to work extremely long hours.

The official restrictions placed upon the employment of (foreign) migrant workers also contributed to their labour market position, not only in terms of limiting the length of contract, but also by restricting changes in occupation and internal mobility. As noted above, these restrictions were aimed at providing labour market flexibility so that, in the case of unemployment, migrant workers would be the first to lose jobs and be expelled from the country. While it was to prove difficult to enforce such expulsions (notably in France and Britain), it was the case that, despite their youth, higher levels of activity and their willingness to take jobs others had rejected, migrants suffered higher levels of unemployment than indigenous workers. Moreover, this vulnerable position within the labour market was reinforced by discriminatory practices among employers, other workers and sometimes unions, to avoid recruiting migrant workers or to maintain them in subordinate posts. Significantly, it was argued that such discriminatory practices in the UK were based upon an assumption that migrant workers were 'undesirable and their employment is merely an unfortunate necessity . . . [and] . . . that they are not regarded as suitable for better work' (Castles and Kosack, 1973: 108–109).

By examining the labour market position of migrant workers from a comparative perspective, Castles and Kosack provide a useful framework for historical analysis, focusing upon the characteristics of the migrant workers, their employment patterns and location within job hierarchies (of segmented labour markets) and the way in which their position is determined both by state migration policies and, in many cases, by negative perceptions of migrant workers. Using this framework, the following section will examine contemporary migration trends that affect the UK within the European Union.

## 8.4 Migration to the UK from the European Union: Contemporary developments

Before examining in detail developments in migration patterns since the accession of the A8 countries to the European Union in 2004, it is important to provide some overview of the changes that occurred in the interim period from the end of the economic boom. While it is impossible to provide any detailed analysis within the confines of this chapter, it is necessary to highlight a number of developments that helped to shape the contemporary period.

First, the period of economic boom, like all good things, came to an end, as the international economy experienced the oil shocks of the 1970s and the end of the Bretton Woods system of exchange rate controls. National governments struggled to maintain the 'holy family' of economic growth, high levels of employment and welfare capitalism and the Keynesian economic policies that dominated the post-war political settlement came under attack from a resurgent free market approach, championed by the Chicago School (Harvey, 2007). Consequently, neo-liberal economic doctrines have increasingly influenced policy-makers, especially following the collapse of the communist regimes of the Soviet Union and Eastern Europe. Without an alternative economic model, there has been a widespread, if gradual, shift towards policies of deregulation at international ('free' trade agreements and the internationalisation of financial services) and national (marketisation and privatisation) levels within an international framework (e.g., the Single European Market).

Within this wider liberal economic framework – and facilitated by the phenomenal advances in transport, technology and communications – there have been significant pressures placed upon employers to restructure their production or service provision, and upon governments to provide competitive business environments within which these employers operate, for fear of the relocation of production and, increasingly, services overseas (Eironline, 2006). However, within this process of intensified market competition, an important set of analyses have emerged which highlight the different ways in which national capitalisms have adapted to this business environment (Crouch and Streeck, 1997), focusing upon the 'varieties of capitalism' debate (Hall and Soskice, 2001) and the scope for distinctive institutional and public policy responses. This is important, to the extent that the economic structures of west European states, following a broadly similar expansion of manufacturing in the post-war boom period, may (within an overall trend toward a service based economy) retain or relinquish sections of the industrial base and are more likely to experience differences between each other in terms of short-term economic cycles.

Second, the economic crises of the 1970s led to the ending of mass migration into Western Europe based upon the migrant worker model. However, as analyses of the ethnicities and 'foreigners' within the structure of west European states indicate, the process of migration became one of immigration and settlement, with subsequent migration into west European states following patterns of family reunification. Subsequent studies highlight the continuing disadvantage of ethnic minorities and those of foreign birth (and the second and third generations of these groups) within the labour market and wider society (see, for example Wrench and Solomos, 1993).

At the same time, the growth of the EEC to twelve states by 1986 saw the inclusion of former emigration (Ireland, Spain, Portugal and Greece) and destination (the UK) states within the freedom of movement provisions, changing the status of immigrants from these countries within their countries of settlement (within the EEC). It was also the case that with the expansion of the economies, some new member states have 'experienced mutating in status from being predominantly a sending to being a receiving country' (Menz, 2010: 27). Following the creation of the European Union, upon the ratification of the Maastricht Treaty in 1993, three further states (Sweden, Finland and Austria) also joined the EU in 1995. The free movement of workers also applies to the countries outside the EU, but within the European Economic Area (Iceland, Liechtenstein and Norway) as well as Switzerland. Thus, to a significant extent intra-European migration now falls within the scope of the freedom of movement articles of the EU, and is frequently referred to as mobility (within the single market) rather than migration. The collapse of communism also led the EU to adopt policies of further enlargement and to address the issues of freedom of movement for new member states including those from central and Eastern Europe.

Finally, it is important to note a shift in EU policy in respect of political and economic migration, reformulated to emphasise the need for extra-EU migration to address bottlenecks in labour supply, and contribute to the promotion of competitiveness. This, Menz (2010: 30–35) argues, is cast in terms of attracting more highly skilled migrants into the EU, but effectively means acquiring the skills these migrants have developed in their country of origin (sometimes referred to as 'brain drain') and relieving some of the pressures on the funding of higher education, vocational education and training systems. At the same time this does not preclude the continued use of migrant workers from outside of the EU to address low skilled, low wage work where shortages may appear. However, the key shift in policy within the EU, is to promote economic migration while also denigrating 'noneconomic channels of migration, including largely humanitarian avenues of access' (ibid.: 31), reflecting a reactionary response to the pressures of asylum claims following protracted conflicts in the Middle East and Africa.

It is against this political and economic background that the second substantive phase of migration within Europe occurred. Following the succession of the A8 countries to the EU in 2004, only three of the 15 established member states (EU15) opened their labour markets up to citizens from these countries (UK, Ireland and Sweden)[7] with other countries using transitional measures for up to up to seven years to limit migration from the A8 states. In view of the limited opening up of EU15 labour markets at the point of accession and the complexities surrounding migration patterns since the end of the 1970s, the remainder of this section will focus upon the relative impact of A8 migrants on the UK labour market. The UK is the country that has absorbed the largest number of A8 workers, with estimated numbers rising from around 200,000 in 2005 to 600,000 during the economic crisis in 2008, and increasing again to over 700,000 by 2010 (Galgóczi et al., 2012: 11). However, it should also be noted that A8 migrants still constitute a minority in the UK, smaller in proportion than both EU15 and non-EU immigrants (Bettin, 2012: 52).

It should be noted that at the time of accession, the UK economy was in a strong position. During 2004 the economy grew by 3.1 per cent, with fourth quarter data indicating an inflation rate of 3.4 per cent (RPI), wage growth at 4.3 per cent (average earnings) and economic activity levels at 74.9 per cent. The economy was also experiencing low unemployment rates (4.7 per cent using the ILO unemployment rate) leading the ONS (2005: 6) to report that 'the labour market is tight by recent historical standards [and] . . . there continues to be little sign of much change in the overall market'. These conditions explain the support for the opening up of the labour market to workers from accession states, as migrant workers could be used to fill gaps created by skill or labour shortages.

Returning to the themes explored by Castles and Kosack (1973) above, the structure of the A8 migrant population in the UK can now be explored. First, in relation to the characteristics of migrant workers, Bettin (2012: 51–61) uses quarterly Labour Force Survey (LFS) data for the UK between 2006 and 2010 to observe that A8 nationals were predominantly young, with those under 35 constituting 82.6 per cent of migrants in 2006 and 75.1 per cent in 2010. However, in contrast to the period examined by Castles and

Kosack, there was a high degree of gender equality among migrants, with females constituting 47.1 per cent of A8 migrants in 2006, rising to 51.0 per cent in 2010. In terms of economic activity, A8 migrants had persistently high activity rates over 80 per cent, being relatively unaffected by the economic crisis. This was higher than UK nationals, which fell from 73 per cent in 2006 to 70.5 per cent in 2010, and non-EU nationals whose activity rates were around 10 per cent below those of UK nationals. While activity rates mirror the findings of Castles and Kosack, a striking difference emerges when estimating for the skills and qualifications of A8 migrants. Using the length of formal education as a measure, a higher proportion of A8 nationals completed their formal education after the age of 21 years, compared to UK nationals (25.8 per cent).

In relation to the labour market, a similar argument can be made to that of Castles and Kosack relating to the importance of A8 migrant workers to the UK based upon the occupational structure of their work. McCullum and Findlay (2011) undertook an analysis of the WRS data available.[8] They found that there were concentrations of A8 workers in certain sectors, notably construction, hotels and catering, agriculture, and food processing, and manufacturing. Unfortunately, the largest category recorded under WRS was administration, business and management, but this category is highly problematic as it is contains employment agencies, which employ many A8 workers in organisations in different sectors (frequently those listed above). When controlling for this distorted data, McCullum and Findlay assess the relative importance of A8 workers to each sector, highlighting a number of 'migrant dense' sectors. For while A8 workers, based upon WRS registrations, constituted 3.8 per cent of total employee jobs in June 2010, they constituted 40.3 per cent of jobs in agriculture and 10.4 per cent of jobs in hospitality.

These data are supported by other research using the LFS. In a report to the TUC *Commission on Vulnerable Employment*, Jayaweera and Anderson (2008: 20) highlighted that A8 migrants were disproportionately concentrated in manufacturing and within the low wage and low skilled sections of the labour market. While 22 per cent of recent migrants were in elementary occupations (compared to 12 per cent in the entire LFS sample), 37 per cent of migrants from A8 countries were in elementary occupations. Further, when examining WRS data (2004–2007) for occupations, rather than sector, they found the largest numbers of registrations were as process operatives, followed by warehouse operatives, packers and kitchen and catering assistants.

Echoing the work of Castles and Kosack (1973), these data highlight that the work undertaken by A8 migrant workers falls within a number of key sectors, is usually unskilled, and is located in the lowest segments of the labour market (see, for example, Hamilton and McCabe, Chapter 7 this volume); representing either temporal labour shortages as in agriculture, or full time positions which employers had difficulty filling from the existing labour force. Crucially, there has been a significant mismatch between the education and skills of A8 migrant workers and the work they undertake. According to Bettin (2012: 59) in 2010 the LFS indicated that 56 per cent of UK nationals undertook white collar work, whereas those workers from A8 countries, despite higher education levels, were disproportionately located within blue-collar jobs (82 per cent).

When looking at working hours, Jayaweera and Anderson (2008: 29) – interpreting LFS data – argue that (all) migrants worked longer hours per week; 55 per cent of recent migrants worked 31 to 48 hours (compared to 48.3 per cent in the whole sample) and 15.4 per cent (compared to 13 per cent) worked more than 48 hours. However, they also identify that recent migrant workers on temporary contracts were more likely to work fewer than 31 hours per week. When analysing data from a range of sources they argue 'that there are important differences between A8 nationals and others, with recent entrants from A8 states nearly twice as likely to work more than 48 hours, and nearly four times less likely to work less than 31 hours' (ibid.: 32). While the evidence of long working hours resonates with the arguments of Castles and Kosack, the potential under-employment of A8 workers in terms of working hours could highlight the different economic conditions post-accession. In particular, employers in the UK are able to legally utilise migrant workers on a range of flexible contracts to reduce costs and link employment (in terms of levels and hours) closely to patterns of labour demand.

Castles and Kosack observed that a combination of legal regulation and collective bargaining through unions has meant that migration into Western Europe had not driven down pay levels in the period under investigation, but there is evidence to suggest the vulnerability of A8 migrant workers in respect of pay. Here Jayaweera and Anderson (2008: 39), recognising that WRS data is prone to underestimate under-payment, still observe that in the period January to September 2007 of the 157,410 new registrations 5,655 reported (3.6 per cent) being paid under the applicable National Minimum Wage (at that time £5.35 an hour for workers aged 22 and over). More significantly, they observe that following the Low Pay Commission's investigations into a sample of firms between November 2004 and December 2006, 20 per cent of those selected were found to be non-compliant with minimum wage legislation and arrears of £144,000 were identified for 1,171 workers. These data, taken with smaller data sets lead Jayaweera and Anderson to argue:

> The likelihood of getting paid less than the minimum wage was greater for younger migrants, those from A8 and A2 countries, those with lower levels of English proficiency, women and those in more 'migrant dense' sectors such as hospitality, agriculture and construction. Given that large proportions of migrant workers fall into these categories, these patterns reinforce their vulnerability in employment (ibid.: 40).

While the official restrictions placed upon the employment of A8 migrant workers could not be enforced under EU freedom of movement provisions, an important development in the employment of migrant workers was the extensive use of temporary contracts and employment agencies by employers utilising A8 workers (MacKenzie and Forde, 2009). In many ways the ability to maintain temporary contracts or to delegate responsibility for employment to employment agencies has provided the flexibility in employing A8 workers that previous (and continuing) legal restrictions for migrant workers ensured. The weakness of regulations in respect of agency working have been highlighted by the TUC (2013), while there are examples of incorrect payments and additional deductions from wages for A8 workers employed through agencies (Jayaweera and Anderson, 2008) especially where the employment also included accommodation (French and Möhrke, 2007).

Despite evidence of the concentration of employment in specific sectors and the poor employment conditions applied to A8 workers, it is important to note that in stark contrast to the evidence of the taste for discrimination highlighted by Castles and Kosack (1973), employers have frequently praised the work ethic of A8 workers (and exhibited preference in selecting A8 workers over existing unemployed British nationals and other available migrant workers) as well as their transparent legal status (French and Möhrke, 2007). This may help explain, in part, why activity rates among A8 nationals have remained high despite the economic crisis in the UK (Bettin, 2012).

The recession has, however, had an impact upon migration patterns. While activity rates among A8 nationals have remained high, there is evidence of a change in the relative levels of A8 migrants between countries. While data sources in the UK are unable to accurately measure migrants leaving the country – and have had to rely upon observing the fall in new WRS registrations and national insurance numbers (McCullum and Findlay, 2011) – LFS data for Poland indicates significant return migration, reflecting the improved economic position in Poland, unemployment in the UK or the lack of opportunities of skilled migrants to secure better jobs and conditions within the UK (Anacka and Fihel, 2012). However, deteriorating economic conditions in Lithuania and Latvia have led migration to continue to the UK, while recent data also highlights the increasing use of Romanian and Bulgarian (A2) workers, even though their documented employment is limited to self-employment or alternative migration schemes under the period of transitional measures (Bettin, 2012).

## 8.5 Employers, the 'function' of migrant workers and the neo-liberal state

The historical overview provided by comparing A8 migrants to aspects of earlier migration into the UK highlights a number of key issues that help to develop a more nuanced understanding of policy objectives, employer aims and migration patterns. The comparison underlines the importance of the economic conditions in influencing public policy on migration due to problems in meeting demand for labour, and helps explain the decision to open the UK labour market to A8 nationals in 2004.

However, the impact of migration in the 1950s and 1960s and in the case of A8 migrants appears to be limited to key sections on the labour market, where labour shortages, rather than skill shortages, increase the demand for labour. The analysis of migration in both periods highlights the concentration of migration within specific sectors, with the jobs taken in these sectors typically low-skilled and low wage jobs. While it is important to note additional migration routes into the UK for skilled migrants do exist, the extensive use of A8 migrants in these sectors and jobs raises wider theoretical issues about the policy objectives of migration.

Here the relevance of Castles and Kosack's (1973) concept of the 'function' of migrant workers within international capitalism regains saliency. Migration policy is key to securing workers to meet labour demand and crucially to maximise productivity, at least in the short-term. While maximising productivity was harder to secure for UK employers in the earlier period under investigation, in large part due to the effective regulation of labour markets through trade unions, the liberalisation of labour markets and the decline in the regulatory capacities of trade unions now provide employers with more scope to achieve this objective. Jayaweera and Anderson's (2008) research, notwithstanding its focus upon official data sources, highlights how a more flexible workforce can be achieved utilising temporal flexibility, minimal employment rights, long working hours and low, if not illegal, rates of pay. Even where employers do meet legal requirements, the scope to remould the workforce is significant. As French and Möhrke (2007) argue, a crucial factor for employers is not simply pay and conditions but reliability of migrant workers. With tight labour markets, employers have repeatedly raised the problems they perceive in securing reliable and hard-working British nationals to fill their vacancies and have embraced A8 workers and highlighted their work ethic. This not only secures increased productivity from the use of migrant workers, but should also be seen as a mechanism to 'rehabitualise' British nationals to employer norms of behaviour and effort: a significant function of A8 migrant workers.

While this analysis can clearly be related to the economic model of migration linked to push and pull factors, the issue of productivity raises more important issues of political economy. Further, as the chapter has outlined, the narrow economic model of migration does not fit closer scrutiny: historical migration patterns and the tensions that emerge within state policy (including EU policy) highlight the complexity of migration. Perhaps this is most apparent when considering the issue of the skills of migrant workers.

A distinctive issue to emerge from the study of A8 migrant workers is the apparent mismatch between the jobs they do and their education and skill levels. French (2012) has indicated that employers and employment agencies have shown little interest in assessing the skills of the A8 nationals, with a preference to use them to fill low-skilled jobs that meet immediate demands for labour. Similarly, the scope for recognising the skills and educational attainment of A8 workers is limited, with the body for assessing these (NARIC), run on a profit-seeking basis and charging for assessments. This lack of interest in migrant workers' skills appears difficult to explain given the traditional skills gap and productivity problems of British industry, and the explicit attempts to secure highly skilled migrant workers to address acknowledged skill shortages. It would appear to be characteristic of the uncoordinated approach of a liberal market economy, following the varieties of capitalism argument, with short-term employer interests in the productivity of over-skilled and educated workers pursued at the expense of utilising available skills across sectors and through capital investment and rationalisation.

This also has wider implications for labour market and public policy. Anderson and Rues (2010: 34–46) argue that employers' utilisation of migrant workers within low-wage and low-skilled sectors reinforces the current trajectory of the economy at the expense of alternative strategies: upskilling and improving pay and conditions for more productive workers; investment in technology to create less labour intensive production and service processes; and innovation in new products and sectors. Further, the implications of high activity rates for A8 workers post economic crisis (notwithstanding return migration to Poland) suggests that employer preferences for these migrants will influence employment patterns in migrant dense sectors. This has important consequences for addressing unemployment among UK nationals as well as skills policy within the UK, as the CIPD (2013) have recently pointed out. It also raises important social questions about the severe attacks upon benefits, notably those related to unemployment currently pursued by the coalition government, in terms of what the realistic opportunities for employment are during a persistent recessionary period and one where sectors previously requiring additional labour can source this from within the EU.

However, such strategies are also vulnerable to changes in migration patterns. The current evidence of return migration to Poland of higher educated workers highlights not only the potential loss of skills from the economy given high education levels across A8 migrants, but also suggests a more extensive process of return migration if, and when, other east and central European economies recover. Further, any assumptions by employers that A8 workers who remain in the UK will retain their 'work ethic' and culture of long working hours have to be questioned. With settlement, the establishment of families and a growing realisation that hard-work may not offer a passport to better jobs, the current working practices and norms may also change over time.

## 8.6    Conclusions

In this chapter the complexities of migration have been explored, highlighting a common theme within this book of the difficulties in developing clear and coherent explanations of an increasingly 'messy reality'. However, it is argued that these complexities can be better understood if contextualised through historical analysis and by engaging with wider economic, legal and labour market debates. This is important for the discipline of management studies, which is often overly focused upon 'the organisation' and, following the postmodern turn, frequently weak in examining and valuing the material contexts that shape the activities of managers and workers.

By taking such an approach to the study of migration, comparative analysis has identified labour market practices that appear to be consistent over time, notably in relation to the sectoral concentration and the low-skilled nature of migrant workers' jobs as well as the limited prospects for advancement. A key distinction to emerge from analysing the contemporary migration of A8 workers is, however, the increased scope for employers to secure productive labour through utilising migrant workers in a deregulated liberal market economy. In this sense, employers in migrant dense sectors are able to extract profit by intensifying exploitation, at least in the short-term from their workers by utilising cheaper, more reliable and flexible migrant workers. Crucially, the use of migrant workers in these sectors also helps management shift the 'frontier of control' (Goodrich, 1921) further in their favour, by using coercive comparisons with migrant workers to 'instill' into their workers new expectations in terms of behaviour and effort. This is a significant development within sections of the UK labour market, but as the chapter also argues these strategies place short-term aims ahead of more strategic utilisation of skills and productive forces, with wider political economic implications for the UK.

The potential for Polish migrants to leave the UK is a significant development in terms of migration to Western Europe, though not in the history of Poland itself (Anacka and Fihel, 2012). However, the growing availability of new migrant workers under the freedom of movement provisions, immediately from the A2 states, does provide employers with an alternative to employing A8 migrant workers, whether as a result of return migration or if the work ethic of A8 migrants is perceived to be faltering. In the absence of restrictions on migration within the EU and weak labour market regulation, this may explain the uncertainty and different estimates highlighted at the beginning of the chapter in relation to Romania and Bulgaria. While the chapter has not been able to provide more reliable estimates, it has hopefully provided a better explanation for such uncertainty!

**NOTES**

1. Transitional measures can, however, be applied by existing member states to limit the entry of workers from the newest, and 28th, member state Croatia (which joined the European Union on 1 July 2013) for up to 7 years.
2. The eight central and east European states that acceded to the EU in 2004 were Poland, the Czech Republic, Slovakia, Hungary, Slovenia, Lithuania, Latvia and Estonia.
3. Anderson and Ruhs (2012: 13) stress the importance of the distinction between foreign born and foreign national in such a definition as the latter group will contain those who do not have long-term residence rights and are not necessarily able to move freely within the labour market.
4. At the end of the Second World War, and following the agreement reached between the allied forces at the Yalta conference, Europe was effectively divided into two: the west European states, supported by the United States, developed capitalist market economies and liberal democratic political systems; the east European states, support by the Soviet Union, developed planned economies and political systems based upon the rule of the respective communist parties. The building of the Berlin Wall in 1961 to stop East

Germans fleeing west (or to protect East Germans from the evils of capitalism, depending on your perspective) became a potent symbol of this division but also highlighted the end of a significant post-war migration trajectory.

5. By contrast, the more problematic economic position in the UK reflected, in part, that this period of restructuring had already been completed, so there were limitations to possible economic growth and expansion of industries to secure economies of scale.

6. The impact of migration on the Swiss economy was more apparent, with migrant workers constituting 29.8 per cent of the total labour force (Castles and Kosack, 1973: 61).

7. Malta and Cyprus also joined the EU on this date, but the small size of their respective populations meant that transitional measures were not applied to these economies in terms of freedom of movement.

8. The WRS was a scheme set up by the UK government under the transitional measures to register A8 migrants who were employed (rather than self-employed) and was used to limit certain entitlements to benefits until a specified period of work had been undertaken. While there are questions as to the coverage of WRS data in terms of total A8 migration and issues of data sets remaining up to date (to track changes in jobs), the data remained 'the most detailed information source on the temporal, spatial and sectoral trends in A8 labour migration' (McCullum and Findlay, 2011: 11) prior to its closure in April 2011.

 **REFERENCES**

Anacka, M. and Fihel, A. (2012) 'Return migration to Poland in the post-accession period' in Galgóczi, B., Leschke, J. and Watt, A. (eds), *EU Labour Migration in Troubled Times: Skills Mismatch, Return and Policy Responses*, Basingstoke: Ashgate.

Anderson, B. and Ruhs, M. (2010) 'Migrant workers: who needs them? A framework for the analysis of staff shortages, immigration and public policy' in Ruhs, M. and Anderson, B. (eds), *Who Needs Migrant Workers? Labour Shortages, Immigration and Public Policy*, Oxford: Oxford University Press.

BBC News (2006) *Nearly 600,000 new EU migrants*, 22 August 2006. Accessed at: http://news.bbc.co.uk/1/hi/uk_politics/5273356.stm (retrieved 16 September 2013).

Bettin, G. (2012) 'Migration from the accession countries to the United Kingdom and Italy: Socio-economic characteristics, skills composition and labour market outcomes' in Galgóczi, B., Leschke, J. and Watt, A. (eds), *EU Labour Migration in Troubled Times: Skills Mismatch, Return and Policy Responses*, Basingstoke: Ashgate.

Böhning, W. (1972) *The Migration of Workers in the United Kingdom and the European Community*, Institute for Race Relations London: Oxford University Press.

Castles, S. and Kosack, G. (1973) *Immigrant Labour and Class Structure in Western Europe*, London: Oxford University Press.

Castles, S. and Miller, M. (2003) *The Age of Migration: International Population Movements in the Modern World* (3rd edition), Basingstoke: Palgrave Macmillan.

CIPD (2013) *The State of Migration: Employing Migrant Workers*, Chartered Institute for Personnel and Development, London: CIPD.

Crouch, C. and Streeck, W. (1997) *Political Economy of Modern Capitalism: Mapping Convergence and Diversity*, London: Sage Publications.

Eironline (2006) *Relocation of production and industrial relations*, European industrial relations observatory online, February, TN0511101S. Accessed at: http://www.eurofound.europa.eu/eiro/2005/11/study/tn0511101s.htm (retrieved 18 September 2013).

French, S. (2012) 'Beyond ESOL? Assessing the propensity of east European migrant workers to undertake further and higher education', *Research in Post-Compulsory Education*, 17(1), 125–142.

French, S. and Möhrke, J. (2007) *The impact of 'new arrivals' on the North Staffordshire labour market'*, Report to the Low Pay Commission, London: Low Pay Commission.

Galgóczi, B., Leschke, J. and Watt, A. (2012) 'EU labour migration and labour markets in troubled times' in Galgóczi, B., Leschke, J. and Watt, A. (eds), *EU Labour Migration in Troubled Times: Skills Mismatch, Return and Policy Responses*, Basingstoke: Ashgate.

Goodrich, C. (1921) *The Frontier of Control: A Study in British Workshop Politics*, Orlando, FL: Harcourt, Brace and Company.

Hall, P. and Soskice, D. (eds) (2001) *Varieties of Capitalism. The Institutional Foundations of Comparative Advantage*, Oxford: Oxford University Press.

Harvey, D. (2007) *A Brief History of Neo-Liberalism*, Oxford: Oxford University Press.

Jayaweera, H. and Anderson, B. (2008) *Migrant Workers and Vulnerable Employment: A Review of Existing Data*, Report for TUC Commission on Vulnerable Employment, Oxford: Compas. Accessed at: http://www.vulnerableworkers.org.uk/wp-content/uploads/2008/08/analysis-of-migrant-worker-data-final.pdf (retrieved 18 September 2013).

Korkiasaari, J. and Söderling, I. (2003) *Finnish Emigration and Immigration after World War II*, Siirtolaisuusinstituutti – Migrationsinstitutet, Turku. Accessed at: http://www.migrationinstitute.fi/articles/011_Korkiasaari_Soderling.pdf (retrieved 19 September 2013).

Lucas, R. and Mansfield, S. (2008) *Staff Shortages and Immigration in the Hospitality Sector*, A paper prepared for the Migration Advisory Committee. Accessed at: http://www.ukba.home-office.gov.uk/sitecontent/documents/aboutus/workingwithus/mac/239769/lucasandmansfield2008 (retrieved 18 September 2013).

MacKenzie, R. and Forde, C. (2009) 'The rhetoric of the "good worker" versus the realities of employers' use and the experiences of migrant workers', *Work, Employment and Society*, 23(1), 142–159.

McCullum, D. and Findlay, A. (2011) *Trends in A8 migration to the UK during the recession*, Population Trends 145, Autumn 2011, London: Official for National Statistics.

Menz, G. (2010) *The Political Economy of Managed Migration: Nonstate Actors, Europeanization and the Politics of Designing Migration Policies*, Oxford: Oxford University Press.

ONS (2005) *United Kingdom: Economic Accounts Quarter 4 2004*, Office for National Statistics, London: The Stationery Office.

Phizacklea, A. and Miles, R. (1980) *Labour and Racism*, London: Routledge & Kegan Paul.

Ruhs, M. and Anderson, B. (eds) (2010) *Who Needs Migrant Workers: Labour Shortages, Immigration and Public Policy*, Oxford: Oxford University Press.

Salt, J. (1976) 'International labour migration: The geographical pattern of demand', in Salt, J. and Clout, H. (eds), *Migration in Post-War Europe: Geographical Essays*, London: Oxford University Press.

Salt, J. and Clout, H. (1976) 'The demographic background', in Salt, J. and Clout, H. (eds), *Migration in Post-War Europe: Geographical Essays*, London: Oxford University Press.

Scott, S. (2008) *Staff Shortages and Immigration in Agriculture*, A paper prepared for the Migration Advisory Committee. Accessed at: http://www.ukba.homeoffice.gov.uk/sitecontent/documents/aboutus/workingwithus/mac/239769/scott2008 (retrieved 18 September 2013).

Sjaastad, L. (1962) 'The costs and returns of human migration', *Journal of Political Economy*, 70(5), 80–93.

Temin, P. (2002) 'The Golden Age of European growth reconsidered', *European Review of Economic History*, 6, 3–22.

*The Observer* (2013) 'Romanian and Bulgarian migration estimates are "unfounded", says report', 18 August 2013. Accessed at: http://www.theguardian.com/uk-news/2013/aug/18/estimate-romanians-bulgarians-unfounded (retrieved 16 September 2013).

Toniolo, G. (1998) 'Europe's Golden Age, 1950–1973: Speculations from a long-run perspective', *Economic History Review*, 51(2), 252–267.

TUC (2013) *TUC lodges complaint against the UK government for failing to give equal pay to agency workers*, Press Release 2 September. Accessed at: http://www.tuc.org.uk/workplace/tuc-22536-f0.cfm (retrieved 18 September 2013).

Wrench, J. and Solomos, J. (1993) *Racism and Migration in Western Europe,* Oxford: Berg Press.

# 9

# Interpreting technology: Telework and the myth of liberation

*Emma Surman*

## 9.1 Introduction

Technology is central to modern life (Grint and Woolgar, 1997) and hence of vital concern to managers. In the attempts to understand and explain the organisation of work, technology is often presented as separate to, distinct from and in opposition to the social and cultural or more human elements (Corbett, 2009). Conceived of in this dualistic manner, technology is often depicted as having a particular predetermined effect on the organisation and the working lives of people within it. In applying the technology, it is seen to alter the way in which the organisation functions and is structured. This in turn alters the type of work required, the manner in which it is conducted and the way in which organisations and work are experienced. From a management perspective this effect has invariably been presented as positive, delivering assumed benefits and ultimately leading to improved organisational performance. As a result, managers have been encouraged to adopt new technologies in order to enhance performance, increase customer satisfaction and provide a greater return on investment, a move which has resulted in a managerial discourse surrounding the introduction of new technology which associates it with efficiency, progress and remaining 'cutting edge'.

From the perspective of an employee, the introduction of new technologies has frequently been perceived and presented as having a destructive effect on their experience of work. It has been associated with the deskilling and alienation of the workforce and as a means of placing increased control in the hands of management (Burnes et al., 1988). For example, the introduction of the automated assembly line dictating the pace of work or the use of information and communication technologies in call centres that make the individual highly visible and enable continual and detailed levels of monitoring.

Ascribing certain effects to the introduction of technology, whether positive or negative, assumes an inherent quality residing in the technology which is subsequently realised when applied in a particular context. However, as Grint and Woolgar (1997: 10) state, 'technologies do not exist independently of human interpretation'. Any effect is down to the interaction between the technical and the social and rather than the social and the technological standing in opposition to and aside from one another, they should be viewed as highly interwoven elements in the complex fabric of organisational life. It follows, therefore, that if we wish to understand the role that technology plays within organisations, we need to understand the 'interpretative activities' (Grint and Woolgar, 1997) of those working with it and explore the ways in which people interact with, relate to and incorporate technology into their working lives.

This chapter focuses on the particular application of technology that enables people to 'telework' and explores whether it leads to new and different ways of living and working. Adopting the approach that the effects of technology 'depends on the mediating effects of the interpreter' (Grint and Woolgar, 1997: 136) it explores the mythical claims that information and communication technologies liberate users from the vagaries of the workplace by looking at the lived experience of telework, and the ways in which this technologically enabled way of working is integrated into the lives of users.

While no single definition of telework has been found (Sullivan, 2003) and this term covers a very wide range of work experiences, it always involves 'working at a distance from the people who pay you' (Bertin and Denbigh, 2000: 1). While working at a distance is not a new phenomenon, new technologies have altered the types of work that can be done remotely. For many years, people referred to as homeworkers have typically carried out low skilled manual work from within their own homes, working at tasks such as packing, sorting and assembly work. Those conducting these tasks have mostly been subject to poor working conditions, few or no employment rights, unpredictable workloads and very low wages. The introduction of new technology has raised the profile of remote working and it is no longer something only done by those on the margins but has now ostensibly become a perk available to highly trusted professional staff (see, for example, Stanworth, 1997; Sullivan and Lewis, 2001; Tietze and Musson, 2002). But the relative status of homework is fraught with paradoxical understandings of space, time and activity, as will be clear in this chapter.

The discussion that follows is based on research conducted into two pilot telework projects that were run at a UK High Street bank, referred to here as Any Bank. The teleworkers, who were all women, have been given pseudonyms in this text to ensure anonymity. They had all previously worked on company premises as part of the call centre operation and had volunteered to take part in the pilot project. This chapter will look at the day-to-day experiences of these teleworkers as they used technology to work away from the office. In particular, it will focus on the ability of telework to liberate the workforce from the centralised place of work and the associated discipline and restrictions. As such, the starting point of this chapter is the distinction or boundary that has assumed a significant presence in modern life; that between work and home. Although, as this chapter will explore, these two places are not always as separate and distinct as they might seem, or as we might like them to be, it is a distinction that has both a spatial and temporal relevance to people's lives. Many people leave their homes on a daily basis and travel to do a 'day's work' before leaving the workplace to return home and the appeal of telework, by contrast, lies in the potential to blur this distinction. After discussing the history and nature of this boundary, the experience of the teleworkers at Any Bank will be considered. This reveals that despite moving work into their homes, the interpretative actions of the teleworkers served to replicate and strengthen the boundary between home and work rather than eradicate it.

## 9.2 The separation of work and home

In order to understand the myths that have become associated with telework, it is necessary to spend some time discussing the boundary that separates work and home. This distinction has not always been meaningful in people's lives. For example, in feudal times, the peasant home was a site in which activities which we might now categorise as either labour or leisure co-existed (Pollard, 1965 as cited in Fleming, 2005) and the dwelling place was also the place from which all productive activity would have been carried out. As a result, little distinction was made between what we might see as domestic activities, for example eating, sleeping, socialising and those which related to production or exchange (Hall, 1995). It was only with the advent of the Industrial Revolution that a spatial separation developed between where people lived and where they worked (Cott, 1977; Hall, 1995).

The arrival and spread of factories as part of the process of industrialisation meant that people were drawn out of the countryside and into the spreading towns. Workers exchanged a subsistence existence for a paid job which imposed both a spatial and temporal discipline (Thompson, 1967). Space became segregated with different places for working and living but also within these different places, specific activities were allocated to specific locations (Sack, 1986). Time also became compartmentalised. Whereas within the agrarian economy activities were closely linked to the changing seasons, the spread of the factory system produced the requirement to be in a set place for a set number of hours in order to obtain a wage. The notion of separate work and leisure time was introduced and a new pattern of living emerged.

Although reference to a boundary between home and work might suggest complete separation between the two, they have never been fully separated, as each flows into (du Gay, 1996) and influences the other. The home was and is often sentimentalised, seen as a haven, a place of sanctuary and an escape from the pressures of modern living (Cott, 1977; Lasch, 1977; Saranceno, 1987). However, despite its associations with rest and relaxation, the home is the site of a great deal of labour. This often goes unrecognised as it is frequently carried out by women, receives no wage and as such it is devalued and disappeared (Fletcher, 2001). This permeability between the world of home and work is further evidenced in current times through the spread of mobile and digital technologies. The presence of these devices has meant employees may be (or feel they are) under pressure to make themselves available outside of work time, during evenings, weekends and holidays leading to an 'always on' culture which eats into leisure time (Wall, 2012). Attendant with this phenomenon is a wealth of literature surrounding the struggle of 'work–life balance'; suggesting that it is the role of the worker to do this management themselves (for example Land and Taylor, 2010).

Despite the leakiness of this boundary and even though it is 'by no means impermeable' (Fleming, 2005: 289) the distinction between home and work has persisted as a meaningful reference point and retains a relevance for modern living, with the home seen as a place where the individual is free to determine their own activity (Fleming and Spicer, 2004).

## 9.3   The myth of telework

The supposed qualities, capacities and effects attributed to technology have resulted in the creation of certain myths which have either become associated with the introduction of new technologies in general or with a specific application. In some cases these myths focus on technology as destructive, for example, the case of the Luddites in the 19th century textile industry in the United Kingdom. In other cases, such as the telework being discussed here, the myths focus on the positive potential of technology.

For futurists such as Toffler (1980), telework, encapsulated in his notion of an 'electronic cottage', has the potential for change on a par with the transition witnessed during the Industrial Revolution, rewriting 'the ground rules that once governed us' (Toffler, 1980: 264). Similarly for Handy (1980), new technologies would enable a 'flexi-life' (1980: 120) whereby people would be freely able to determine how and when they would work. For both of these authors, the opportunity for radical change revolved around the possibility of blurring or erasing the boundary between home and work, an appeal so alluring that in the early 1990s there were enthusiastic predictions that large swathes of the population would soon be working this way (NEDO, 1986; Olson and Primps, 1984). From an employee's perspective, the appeal lies in the possibility that we might be able to better integrate two seemingly distinct spheres of our life. Without the need to travel to and from work on a daily basis and being able to work at times that might fit with other commitments, telework provides the potential to obtain a more rewarding existence: to live and work, where, how and when we want to. Benefits are also seen to extend beyond the individual; reducing traffic congestion, lowering levels of pollution and leading to a resurgence in 'local' communities. It would also offer equal employment opportunities for working mothers, the disabled and long-term sick (Deeks, 2000). Organisations would also benefit from a reduction in fixed costs and a more flexible and committed workforce.

Many of these benefits of telework emerged during the research at Any Bank as reasons for instigating or participating in the project. The bank's reasons for running the project included: containing and reducing costs of running the call centres and seeking to expand the catchment area for the recruitment of new staff. Managers also hoped that staff would be more willing to do extra shifts because work would become that much more convenient, something that many office based staff were unwilling to do. Another important reason was the opportunity to expand the size of the call centre without having to acquire another building. The current building was full to capacity and taking on extra office based staff would mean acquiring or renting new premises.

Among the employees at Any Bank, the reasons given for wanting to take part in the project included: the difficulty and cost of parking, avoiding the commute (which in the case of one employee was an hour and a half each way) and being in a better position to combine work with other commitments including caring responsibilities for children and other relatives.

## 9.4 Technology and boundary work: The life of the Any Bank teleworker

Any Bank chose two call centres as the sites from which to conduct their pilot projects. The teleworkers were each given a workstation, computer, fax machine and had an ISDN line installed in their house to enable them to receive inbound calls and were therefore able to operate in the same way as their office based colleagues. There were 24 staff taking part in the pilot project, the majority of which were 'information receivers' (Korczynski, 2005), taking in-bound telephone calls either dealing with applications for loans or servicing bank accounts. This call centre work was highly reliant on technology, as calls were distributed to an available customer service representative via a call distribution system. In addition, the interaction with the customer was dictated via a series of screens which clearly set out the questions to be asked. This technology also enabled the call centre supervisors to closely monitor the work of the staff, as at any point they could identify who was signed into the system. They could also obtain information regarding length of calls and were able to record calls, which they did on a regular basis. All this information was used to tightly monitor staff performance which, if it did not meet the required targets, would result in disciplinary action.

As the earlier discussion has revealed, despite being somewhat 'leaky', the boundaries between home and work have had a spatial and temporal relevance to people's lives for a significant period of time. Through the use of new technologies, the teleworkers at Any Bank had the physical boundaries between home and work removed and they were now living and working in the same place. What is of interest here is the ways in which the teleworkers interpreted this change and the practices they adopted as they interacted with the technology to commence this new way of working.

The interviews conducted with the teleworkers revealed a variety of reactions and experiences. Many were relieved at not having the daily commute to work and the associated struggles with parking. Others felt that their home lives had benefited. While the teleworkers felt that the changes telework had enabled had undoubtedly improved their lives, they did not report adopting practices which suggest the kind of transformatory experience predicted by Toffler (1980) or Handy (1980). Indeed, rather than releasing them from established patterns of living and enabling an alternate existence that they were free to determine themselves, having home and work in one place posed a number of dilemmas with which the teleworkers felt they had to find a way to cope with. This is nicely encapsulated in a quote from Barbara:

> I said to them at work, 'Now do I wear my shoes or my slippers at home?' [. . .] I know it's really weird but I really found it a strange thing at first, to know whether to wear shoes or slippers. [. . .] because, I mean, I've been working since I left school at 16 and I'm 50 next year, so I've worked for 34 years and I've always gone to work in my shoes haven't I? (Barbara)

For all Barbara's working life, footwear has been a way to distinguish between work and home. Through understanding the two as different, she was able to make sense of the situation and understand how to behave appropriately. Thus, the distinction between home and work provided a common framework, and it was through reference to it that she was able to generate meaning and understand actions. Barbara went on to discuss the how she dealt with this dilemma, whereby in the absence of a spatial distinction between her home and work she maintained a mental one.

> I go to work, it's really weird. If I talk to anyone I go 'I'm going to work' and they go 'but you work from home'. I know but I have to say in my mind, I go to work [. . .] it's no different to me, coming in here to go to work than to go into the office, in my mind. It's a discipline thing for me. (Barbara)

This socially constructed distinction served a real and useful purpose in Barbara's life. Although she did not leave home to go to work, she still found it useful and meaningful to maintain the distinction between the two places. Other teleworkers similarly reported the need to retain this division. For some it could continue to have a spatial dimension as their workstation and computer were in a separate room, a spare room or study into which they would only go when they were working and on which they were able to close the door at the end of their shift. For others, it was not possible to gain this physical separation, as they had to work in the living room, dining room or frequently their own bedroom. For these women, other more symbolic means of dividing home and work were utilised. Part of the equipment provided by Any Bank for the teleworkers was a workstation. This was designed so that everything, including the chair, could be shut away inside and when closed, one had no indication as to what was inside; it simply looked like a large cupboard or wardrobe. For some of the teleworkers, the ritual of opening up and then closing down the cupboard, served as a marker of the start and end of their shift respectively.

Other rituals and practices had also developed to help maintain the distinction between home and work. For Shirley, one such ritual involved the provision of drinks whilst working her shift. When at home, her usual routine involved going to the kitchen and helping herself as and when she was thirsty. Working in her bedroom, she felt unable to wander downstairs whenever she wanted a drink and her teapot became an important part of her working routine. She filled it up and took it upstairs with her so that she could still have a drink but would not have to leave her workstation until her next permitted break.

> I never come down here [to the kitchen] and make a drink [when working]. I take my teapot upstairs on a tray. I've got a tea cosy so it keeps it quite warm, so if I do want a drink in between [breaks], even if I've made the tea half an hour or an hour ago it's still warmish. (Shirley)

Due to the confidential nature of the data dealt with by the teleworkers, the bank required that they were always alone in the room while they were working. Therefore, the distinction between home and work was important and relevant not only for the Any Bank staff but also for their families and the teleworkers went to great lengths to ensure that their families respected the distinction. One teleworker told of how, if a family member made her a drink while she was working, they would not bring it into her but would knock and then leave it outside the living room door. Another told of how her daughter had made a sign which would hang on the room she was working in. On one side was a sad face and the word 'working' and on the other was a somewhat happier looking one accompanied by the words 'not working'. This sign was used to indicate to the rest of the family whether or not they were able to enter the room. Other teleworkers took this even further constructing rules for how the family was to behave even when in other parts of the house. For example, asking their children's friends not to ring the doorbell when they were working, as it made the dog bark or having to talk to their visiting friends outside of the house rather than inviting them in.

By incorporating these practices into their home lives, rather than blurring the boundary between home and work, the teleworkers can be seen to reproduce the division between work and home *within* their own home. For them, the divide between home and work was not erased and the move to telework did not lead to a radical transformation in their lives. Any consensus as to the 'effect' technology will not be imposed on working lives but will be socially constituted (Grint and Woolgar, 1997) and of course, the teleworkers did not exist in isolation but continued to interact with others, both in and out of work. For the most part, these others still followed a pattern of living which distinguished between home and work. Hence, the teleworkers still lived and operated in a world in which the divide between home and work remained meaningful and significant. Therefore, it made sense and was also meaningful to them to retain this distinction in their own lives. Given that home and work were no longer spatially distinct, they were encouraged and felt a need to symbolically recreate it. Although they did report some small but significant changes, for example; being able to have tea with their families before starting work, kissing their children goodnight during their break, saving the frustrations and time associated with sitting in the traffic and struggling to find a place to park that was near to work and reasonably priced, practices adopted reinforced established patterns of living rather than presenting any radical transformations.

A quote from Sally also shows that for her, not only had the divide between home and work been retained but the distinction between the two worlds had intensified. The removal of the commute had removed the 'in-between zones' both mental and physical that were encountered whilst traveling to and from work. Without this transition time, you were either now at work or at home. Rather than blurring the divide between home and work, for Sally, the distinction had become even sharper.

> Rather than your whole life being taken over by your job, it does only occupy seven hours of your day. You can put it away and forget it. (Sally).

## 9.5    Discussion and conclusion

In the world of organisation studies there has been a move to question and seek to deconstruct binary divisions, to highlight the unstable and socially constructed nature of these separations. This critical approach is done for good reason, for inevitably one side of the division is privileged and therefore valued above the other. In a paper arguing for the 'eradication' of dualisms, Knights (1997) argues that although distinctions are important in order to enable communication, the undesirable result of the division is that 'what is distinguished as 'this' or 'that' is reified as an ontological reality rather than merely a provisional, subjectively significant and hence contestable ordering of 'things'. Which he states will result in 'mis-placed concreteness' (p. 4).

The technologies that enable telework were associated with the possibility of removing or blurring the dualism of home and work. However, the teleworkers at Any Bank interpreted their relationship with technology and work within the existing frame of reference. It served to provide a reference point that made situations meaningful and enabled them to account for their own actions and those of others. It also helped them to know what was appropriate in a particular situation, for example in terms of clothing, behaviour and attitude by establishing a difference between the two. The clearer and more obvious the differences were, the simpler it was to define meaning and behave in an appropriate way. Difference is created through a process of separation and the construction of boundaries and it is through reference to these constructions that a situation is transformed from one that is unclear and ambiguous into one in which a familiar order prevails (Cooper, 1993). For the teleworkers at Any Bank, the transfer of the workstation into the home posed a number of dilemmas and was at times a source of anxiety which they needed to manage and cope with. After a period of having to leave home in order to *go* to work, in some cases for many years, they were able to cope with the new circumstances by recreating and sharpening the boundary between home and work and restoring a familiar order in their lives. Although 'leaky', this reference point was too useful for them in both their social interactions and as a way of making sense of their activities (Cohen, 1989) to be lost. Its continued presence ensured that differences, meanings and order were retained, it also enabled them to comply with social norms and served as 'working consensus' (Goffman, 1990) around which the teleworkers could construct and maintain their identities. Thus although the boundary between home and work may have shifted, it remained useful and meaningful in interpreting the new situation in which they found themselves. The change in workplace resulted in the adoption of practices which replicated the existing order and frequently meant that they exerted stricter controls on themselves than they were subject to in the workplace.

In addition to the spatial constraints, the teleworkers at Any Bank also experienced temporal restrictions on their activities too as they were not permitted any freedom in terms of the times when they worked. They were still required to work a set shift with a clear start and end time and were only permitted to take the permitted level of breaks. The technology enabled the same levels of monitoring whether the employee was in the office or at home, and deviation from the required hours of work, or any tea breaks that were slightly longer than they should be were quickly identified. Similar findings have emerged from other studies of telework where, far from leading to a variety in working patterns, it has been found that for teleworkers, traditional working hours remain the rule and other schedules the exception (Valenduc and Vendramin, 2001; Dimitrova, 2003). The split between home and work has developed and entwined itself in the lives of workers over a long period of time and in the words of Fleming (2005: 298) 'history cannot be so easily erased from the collective memory of workers'.

This chapter has explored one very specific incidence of the interaction between the technological and the social in the workplace. The use of new technologies within organisations will not be uniformly similar across different societies, industries or companies and this chapter reveals the lived experience of technological change and how it was experienced and interpreted by one particular group. As highlighted at the start of this chapter, all of the teleworkers in this study were women. The constructed boundary between home and work is also gendered, with women associated with the private world of the home and men the public world of work. Further work is required to explore and discuss the role of these associations in the interpretative actions of teleworkers. Age may also be a relevant factor in this respect. The women in this study had not grown up immersed in the plethora of digital technologies that surround us today. Some had not even used a PC (only a dumb terminal) prior to taking part in the project. For future generations, or different workforces in other industries, the experience may be different. For example, recent news stories have revealed a reversal of policy amongst some Internet organisations that had previously permitted and encouraged employees to telework. Yahoo banned employees from remote working (Ryan, 2013) and in a memo which was leaked to media outlets by disgruntled employees, the CEO Marissa Mayer stated 'We need to be one Yahoo!, and that starts with physically being together' (Swisher, 2013). This sentiment is echoed in the comments of Google's Chief Financial Officer Patrick Pichette who is reported as saying 'There is something magical about sharing meals, there is something magical about noodling on ideas' (Ryan, 2013). Further, in a story which appeared on the BBC website, it was reported that a software developer employed by a company in the US outsourced his own job to a company in China. He paid them a fifth of his salary and reportedly spent his time surfing the web and watching YouTube. The technology which enabled him to work remotely also enabled the outsourcing of his job. According to the report the employee has subsequently lost his job (BBC, 2013). It seems in this case the interaction between the social and the technological did lead to new practices and radical interpretations but these were not approved of by the employing organisation.

In an interesting study of hobbyist software developers who improved and developed commercially available video games, increasing the levels of sophistication, Postigo (2003) found that the 'gamers' did not seem to mind completing unpaid work for the company making the games and effectively gave away their intellectual property. For these individuals, who supply what Postigo refers to as 'passionate labour' (2003: 605), the divide between work and leisure can already be seen to be ambiguous and may lead to different practices and interpretations. Likewise, the continued development of the application of technology within the workplace has also meant that in some instances organisations have been able to dispense with the employee altogether, requiring the consumer to provide the labour instead. In the supermarket, the library or the airport, the need for some staff has been removed as we are now able to check out our shopping and library books or check ourselves onto a flight or pick up our cinema and theatre tickets or get money out of the bank without the help and assistance of another person. It is done either via a dedicated on-site machine or increasingly remotely via an Internet connection from our PC, laptop, tablet or mobile phone. The increasing involvement of the customer in the work of the organisation, in which they themselves become part of the production process at the expense of the employee, has been referred to as the process of 'co-creation' (Zwick et al., 2008; Echeverri and Skålén, 2011), and leading to terms such as the 'prosumer' (Ritzer et al., 2012) or the 'working consumer' (Rieder and Voss, 2010). Such changes to the processes of consumption as well as production of work and leisure may pose further challenges to the boundary between home and work and lead to new and alternative interpretations as the social and the technological interact.

 **REFERENCES**

BBC (2013) 'US employee 'outsourced job to China'', BBC News online, http://www.bbc.co.uk/news/technology-21043693 (retrieved 18 January 2013).

Bertin, I. and Denbigh, A. (2000) *The Teleworking Handbook: New Ways of Working in the Information Society*, Kenilworth: Telework, Telecottage and Telecentre Association.

Burnes, B., Knights, D. and Willmott, H. (1988) 'Introduction', in Knights, D. and Willmott, H. (eds), *New Technology and the Labour Process*, Basingstoke: Macmillan Press.

Cohen, A.P. (1989) *The Symbolic Construction of Community*, London: Routledge.

Cooper, R. (1993) 'Organization/disorganization', in Hassard, J. and Pym, D. (eds), *The Theory and Philosophy of Organizations*, London: Routledge.

Corbett, J.M. (2009) 'Technology', in Hancock, P. and Spicer, A. (eds), *Understanding Corporate Life*, London: Sage Publications.

Cott, N. (1977) *The Bonds of Womanhood: 'Woman's Sphere' in New England 1780–1835*, New Haven: Yale University Press.

Deeks, E. (2000) 'Petrol shortage fuels teleworking mini-boom', *People Management*, 28 (September), 14.

Dimitrova, D. (2003) 'Controlling teleworkers: Supervision and flexibility revisited', *New Technology, Work and Employment*, 18(3), 181–195.

du Gay, P. (1996) *Consumption and Identity at Work*, London: Sage Publications.

Echeverri, P. and Skålén, P. (2011) 'Co-creation and co-destruction: A practice-theory based study of interactive value formation', *Marketing Theory*, 11(3), 279–301.

Fleming, P. (2005) 'Workers' playtime? Boundaries and cynicism in a "culture of fun" program', *The Journal of Applied Behavioral Science*, 41(3), 285–303.

Fleming, P. and Spicer, A. (2004) 'You can check out any time but you can never leave: Spatial boundaries in a high-commitment organization', *Human Relations*, 57(1), 75–94.

Fletcher, J. (2001) *Disappearing Acts: Gender, Power and Relational Practice at Work*, London: The MIT Press.

Goffman, E. (1990) *The Presentation of Self in Everyday Life*, London: Penguin.

Grint, K. and Woolgar, S. (1997) *The Machine at Work: Technology, Work and Organisation*, Cambridge: Polity Press.

Hall, C. (1995) 'The history of the housewife', in Malos, E. (ed.), *The Politics of Housework*, Cheltenham: New Clarion Press.

Handy, C. (1980) 'Through the organizational looking glass', *Harvard Business Review*, January/February, 115–121.

Knights, D. (1997) 'Organization theory in in the age of deconstruction: Dualism, gender and postmodernism revisited', *Organization Studies*, 18(1), 1–19.

Korczynski, M. (2005) 'Skills in service work: An overview', *Human Resource Management Journal*, 15(2), 3–14.

Land, C. and Taylor, S. (2010) 'Surf 's up: Work, life, balance and brand in a new age capitalist organization', *Sociology*, 44(3 ), 395–413.

Lasch, C. (1977) *Haven in a Heartless World: The Family Besieged*, New York: Basic Books.

NEDO (1986) 'IT futures surveyed: A study of informal opinion concerning the long term implications of information technology', HMSO, London: Technology & Society.

Olson, M.H. and Primps, S.B. (1984) 'Working at home with computers – work and non-work issues', *Journal of Social Issues*, 40(3), 97–122.

Pollard, S. (1965) *The Genesis of Modern Management*, London: Arnold.

Postigo, H. (2003) 'From pong to planet quake: Post-industrial transitions from leisure to work, *Information, Communication and Society*, 6(4), 593–607.

Rieder, K. and Voss, G. (2010) 'The working customer – an emerging new type of consumer', *Psychology of Everyday Activity*, 3(2), 2–10.

Ritzer, G., Dean, P. and Jurgenson, N. (2012) 'The coming of age of the prosumer', *American Behavioral Scientist*, 56(4), 379–398.

Ryan, M. (2013) 'Teleworking: The myth of working from home', *BBC News Magazine online* http://www.bbc.co.uk/news/magazine-21588760 (retrieved 4 March 2013).

Sack, R. (1986) *Human Territoriality: Its Theory and History*, Cambridge: Cambridge University Press.

Saranceno, C. (1987) 'Division of family labour and gender identity', in Showstack Sassoon, D. (ed.), *Women and the State*, London: Hutchinson Education.

Stanworth, C. (1997) 'Telework and the information age', paper presented at *International Labour Process Conference*, University of Edinburgh, Scotland: 25–27 March.

Sullivan, C. (2003) 'What's in a name? Definitions and conceptualisations of teleworking and homeworking', *New Technology, Work and Employment*, 18(3), 158–165.

Sullivan, C. and Lewis, S. (2001) 'Home based telework, gender and the synchronisation of work and family: Perspectives of teleworkers and their co-residents', *Gender, Work and Organization*, 8(2), 123–145.

Swisher, K. (2013) '"Physically together": Here's to the internal Yahoo no-work-from-home memo for remote workers and maybe more', *AllThingsD* http://allthingsd.com/20130222/physically-together-heres-the-internal-yahoo-no-work-from-home-memo-which-extends-beyond-remote-workers/ (retrieved 4 March 2013).

Thompson, E.P. (1967) 'Time, work discipline and industrial capitalism', *Past and Present*, 38(1), 56–97.

Tietze, S. and Musson, G. (2002) 'Feeling groovy: The times and temporalities of telework', paper presented at the *20th Standing Conference on Organizational Symbolism*, International Business School, Budapest, Hungary, 10–13 July.

Toffler, A. (1980) *The Third Wave*, London: Pan.

Valenduc, G. and Vendramin, P. (2001) 'Telework: From distance working to new forms of flexible work organisation', *Transfer*, 7(2), 244–257.

Wall, M. (2012) 'Is telework driving us crazy?' BBC News online http://www.bbc.co.uk/news/business-19594518 (retrieved 18 January 2013).

Zwick, D., Bonsu, S.K. and Darmody, A. (2008) 'Putting consumers to work: "Co-creation" and new marketing govern-mentality', *Journal of Consumer Culture*, 8(2), 163–196.

# 10

# Media as mediation: Uncertainty and representation in the construction of news

*Barry Schofield*

## 10.1 Introduction

Given the monumental amount of attention that has been devoted to expos-ing the sundry sins of the British press, it may seem perverse to suggest there is anything more that can be usefully gained from further exploration in this direction. Yet for all the effort that has gone into cataloguing the sordid tales of phone hacking, press intrusion and illegal payments to police officers, there has been little scrutiny of the staple product of all media life: *News*.

Current research into media effects has, instead, drawn upon a diverse range of subjects including economics, political science, sociology, psychology and communications studies and has incorporated a number of theoretically informed methods from 'public choice theory', the statistical analysis of data sets (for example, identifying relationships between media consumption and polling data) to interviews and discussion groups (for a good review, see Ofcom.co.uk). Running through much of this research and literature is the idea that the media has an ability to influence the topics that audiences think about, what some have termed the 'agenda-setting' effect (McCombs, 2002; Norris, 2005) Opinions differ, however, as to the exact nature of these effects and there has been insufficient time for the implications of the recent scan-dals over press behaviour to be fully theorised in this regard.

Any inquiry into press behaviour needs to concern itself with what consti-tutes 'news' – how it is selected, shaped, interpreted and disseminated as a cultural artefact. It is 'news' that forms the *raison d'être* of the press and which links the world of journalists to their readers according to some unstated theory of cause and effect. The problem of 'news' goes to the heart of press activity and raises questions about *how* information and other materials are used to construct narrative stories that can be deployed for persuasive effect (see also French, Chapter 8 this volume).

This chapter attempts to address this shortcoming by exploring some of the organisational mechanisms that delineate the everyday production of news. In this exercise I am not concerned with further tracing the ethical arguments about press behaviour or discussing the merits of regulating newspaper practice. Nor am I interested in presenting a narrowly ideological conception of news, as a discourse that serves vested political or class interests. Politics here is construed as more than the party system, electoral manoeuvrings, ideological labels, governmental power struggles and the machinations of media moguls. Instead I give much wider latitude to the term 'political', treating it as a struggle to compose and stabilise an identity for 'news' from the resources available.

## 10.2 The taming of uncertainty

In what follows, I argue that the discourse of 'news' is the engineered outcome of processes that are shaped, ordered and assembled from a complex range of socio-technical materials. When confronted in its raw, shapeless condition – prior to any assemblage – 'news' has no essential meaning, no 'natural identity' that makes it recognisable as such. Instead 'it' is manufactured in contexts of uncertainty in which there is no natural coherence between events, people, technologies and meanings. This is a condition that I have elsewhere described as 'vague' (Schofield, 2003), to describe a situation of radical uncertainty in which no essential identity exists, or at least one in which meanings have yet to be established and identities stabilised. Vagueness, as I have described it, is not treated in its usual pejorative manner, however, as a condition of tangled confusion or woolly minded chaos. Rather, it refers to a more primitive condition of *dis*-order, one in which meanings have yet to be constructed and fixed.

This is similar to the early 20th Century term 'meaningless infinity' which the German social philosopher Max Weber coined to describe a situation in which meanings do not appear to us naturally or in their familiar form, but instead have to be shaped actively. By 'meaningless infinity' Weber was suggesting that the world does not present itself to our everyday understanding as already formed, that it is intrinsically unreadable and that we have to convert its inarticulation into meaningful signs and symbols. For Weber this process of rationalised meaning making was part of the constitutive character of modernity. Weber's 'meaningless infinity' is also reminiscent of the swirling mass of unformed drives and emotions that Sigmund Freud described in the same period to theorise the subconscious strata of thought in his model of the human psyche. For Freud these dynamic forces are typically brought under partial control by the censoring pressures that try to align them with society's norms.

Radical uncertainty is also a condition that, I suggest, confronts journalists and media organisations when they are required to produce 'news', and often acutely so in situations where they are constrained by pressures of time and in fierce rivalry with commercial competitors. In their reporting of new events, newspapers impose structures that try to 'cure' the world of events of this indeterminacy. New occurrences that, by traditional definition, constitute our customary understanding of news, are never laid out before newspapers as a landscape composed of neat and tidy entities. Instead they are better understood as a messy, unformed and random reality which has to be tamed and cleansed by media intervention in order to produce a specialised form of knowledge called 'news.' In other words, news has to be made before it can be discovered.

According to this mode of thought, uncertainty need not be seen as a necessarily negative or adverse condition but instead one of open possibilities, a creative well-spring that can invite or provoke active translation. Newspapers perform this work of translation by acting as sense-making mediators, trying to reduce the uncertainty by giving 'it' an acceptable shape and form – *an identity* – that can then be held sufficiently still and be rendered useful in order to fulfil the demands of everyday production.

The sensibility that I have outlined so far, and in what follows, draws inspiration from a broader theoretical perspective that treats organisation as a generalised social strategy of representation and control that has as its impulse a drive to stabilise, classify and locate the remote and intractable character of the world. This view of organisation – as a *process* rather than a ready-made entity – is typified in the writings of Weber, Michel Foucault and Robert Cooper who share a common concern with tracing and understanding the tensions, ambiguities and contradictions in the continuous structuring of modern society (for a fuller exploration of this perspective see Cooper 1987, 1989, 1993 and 1998).

Drawing on this perspective, I show how newspapers perform the task of converting disordered events into the ordered identity of news to enable the construction of an object of knowledge. Creating a knowable object – an identity – is made possible through acts of representation and is typically achieved by differentiating and detaching the putative object from the field of uncertainty and flux of its context. As I argue below, newspapers conduct this organising function by imposing bureaucratic protocols, routines and definitions, as well as by constructing more informal mechanisms that shape the professional behaviour of journalists. These mechanisms act as an organising grid that reduces uncertainty by providing the generative principles and practices of news production. As I show below, it is also a process that has direct, and occasionally uncomfortable, repercussions for journalists themselves.

## 10.3 The *re*-presentation of events

In the construction of news, the ultimate goal is the re-presentation of actual events occurring in the real world in a particular form of knowledge comprising words, stories, images and photographs. To achieve any plausibility news must be made to resemble the real-world event as closely as possible. To do so, however, the work of constructing a representation must undertake a kind of journey, in which, paradoxically, it has to become independent of the reality it purports to reflect.

This process enables subsequent translations to take place in a process that is typically concealed from view as the emerging representation takes shape. In this process of successive translations multiple acts of mediation occur as reality is presented again and again – that is *re*-presented – as an image of the real. Through this work of mediation the representation of 'news' achieves its persuasive effects not so much by denying or renouncing the real-world event, but by substituting for its role by 'speaking for it' and for other human voices. The construction of news thus depends fundamentally on the way the media performs these acts of mediation.

By juxtaposing 'event' with 'representation' in the way suggested here, however, there is a danger of portraying their relationship as a simple case of 'real' versus 'copy', a mimesis with just two opposing terms. But, as I try to show below, this relationship is neither simple nor straightforward. Often several degrees or levels of representation are necessary to fix and stabilise a narrative before its distinctive identity as a 'news' story can be accomplished. These processes take place in a median space between the poles of the real and its copy. This intermediary zone between reality and representation is a highly problematic and contested space in which considerable labour is deployed. Much of this labour of mediation is performed invisibly and in silence, according to practices of progressive editing that customarily elide their moments of manufacture. In what follows I try to locate and give 'voice' to some of the moments of mediation – those hidden levers, locks and keys – that ordinarily escape attention in our daily consumption of news.

I do so by focusing initially on some of the routine administrative mechanisms that impose order on the uncertainty of events by providing a bureaucratic logic to the production of news. These processes help to reduce the uncertain timing and frequency of occurrences by constructing 'news' in such ways that they are made to conform to the exigencies of production. Anticipation and predictability thus have to be built into the process of news construction to manage the inherent indeterminacy of its contexts.

These everyday acts of mediation also occur less formally, but with equally potent effect, whenever the human agents of newspapers – journalists – are despatched to the scene of new events. Here 'in the field' other structuring devices are deployed as journalists are thrown on to themselves to produce narrative order out of the randomness of events. This is illustrated in an incident drawn from personal experience in which the activities of journalists were shaped in decisive ways by the organising activities of their professional 'pack'.

Through both the everyday reality of bureaucratic procedures as well as in the more informal milieu of professional journalists, newspapers perform their mediating functions as cultural gatekeepers, attempting to re-write the disordered vagueness of the world into the narrative of news. If the impact of these processes of mediation is to be properly appreciated, however, it is necessary to confront some of the guiding myths that customarily inform our common-sense understanding of news. This means challenging some of the core assumptions that portray news as the simple and natural occurrence of events happening in the real world.

## 10.4  News as natural and obvious

Questions about what constitutes 'news' often elicit evasive responses from journalists who are confronted by them. Frequently reporters, sub-editors and photographers will dismiss such inquiries as so much navel-gazing nonsense. The 'news', they assert, is simply what it is: people and events happening in the real world. According to this self-evident logic, 'news' just happens 'out there' as facts of life and the journalist is merely a passive receptor of phenomena and one whose simple function is to report what he or she observes with objective neutrality.

The image here is of news as natural with the role of the individual journalist and his or her organisation as convenient conduits for the throughput of data, detached witnesses or faithful stenographers of events, who simply observe and chronicle things that occur in the world 'out there', beyond their direct control. Even the names of some of our most popular newspapers – *Mirror, Observer, Times, Express, Echo, Messenger* – reinforce the pervasive image of news media as detached witnesses to history engaged merely in the task of delivering the news with a breathless, but essentially unbiased urgency.

With such imagery, the suggestion, then, is that news is simply a mirror of reality and one that requires, at most, only a minimal effort of labour to bring it to the attention of its readers; anything more elaborate would distort the reality it purports to represent. What such an image most forcefully repels, of course, is the very idea of news as something that is actively produced as an outcome of human activity. For it to be regarded as something that is overtly 'made' would necessitate recognition of the systematic work that goes into its construction, a recognition that would inevitably connect it with a whole network of places, times and acts. All such cultural operations are necessarily erased in the conception of 'news as natural'. Even the application of the name of an individual journalist, in the form of an author's by-line above a story, is not enough to dislodge the dominant image of the reporter as a detached observer of events. The force of the 'news as nature' conception is so strong, indeed, that it is able to reabsorb such ironic reminders of human intervention back into the naturalness of its overriding myth.

Within busy newsrooms, difficult questions about the nature of news can also be sidestepped easily by recourse to a journalistic discourse that typically privileges technical questions over ones that demand any rigorous self-scrutiny. There is a routine use of terms such as *'copy'*, *'angles'*, *'intros'* and *'deadlines'* to refer to technical aspects of story construction and their timing within the production system, while categories such as *'hard news'*, *'features'*, *'backgrounders'*, *'breaking news'* and *'human interest'* stories are shorthand phrases that define different types of news. These terms denote, classify, demarcate and categorise content and also help to organise and simplify administrative systems, roles and practices in the form of diverse and specialised functions. They operate, in other words, as key signifiers of institutional and professional identities.

The use of such an institutional lexicon is not, of course, unique to newspapers. Such a vocabulary operates in many institutional milieu (see, for example, Erving Goffman's (1961) focus on life in mental hospitals and Aaron Cicourel's (1968) account of the working lives of police and probation officers). What is different in the case of newspapers, however, is that their professional language is related directly to their cultural role as knowledge-making institutions. Newspapers actively insinuate themselves into the culture of their societies, arranging and ordering their materials according to the putative tastes and preferences of their audiences and serving as significant producers of a specialised type of knowledge that guides and shapes social reality. By telling us what we don't know they thus perform a world-constituting role.

This specialised form of knowledge is also shaped by different types of information which acquire their meanings through specific categories and which occupy predetermined slots in the production schedule. These categories function as explanatory schemas, and through their repeated use, construct de facto spaces in the public mind which then have to be filled. Such categories crucially reflect professional and corporate 'news values', the usually unspoken understanding that guides journalists in deciding what is and is not news. News values also have to be attuned to the schedules of production operating within different media institutions and keyed to the particular interests of different editors, proprietors as well as readers.

Allocating discrete spaces in newspapers – which may be designated as 'politics', 'environment', 'science' or some other category – provides a further remedy to the randomness and uncertainty of events. This bureaucratic response to uncertainty, in turn, constructs a specialist division of labour among journalists with the creation of roles, such as the political correspondent, the crime reporter and the sports commentator. Such specialists are occupationally committed to producing a continuous output of knowledge about their respective worlds, typically by cultivating contacts who can be relied on as regular sources of information. Journalists have their constituencies in much the same way as politicians.

Most importantly, however, such specialist functions also provide newspapers with one solution to the ever-present condition of uncertainty that would otherwise continue to haunt them. Events in the real world cannot be guaranteed to occur within the timetabled frequencies of editions and the production of specialist news is one way of managing this uncertainty through the supply of a continuous flow of information. News can thus be anticipated in advance of any actual occurrence. In this way, *production* follows *prediction*.

Such ordering technologies provide an important interpretative framework guiding the expectations and assumptions of journalists and readers alike and helping to shape and influence attitudes that make it easier to recognise 'news' in its varied and distinctive forms. Such devices work, in other words, as mediating structures that help to define and shape an organising matrix that cleanses the social world of its intrinsic uncertainty while also serving as a hidden constraint about what can and what cannot be reported.

What is being described by these mediating structures are the organisational and professional codes, the protocols, expectations and generic rules that govern the treatment of information, almost in abstraction from its empirical objects. This treatment does not proceed randomly, but follows pre-established formats. Information and other material arriving at newspapers is thus made to flow into the production system via the familiar grooves of professional and corporate systems. The network of rules, places, times and expectations act as simplifying mechanisms that shape built-in assumptions and values and become so enshrined over time that they are largely accepted without any awkward self-questioning by those engaged in its production. What may appear unregulated is, in fact, highly controlled.

This panoply of formal and informal structures provides journalists with a largely pre-formed and institutionalised ethos about what constitutes 'news'. News emerges, then, not simply as a cultural construct: it is also the product of a set of organisational practices, definitions and meanings which reflect the values and pressures operating within different media institutions.

The characteristic defensiveness of the journalist when confronted by questions about the identity of news and its status, as well as their own roles in its production, is thus instructive and intriguing precisely because it overlooks what is routinely taken for granted. But news is a problem precisely because it is treated so unproblematically. It's taken-for-granted status masks the possibility that journalists are involved inextricably in the construction of 'news' as something *produced* in circumstances that are particular and from materials that are frequently mundane. What is characteristically dismissed as 'natural' and 'obvious' by journalists and their audiences – as well as those charged with conducting official inquiries – is of vital interest and consequence precisely because it disguises the apparently mysterious ways that news is actively shaped and constructed.

Such mechanisms also provide us with some important clues to the material conditions that constitute the possible resources used in the construction of *any* identity, whether that of the professional journalist or the identity of the news stories they generate. It is here – *in the engineering of an identity* – that we get an important insight into the labour of mediation that goes into the construction of news.

# 10.5 Groupthink and 'pack journalism'

To explicate these mediating processes more fully, I turn now to an episode of news construction which occurred on 22 October 1972 when the then England goalkeeper Gordon Banks lost most of the sight in his right eye following a road accident. At the time Banks was the first-choice goalkeeper of the English national team and had recently been voted as the game's footballer of the year. News of his accident thus took on a significance that elevated it to front page news for most of Britain's national press for the next 24 hours and beyond as they reported the progressive decline in Banks's sight which culminated in his eventual retirement from the game.

As a young journalist, I was sent by my employers at a freelance news agency to cover the story and soon found myself immersed for the first time in the professional culture of the tabloid 'pack' who had set up camp in the foyer of the North Staffordshire Royal Infirmary. It was the first time that I had seen a cluster of journalists congregate as a professional group. Despite their diverse backgrounds, they had come together at the same location and with the shared objective of covering the same news event. The outcome of their chance juxtaposition provides a revealing insight into the kind of groupthink that often goes into news production.

The assembled group waited inside the hospital foyer for what seemed like an eternity, receiving periodic updates from hospital officials who had promised to inform us of any significant changes in Banks's medical condition. By the end of a long and tedious day, most of the information about the accident had filtered through to the journalists present via the police, though many of the incidental details were still unclear. How had the crash occurred and what of the other driver who had collided with Banks's car head-on?

These were questions that could not be answered readily by the police, ambulance personnel or hospital officials, and their reluctance, unwillingness or inability to speculate only added to a sense of deep uncertainty that I described earlier. The outlines of the accident were known but the personal accounts of the others who had been involved were needed to fill a vacuum in the human interest story that was now demanded urgently by news editors anxious to meet their production deadlines.

As the waiting continued, rumours began to spread among the journalists that the hospital was about to discharge a woman who they believed was the driver of the other car. Soon afterwards an ambulance crew appeared at the entrance to the hospital pushing a stretcher that carried a comatose patient through the crowd of journalists to a waiting ambulance. In her unconscious state, there could be no certainty as to the woman's identity, let alone any realistic prospect of securing a coherent interview with her. But with time pressing and yawning gaps in the story still needing to be filled, one of the most experienced journalists gestured to his colleagues to gather round him. He then addressed the group with the words . . . 'Well, I don't know about you, but I heard her say the following. . .'. For the next five minutes he addressed his colleagues in the assumed identity of the woman driver who they had all just witnessed leaving the hospital on a stretcher and heavily sedated.

Pressured by their editors and now prompted by their colleague's words, the assembled journalists scribbled in unison as the words attributed to the woman spilled out in an unfolding monologue. What emerged was an account of how, in the confusion of the accident, she had been unaware initially that she had collided with Gordon Banks. It was only later, as she regained consciousness in hospital that she had learned about his identity. As the scale of Bank's injuries became known, she described how gradually it began to dawn on her that she may have unwittingly brought an end to the career of the world's finest goalkeeper. By the time this impromptu news conference had ended a story had been constructed in terms that might just satisfy the demands of newspapers and their readers.

The absurdity of this blatant estrangement from truth is recounted here not as a basis for discussion about its rights or wrongs or to suggest that such acts of media delinquency are typical of all journalistic activity, but to illustrate how, in conditions of stress and uncertainty, a news story was constructed. It struck me then as bizarre and is analysed in more detail below as an insight into the considerable labour that went into the work of assembling an identity for what would subsequently become a distinctive news story.

The starting point for the journalists was the need to produce a story within the context of the pressing deadlines and the framework of practices and procedures referred to earlier and in the uncertainty that followed the accident. The gap in the story, as far as the journalists were concerned – *an account of the other driver* – remained unwritten. This omission presented itself as a blankness in their accounts, but it was an indeterminacy that, far from closing off further options, invited active intervention, enticing them into the work of construction. Under conditions of considerable tension, a confusing dead-end became deliciously alive with fluid opportunities.

Faced with the urgent need to meet their deadlines, the most senior of the journalists summoned his colleagues with the words 'I don't know about you?' This apparently throwaway remark, however, contained within its casual indifference an egalitarian appeal to those present that was strengthened by the subsequent declaration . . . 'but I heard her say the following. . .'. This democratisation of the assembled journalists served as an invitation to participate in an act of contrived story-telling that would yoke them together as a 'pack' and would ensure their complicity in the joint endeavour that followed. Thus with a single movement of the head and just a few words he was able to construct a professional pact that could have been paraphrased as: 'We're all in this together'.

The implication of the speaker's invitation was clear: By acting together, the force of their collaboration would produce a news story that would carry much greater authority than if any or all of their accounts were expressed more randomly. In a single sentence and in the comfortable tones of its easy vernacular, the speaker was thus able to turn a diverse group of individuals into a tribal huddle whose members were all committed to the same objective. Once assembled, the journalists' pack provided an important platform for the virtuoso performance that followed as the identity of the story was sutured together from the ingredients available.

The speaker's invitation to his colleagues was, of course, one that few could afford to reject. They knew that turning down the offer of collusion would come at a cost. Not only would it have denied them access to an interesting story, but its awkward omission from their individual reports would have to be accounted for later. Happily for me, these pressures did not apply. As a freelance journalist, my job was to find commercially marketable aspects of the story that would only have a value if they had been missed or overlooked by staff reporters. It was a role that allowed me access to what the other journalists were doing but excluded me from actively participating in the collaboration of the pack, comprised as it was of reporters who were employed as staff journalists by their newspapers and who knew each other well from their shared experience of news gathering at other major events.

Once the initial collaboration of the pack had been forged, it also provided those present with a stronger collective defence that might have to be called on later to resist any challenges from the woman herself – their putative interviewee – if she subsequently objected to the homogenised account that would be attributed to her. The prospects of this happening could be calculated to be minimal, however, because the woman's own blurred recollection of events could quite easily be dismissed as hazy and unreliable. In any event, membership of the pack rewarded them with the insurance of safety in numbers. With these few opening remarks, therefore, the speaker was able to reduce the risk of subversion from inside the group as well as perversion from outside.

After anchoring the emerging shape of the story in the mutual complicity of those present, the journalist then dictated an interpretation of the accident in the form of a first person account that purported to be in the words of the woman herself. From this point onwards, the 'I' of the journalist became the 'I' of the woman. One personal identity – the journalist's – was sloughed off as a necessary precondition for the emergence of a second – the woman's – and then a third, in the form of a news story that could be attributed to her.

Though absent, the woman effectively became present in the journalist's version of events and though still silent and sedated she was given a coherent voice and a script that had been written for her. She had, in effect, been released from invisibility only to be ensnared and made to play a minor supporting role in a much larger drama. The work of inclusion/exclusion that made this possible was further helped by the subsequent design of the story as an account of an otherwise anonymous woman who may have involuntarily ended the career of a famous footballer. Her stigmatisation as the unwitting cause of the accident was further enabled by a process of 'othering', that is, by differentiating her from the other actors in the drama and then imbuing her imaginary words with a negative charge.

The eventual outcome of all this effort was the re-presentation of the woman's putative experiences in the form of a human interest story that would shore up and give added plausibility to the main article. For all its precarious construction, however, what was striking was the very ordinariness of the story itself. An account of the personal experiences of an otherwise anonymous person, who had been thrust into public consciousness following a road accident, was told in a language of moderation and restraint. Its very ordinariness, however, helped to tell the story in a way that conformed to a familiar idiomatic format that could be summed up as: 'How I ended the career of a sporting legend'. It was, of course, a story whose logic 'worked' by ensuring that its formulaic identity would be easily recognisable to readers used to such formatting.

It was a news story that, despite its clearly contrived nature, was also illustrative of how this particular identity was brought into existence through the mediating labour that went into the active translation and progressive re-presentation of the materials at hand. And once the representation had been agreed by all those present, the task of engineering an identity for the news could be relaxed. The gel that held together the pack and their absent/present interviewee dissolved as quickly as it had formed.

The exercise of constructing a news story is analysed above to exemplify the silent but salient work of mediation that went into the construction of a specific news story. The actions of the journalists' pack imposed a structuring logic on events, translating vagueness into an object of knowledge. This is a process that, despite its clearly contrived nature, is nevertheless emblematic of news construction more generally. It can be summed up as a drama in four parts:

*Identity as a problem:* The question about identities – whether related to a news story or any other – invariably becomes a matter of concern when seen as a critical problem requiring intervention. In the case described above, the problem facing the journalists was how to produce an account of the woman's experiences to fill a gap in their reporting that was needed to meet the demands of their organisations. Their reaction to the intrinsic uncertainty that confronted them was as a response to the pressing problem of a *lack* of identity for their story.

*Translating uncertainty:* The task of producing a news story depends on constructing a convincing representation of reality and this takes place in a median space that is always political in the sense of involving an active struggle to secure its achievement. As we saw with the covert actions of the journalists' pack, the manoeuvres that are followed in news production are often concealed from public observation. For those journalists who gathered at the hospital, the starting point was the initial *lack* of information, a situation akin to a condition of radical uncertainty that I alluded to earlier. Rather than acting as a deterrent, however, this indeterminacy proved provocative, enticing – if not actually licensing – the journalists to perform their act of manipulation.

*Assembling an identity:* The identity of a news article, like any identity, never just emerges naturally, but is something that has to be actively shaped and given distinctive form through interaction with other materials, including human agents. In other words, it is something that has to be achieved, *in relation to* an 'other' which, paradoxically, must be attracted and then repelled. In this instance, the journalists contrived their account by constructing one version of events (*the Woman who Ended the Career of a Sporting Legend*) which they then contrasted with another version (*the Agony of Gordon Banks*). In this way, the identity of the narrative was accomplished by differentiating it from the other narrative in a kind of forced marriage of opposites. As a binary pairing they took on their meanings (identities) in so far as each was *not* the other.

*Achieving stability and fixity:* Securing a plausible identity for a news story is the basis for portraying a convincing representation of reality. But fixity and stability can never be guaranteed and considerable effort is necessary to maintain the durability of a news story and so prevent the inherent tendency towards disintegration and disbelief. The activities of the journalists' pack described above reveal the fragile and tenuous condition of the construction work that goes on more generally into producing a coherent narrative suitable for publication.

## 10.6 Conclusion

From what has been described above it would be difficult to refute the contention that news is not only a highly constructed form of knowledge but one that is also arbitrary. All the processes, systems and procedures that are put in place routinely to impose order on the uncertainty of random events serve also to stipulate how information is selected, shaped, interpreted and reported. In this process news emerges as the formatted outcome of a self-fulfilling logic: News is what newspapers say it is.

At every stage in the construction process, newspapers are implicated in such a maze of ways that any attempt to extricate themselves through public protestation to the contrary would lead only to evidence of further and even deeper entanglement. One of the lessons of Leveson and other inquiries into press behaviour is surely that newspapers can no longer luxuriate in the defence that they are merely neutral observers of events happening beyond their control. Their involvement in *making* news, sometimes by resorting to disreputable means, must be by now beyond any reasonable doubt.

In bringing us the news, newspapers, and indeed all media, function as *mediators*, intervening, ordering and reassembling a complex network of socio-technical materials. These systems include bureaucratic procedures, information technologies and taken-for granted rules that provide professional identities and shared ways of thinking for their practitioners. In the examples discussed above, I have tried to locate their often invisible and powerful presence as defining moments that occur in the intercalated space between the real and its representation. And, as with so many structuring processes, the work of mediation can often end up serving the requirements of the systems that produce the news rather than reflecting the more generic nature of the social worlds from which they are drawn.

These acts of mediation are crucially significant to the process of making the news and are achieved through successive acts of translation. This enables the disordered, unruly and often recalcitrant nature of social reality to be re-engineered into a plausible identity called news and in a form that can be produced every day, on time and in neatly ordered packages. In this way news emerges as just another convenient commodity to be consumed alongside all the other corporate products that constitute the character of modern life.

In the era of 24-hour rolling news and with a proliferation of outlets spanning print, radio and digital media, news has become a pervasive presence in contemporary life, a sort of ephemeral background music that is implanted in our heads without the need for too much critical scrutiny. It is expressed, perhaps in its purest form, in the phenomenon of the 'News in Brief' column. Here knowledge is reduced to the irreducible minimum, as scraps of information that flutter into life for fleeting moments and survive only until the next edition. They circulate in our public consciousness as weightless tokens of knowledge and speak of plane crashes, stock markets, political intrigue, climate change and show business scandals: Synopses of the world in 20 words.

The radical over simplicity of these abbreviated forms of knowledge can, however, condition our everyday consciousness to a degree that is perhaps not readily acknowledged, either in official inquiries into press misconduct or within the press and media more generally. For the systems and rules of thinking that make news possible are always only ever the *partial* expression of the more complex social reality they inhabit and purport to serve. Constructing the news – like any act of identity – is always an act of *inclusion* and *exclusion*. These processes invariably entail an editing of reality through processes in which multiplicity and heterogeneity are systematically reduced, disciplined and condensed to produce singularity and homogeneity. The price of producing such truncated versions of reality – and the weight of presumptions they make about human reality – can be felt in an impoverishment of public discourse and a narrowing of the resources that we draw on to understand contemporary life.

In the episode of fabricated story-telling by the newspaper 'pack' described earlier, I showed how, when pushed to the extreme, news construction can mean the suppression and censoring of other voices and other experiences. Despite its blatant contrivance, however, this account is perhaps 'true' in the sense of serving as an emblem of the cultural consequences that are an inevitable outcome of any effort that goes into the forcible construction of news. The pervasive presence of the news in contemporary culture not only allows us know about the lives of remote others, but also structures and constrains the resources available to us to imagine different identities and other ways of being.

 **REFERENCES**

Cicourel, A. (1968) *The Social Organisation of Juvenile Justice*, New York: John Wiley & Sons.

Cooper, R. (1987) 'Information, communication and organisation: A post-structural revision', *Journal of Mind and Behaviour*, 8(3), 395–416.

Cooper, R. (1989) 'The visibility of social systems' in Jackson, M.C., Keys, P. and Cropper, S.A. (eds), *Operational Research and the Social Sciences*, New York: Plenum Press, 51–59, reprinted in Hetherington, K. and Munro, R. (eds) (1997) *Ideas of Differences: Social Spaces and the Labour of Division*, Oxford: Blackwell, 32–41.

Cooper, R. (1993) 'Technologies of representation', in Ahonen, P. (ed.), *Tracing the Semiotic Boundaries of Politics*, Berlin: Mouton de Gruyter, 279–312.

Cooper, R. (1998) 'Assemblage notes', in Chia, R. (ed.), *Organized Worlds: Explorations in Technology and Organization with Robert Cooper*, London: Routledge.

Goffman, E. (1961) *Asylum: Essays on the Social Situation of Mental Patients and Other Inmates*, Penguin: London.

McCombs, M. (2002) 'The agenda-setting role of mass media in the shaping of public opinion', paper presented at *Mass Media Economics Conference*, The Suntory and Toyota International Centres for Economics and Related Disciplines, London School of Economics, London, 28–29 June.

Norris, P. (2005) 'Did the media matter? Priming, persuasion and mobilizing effects in the 2005 British general election', *Elections, Parties and Public Opinion*, September 2005.

Ofcom (2009) 'Local and regional media in the UK: Nations and Regions case studies'. Accessed at: http://stakeholders.ofcom.org.uk/binaries/research/tv-research/lrmannex2.pdf (retrieved 29 February 2012).

Ofcom (2011) 'Communications Market Reports: England, Northern Ireland, Scotland and Wales'. Accessed at: http://stakeholders.ofcom.org.uk/market-data-research/marketdata/communications-market-reports/cmr11/downloads/ (retrieved 29 February 2012).

Schofield, B. (2003) 'Re-instating the vague', *The Sociological Review*, 51(3), 321–338.

# 11

# Care of the underdog: Animals, culture and the creation of moral certainty in the rescue shelter

*Nik Taylor and Lindsay Hamilton*

## 11.1 Introduction

It is already well established that work provides a driving force both for the formation of a person's identity and for managing their interactions with others (Karreman and Alvesson, 2004). Work, it can be argued, provides a 'master status' for many humans, helping them to orient and make sense of who they are and how they relate to other people. When it comes to care professions the powerful culture-building force of work is perhaps even more pronounced because these jobs often rest upon shared ideological values such as a highly developed sense of social justice (Himmelweit, 1999) and meaningfulness (Grant, 2008). This is particularly pronounced in certain environments where 'the underdog' is being cared for (Latimer, 2000). In the current chapter, we examine this in the case of the animal rescue shelter, a place where unwanted and stray animals are looked after and re-homed.

Our broader research with people who work with animals has consistently shown that the ways in which workers interact with animals often provides a key component of occupational and personal meaning-making (see Hamilton and Taylor, 2013). In animal shelters – organisations where 'underdogs' take centre stage – this is a particularly important aspect of workplace culture. By making an ethical commitment to preserving and enhancing animal life, workers often assemble around common values that underline the 'goodness' and the worth of their charges and, by extension, the meaningfulness of their own labour. Often this manifests in the form of the shared ideological belief that commitment to the animals should come before any other consideration. This becomes a fundamental principle by which the organisation functions, a source of collective esteem for those who work there. In this chapter, we will show just a few examples of the ways that this plays out in the multiple tasks and routines of life at a case-study shelter. Indeed, we point out that the majority of work processes in the shelter rest upon an assumption that animals are at the heart of the organisation. In exploring this, our aim is to suggest some of the practical and symbolic ways in which animals are re-coded from undesirable 'rejects' into potential pets.

From the outset, however, we must acknowledge that shelter work (like many other forms of care work) is complicated by the fact that the 'caree' – the receiver of care – is not always able to play a part in setting the agenda. To a degree, this is the case whether one works in the human or the animal care environment. Consider, for example, social work with infants who have not yet learned to speak. Clearly, when dealing with non-humans, however, a specific set of difficulties emerges. Animals do not *talk back*, they do not tell us what they need in ways which are simple to de-code. Above all, they are not like us and we should not presume that they see the world as we humans do. In a shelter, care work is thus made 'messy' by the presence of different species, each existing within different life-worlds with different repertoires of behaviour and modes of communicating. How, then, can humans negotiate the boundaries between the species to determine the 'right way' to do the job? How do they interact with fellow workers to ensure that these 'right ways' are valued across the organisation? And how does this work elevate the symbolic status of animals from 'stray' to 'pet'?

These are difficult and knotty questions which are too broad to answer in a single book chapter but we present them here to provoke some initial thoughts about the complexity of meaning-making when individuals come into contact with animals at work. What we are able to offer in this chapter, then, is an exploration of our own research in animal shelters to better comprehend the methods by which people work together to create and share core values about the care of animals. We seek to shed light on how and why this occurs, both through practical acts of care and also through the development of a degree of moral certainty about the 'good work' of caring for vulnerable 'others'.

Given the subjective and emotive quality of these issues we felt that the best research methods to use would be qualitative rather than survey-based. Thus, we conducted a period of ethnographic fieldwork which consisted of interviews and observations in two shelter organisations, which for practical reasons were based in Britain and Australia. The research was done over a period of six years. The field researcher (NT) worked alongside the carers in both of them, carrying out practical duties of care for the animals, mainly dogs. This involved cleaning the kennels, answering the telephone and work-shadowing other administrative tasks. Data was gathered officially throughout this process with the aid of various field notebooks and by reporting the comments from participants – those interested in the research and willing to share their time through interviews. Staff from several other animal shelters were also interviewed to test out the theories and ideas that we developed. We then considered the emerging themes from this substantial collection of 'raw data' together.

One of our first observations was that something connected all of the shelter organisations that were investigated or visited, irrespective of internal differences in approach, size, ideology and so on; that is, the practice and the discussion of *caring*. In fact, the workplaces that we looked at were very similar, particularly in the ways that workers spoke about their values and ideas around animals. We felt the cultures in both our case study organisations were highly comparable, despite the fact that the research spanned different time periods and different countries. For simplicity, then, and to preserve anonymity we have grouped together all our data and findings as a make-believe organisation called 'Caring Companions'. We talk about this organisation as if it were a single workplace. In the next section of the chapter, we take a closer look at Caring Companions by drawing out some of our main findings.

## 11.2   The work of care at Caring Companions

The shelter workers that we observed and spoke to at Caring Companions agreed that the animals they cared for *mattered*. The work involved taking a range of 'dirty', 'diseased' and 'unwanted' animals into custody; feeding, cleaning and sheltering them, checking their health and resolving acute problems like fleas and skin rashes and – finally – re-homing them to 'adopters', members of the general public who came forward to apply for new pets. At times, we noted that animals arriving at the shelter sometimes appeared to 'resist' the rescue process by behaving in ways that were aggressive, dangerous or threatening. But such episodes of 'violence' and resistance were regarded by the shelter staff as a mundane aspect of the job; just an inevitable consequence of the abuse or neglect that many of their charges had suffered before being 'rescued'. Yet despite the 'anti-social' or neglected physical condition of many of the animals that arrived at the shelter, workers continued to emphasise their importance and value and were rarely willing to compromise the standards that they would accept from those coming to the shelter in the hope of taking a new pet home.

Despite management's stated goal to re-home as many animals as possible, in day-to-day life at the shelter, workers often took satisfaction in turning potential pet owners away on the basis that they were 'bad families' or that they lived in 'bad homes'. In discussing such cases with each other, often out of earshot of management, workers created a specialist way of speaking that elevated the status of the animal while – at the same time – provoked a deep and lasting sense of suspicion relating to the motives and values of outsiders, in this case potential adopters. This emotive and political issue became clearer to us when one worker turned up unexpectedly on her day off. When asked why she had done so, she replied that she had heard a rumour that one of the other staff members was planning to 'give away' a particularly difficult dog who had been in the shelter for a long time. When pressed for details regarding why this was problematic she said: 'He can't go to just any home and Adrian is just trying to get rid of him to make his numbers look good and because he's hard work here barking and aggressive, you know. But I'll let him go back to a crap home over my dead body. This one needs the right place or he will bounce around until he bites someone and we all know where that ends.' Here, the 'difficult dog' that was hard work, aggressive and hard to home was, nonetheless, given heightened value by foregrounding his needs; in this case 'the right place' rather than the 'crap home'. At root, this worker expresses the view that it is unacceptable to re-home a problem animal to make the 'numbers look good'. At the same time, espoused organisational goals – the re-homing of as many dogs as possible – appeared to come second to this culturally embedded 'ethics of care'. These ethics, and not least the apparent purity of the motive for that care, were discussed within the workplace and consistently policed by those employed there.

## 11.2.1 Challenging negative meanings

Through language, then, the shelter staff constantly challenged the taken-for-granted meanings surrounding 'rejected' animals by re-defining 'unwanted' and 'stray' animals into 'pets-in-waiting.' They named the animals and attributed them with mindful personalities (Sanders, 1993), something which they often drew upon when deciding upon the apparent quality of the potential new pet owner. They saw them as individuals, not simply as 'livestock'. These animals were, in their eyes, deserving of a 'forever home' where they would be treated 'properly' meaning, in this case, as members of the family. This turned the exchange between animals and potential new 'owners' into something altogether more meaningful (and tense) than the matching of waiting customers to animals 'in stock'. As one worker explained when asked why she had just turned down an application for a cat from a couple:

**Peggy** (volunteer): I went to their house to meet them because they looked good on paper but when I got talking to them it was clear they didn't want a pet, they wanted a mouser. He kept going on about their mouse problem and how a cat would sort it out for them and she just wasn't interested at all. I had the cat in the back of my car and I'm thinking about her face and thinking 'there's no way I'm leaving her here with them'.

Clearly, then, animals were not re-homed at any cost but – through the language of care – were more positively re-coded as *socially significant*: 'I'm thinking about her face', Peggy reports. Asserting her ability to determine the 'right' sort of home for this particular cat, Peggy dismisses the potential adopters out of hand: 'there's no way I'm leaving her here'. Language like this demonstrated that workers were able to express confidence in their professional ability to judge the good homes from the bad and, in doing this, derived a sense of 'moral goodness'. Interestingly, this involved a degree of judgement about the worthiness of customers, something which informed the shared values of the care team and – by extension – the nature of the organisational culture as a whole. We considered this to be a typical example of the ways in which the animal's desires and care needs were interpreted and articulated by the humans involved. In effect shelter workers acted as 'gate-keepers', holding the power to make the final decision regarding whether a pet could be adopted or not.

Of course, it was not possible for us as researchers to *ask* the cat whether she wished to be a 'mouser' or not. Instead, we relied upon shelter workers to give us *their* interpretation of the animal's needs and desires. In fact it was striking to us just how sure the workers were that they knew what was 'in the best interest' of the animals. It was suggestive of a degree of zealousness that fostered a sense of a clarity on behalf of the animal; a lack of 'ambiguity' in their thinking and approach (see Kelemen, Chapter 2 this volume, for further discussion of this term). Indeed we found throughout our fieldwork that workers often sought to erase 'grey areas' of morality and one of us (NT) has published specifically on this theme elsewhere (Taylor, 2004). In turn, we needed to consider how the certainty of shelter workers affected their decision-making and judgements; the ways in which they used loaded terminology (words such as morals, care, goodness, worth and value) to indicate the depth of their conviction to the job and to their charges. In reporting and interpreting these findings, we hoped to draw out their ways of describing and seeing the world; the ways in which they made sense of their work in context.

## 11.2.2 Challenging species boundaries

The apparent gulf between animals and humans was something that shelter workers chose to work at reducing. All those employed at the shelter took their roles as 'caretakers' of the 'pets-in-waiting' extremely seriously. They felt, generally, that they did a good job under hard circumstances, not least because they were paid little and many of them even worked on a purely voluntary basis. What appeared to compensate, at least partially, for the lack of status were the shared values – a feeling of activism – among the staff who appeared to see themselves as a 'voice-for-the-voiceless'. In practice, they often tried to 'speak for' the animals by attributing them with unique personalities and characteristics. A requisite part of this advocacy was the *assumption of care* that all workers had towards the animals. The animals were seen as their 'charges', as disempowered others who needed protecting from the world outside the organisation, a space where they could be exploited (as 'working' mousers, for example). As such, these animals were seen in ways which went beyond traditional conceptions of animals as 'non-persons' and instead they became 'potential family members'. This perception of animals – as domesticated and vulnerable 'people' rather than workers, objects or things – was shared across the organisation. Their apparent domestication was seen as a starting point from which a transition between traditional animal and human categories was manipulated and readjusted.

It was through a process of adjusting the traditional boundaries between 'pet' and 'owner' by insisting upon the mindful individuality of each of their charges, that the workers felt able to pass judgement upon the worthiness of potential 'adopters'. Yet those we spoke to were keen to point out that this was not a process of anthropomorphism, being 'fussy' or 'too soft'. Likewise, they held that their work was not a matter of extending their 'innate' nurturing capacities in an organisational setting. Instead, we heard on numerous occasions that seeing animals differently – as people rather than objects – was their way of redressing the uncertain status of unwanted or mistreated animals: taking care of society's 'underdogs'. This was at the heart of their motivation for work. By articulating the notion of 'moral goodness', whether this involved questioning traditional barriers between humans and animals (Taylor, 2010), or by challenging the moral values of outsiders, workers were able to demonstrate their commitment to the job. In their way of seeing the world, this was a way (perhaps the only way) of addressing a fundamental social justice issue: the subjugation of the animal by humans. One employee explained this to us during an interview:

> **Tracy**: It's our [humans] fault in the first place, I mean we domesticated them and now we can't even take care of them. It should be our duty to do that at least, seeing as though we did this to them in the first place . . . right now there are about 300 of them are being destroyed on a weekly basis because we aren't dealing with what we've done.

It was understandable, in the light of such emotive comments, that the economic rewards of work often appeared to be secondary to the apparent reward of care. The low pay (and even the absence of pay) did not appear to deter workers from their duty: dealing with society's 'mess'. For most of the workers we interviewed, the experiential act of caring for animals – the emotional, embodied and empathetic connection to the vulnerable other – was all important and overshadowed the low pay and occasionally poor conditions.

## 11.2.3 Challenging the low status of care work

Despite the energy with which they conducted their work, those that we shadowed and interviewed tended to have little explicit interest in developing a formal career structure. This was especially the case in the smaller shelter organisations which were often privately run by one or two key people with several volunteers. This may partly explain the reason why workers framed their motivations in such emotive terms:

> **Mindy**: At least here [at the shelter] I can be sure that this dog or this cat which can't survive on its own gets to live out the rest of its life in plush surroundings. It's the least we can do.

Work was synonymous with an emotional attachment and a deep moral commitment to take care of the animal which 'can't survive on its own'. In expressing such views, almost all of the workers reiterated a shared ethical motive to put the animal first. Yet this was not controlled or prompted explicitly by management, a group whose stated goals were often to ensure that the shelter was economically solvent and, as part of that, stressed a need to re-home as many animals as possible. Indeed, on the rare occasions that managers did try to influence the 'efficiency' of the shelter, their actions were often resisted and challenged by the care workers. This resistance was articulated by recourse to the 'core values' of putting the 'underdog' first. Thus, the values that many workers shared were not handed down by management 'from above' but were decided upon through subtle cultural work on the ground. They related closely to the emotional and ethical drive to care as well as the more philosophical aim to address social inequalities between the species.

As part of this, our field work demonstrated that the shelter workers often enacted motivational purity *to each other* as opposed to (or perhaps as well as) enacting it to the cared for animal. This was a way of making sense of the organisation and their place as individuals within it (Karreman and Alvesson, 2004). Rather than taking the deep moral commitment to animals purely as a sign of personal motivation, then, we took it to be a cultural bonding exercise, functioning here to connect, in a profound way, those who worked at the shelter. In other words, we could not reduce the care process to a dyad between carer/cared-for animal and nor could we consider these to be a collection of like-minded individuals who chose to work at the shelter to express their own deeply personal beliefs about animals. The creation of care was located in a much more complex web of cultural and organisational interactions with fellow humans, and some of these interactions worked to monitor and control the motives and methods of fellow employees.

## 11.2.4 Challenging motives for work

While we noted significant agreement between workers regarding the value and importance of the 'cared for' animals, then, there was occasionally a volatile atmosphere at the shelters we visited. In fact, staff sometimes came to blows and left the organisation altogether; something which has been echoed by other studies (Alger and Alger, 2003: 29–30). When emotions ran high, as they often appeared to do, the staff were prone to internal arguments. At certain points in the fieldwork, this volatility led to a high staff turnover, with many citing differences of opinion, based upon perceptions of others' motivations as morally impure, as a main cause of their leaving work. There were clearly limitations to universal agreement over workplace values, although as King points out, assuming that care workers care out of some innate caring disposition 'is to obscure the *work* involved and undervalue the skills required in providing "good" care' (King, 2012: 54). It also negates the political side of caring work. Popke argues that care should be 'viewed as a fundamentally social, and hence, political relationship' (Popke, 2006: 506). These arguments were borne out by our own findings such that in one interview we heard one staff member claim that she could no longer work with one senior member of staff: 'It does my head in, he's here for the glory and not for them [points to kennels behind the office where discussion is taking place]. He's always in the paper, or on the telly talking about all this good work he does and he couldn't give a shit about the dogs here; he'd give away any that he thinks are hard work and he never checks the homes properly, it's just all about him, him, him, when it should be about them.'

Workers policed each other's motives, consistently vigilant for purity – doing the job for the 'right reasons' – and were quick to point to those who were deemed substandard in this area. We see this as another example of the intolerance for grey areas referred to above; that is, the workers' sense of moral purity was so strong that seeing the world in terms of clear-cut ('black and white') distinctions was endemic. For example, several of the workers adopted vegan lifestyles and saw their caring work for the animals at the shelter as a key component part of this broader identity work. Yet this stance made their lives more complicated at the shelter as they routinely had to deal with the different philosophies of others. As one worker noted 'I just don't get it; how can they [shelter workers] be willing to die for these animals then go home and tuck into a burger?' Clearly, then, for some workers animals held a 'pure' status as human equals, while for others, there appeared to be a more contradictory stance that enabled certain animals to become worthy of care and, at the same time, for others to become food. We do not seek to suggest that either standpoint is 'correct' (one of us is a confirmed carnivore) yet we point to this because it presented a dimension of philosophical complexity which resulted in real and lived tensions between the workers. The result was that vegans often kept their moral and ethical stances to themselves while they were at work:

> **Shelley**: I don't talk about it, it's not worth it. I'm tired of having the same arguments over and over with people who don't listen so I say nothing and just get on with looking after the dogs. Except sometimes I have to speak, you know when I get snide remarks about the food I've brought or when they say things like 'oh Shelley can't come [to the pub for lunch] there's no vegan food for her'.

One worker explained to us that she was tired of being ideologically pinholed by co-workers and members of the public, 'they [potential pet adopters] are always asking me if I'm vegetarian, I mean what difference does it make to how I look after these dogs and how I go about homing them? It's not like I'm only willing to home them with other vegans, although that would be nice (laughs).' These workers seemed disheartened that the caring work offered to the animals at the shelter by other staff did not extend to other species. In some ways, then, this represented a division between humans in the shelter; between those who cared for all species and those who only cared for the cats and dogs in the shelter. This clear bifurcation along moral and ideological lines was found time and again throughout the shelter; for instance between 'good' and 'bad' workers, or between shelter staff and the general public, deemed 'outsiders'. It seemed that the deep-seated emotion and commitment behind much of the care process made it difficult to perceive moral 'grey areas' and complex situations.

Another example of this came when we noted that several workers expressed disappointment that 'outsiders' did not share their zeal for shelter care work. At least half of our research participants explained that they felt that animal care was undervalued and stigmatised. Many had been told by partners and family members that care for other species constituted wasted effort, the sign of being slightly pathological, over-zealous or fanatical about animals. Speaking to the parent of one shelter employee seemed to bear this out:

> **Frank**: I think it's good she's [my daughter's] working at the shelter although she'd be far better getting a proper job that pays well, and I've told her that till I'm blue in the face. There just aren't any prospects in it. She's animal mad though. What can you say to her?

Intriguingly, this apparent parental and social pressure – the taint of 'animal madness' – appeared to have little impact on the career choices of those we interviewed and, in fact, workers often appeared to respond by strengthening their commitment to the ethical values of care. This reinforced our finding that the shelter workers usually valued (what in their view comprised) ethical, meaningful work above the more usual concerns about job security, pay and hours (Grant, 2008).

While at times the staff criticised each other for expressing different values and motives for their work, their shared commitment to the process of caring was something that usually prevented conflicts from getting out of hand. As Alger and Alger noted at a rescue shelter in the US, 'even when conflicts arose between officers and other volunteers, their commitment to the cats kept many volunteers on the job' (Alger and Alger, 2003: 52). Likewise, here the performance of care and rescue helped to bond employees together, connecting the multiple and often disparate factions that might otherwise have developed in these organisations. Crucially, animals forged a link between individuals to resolve (albeit temporarily) the experience of conflict. The volunteers Alger and Alger studied shared a view that if people were 'in it for the animals' other discrepancies (such as being a vegan or a carnivore) could be overlooked. Instead, their volunteers perceived the organisational culture of the cat shelter to be 'committed to life at all costs'. Our findings support this. The feeling of doing 'good' work rather than money, structural authority (or even the respect of outsiders) gave workers reward and helped them to bond together despite their occasionally profound personal differences.

The simple dichotomy (between 'good-for-the-animals' and 'bad-for-the-animals') that we found to underpin much of shelter life was applied by the workers to everything and everyone involved in their working environment and usually took precedence over everything else, even personal feelings and friendships with others. The life-world that was thus created at the shelter was furnished with a selection of moral codes and values that, in turn, justified the hard and often 'dirty' work that the shelter staff did on a daily basis: nothing was 'bad' work as it was all recoded as 'good' for the animals. The lack of structural progression, the absence of financial reward was compensated by the collective strength garnered through the process of care. The rituals of doing this care, including cleaning, feeding and re-homing, became an emotive source of pride and ethical capital in what might otherwise have become mundane, repetitive work.

## 11.3   Concluding discussion: The creation of moral certainty

At Caring Companions, much care work was active and visible; cleaning dog kennels, for example, while other forms of care relied upon intangible responsibilities such as naming animals or making a judgement about the suitability of potential adopters. These seen and unseen acts of caring were of clear importance both in the practical management of the organisation and the development of its distinctive workplace culture (Latimer, 2000). Employees and volunteers worked hard to manage this culture-building process just as they worked hard at the physical labour of care. In repeating these routines and talking about them with peers, they developed a degree of certainty about what was *good for the animal* and, by extension, what constituted *good work*. Moreover, as we have drawn attention to throughout, this led to a 'morally pure' way of seeing the world and a concomitant intolerance for 'grey areas'. Good work was that which was for the benefit of the animal irrespective of all other considerations and, by extension, good people were those who did good work irrespective of outside concerns and pressures. Given that their charges never spoke, however, and inhabited wholly different life-worlds than the humans within the organisation, the development of certainty was both an interesting and precarious process.

In the vacuum normally filled by formal organisational bureaucracy – more common to human settings like the hospital or the care-home – at Caring Companions, workers fell back on informal strategies of sense-making through collective ethical agreement about the importance of animals. It was a self-referential culture, perpetuated by the central motif that throughout their working day, workers were 'in it for the animals' (Pratt and Ashforth, 2003). This process provided the materials for individuals to make sense of their place in the organisation and to regulate their interactions with each other (Karreman and Alvesson, 2004). There was continual discussion and negotiation over the shared set of values which functioned, for the most part, to regulate the behaviours and even the emotions of the fellow *human* workers involved and constituted a form of *normative control* (Karreman and Alvesson, 2004) that did not rely particularly heavily on formal management structure and strategy but upon tacit affiliation to the ethics and codes of conduct that workers decided upon, often quite independently of organisational goals.

Yet these informal values were often hard to 'pin down' or simplify in ways that outsiders could easily relate to. What we could observe, however, was how this normative control played out on a daily basis. In fact, our research suggests that animals took on a deep symbolic significance as a cultural resource; a key part of this organising impulse. Thus, at the same time as human workers were devising ways of thinking, speaking and acting that gave them a sense of connection and ethical purpose in doing the job, the animals turned from 'strays' to 'pets in waiting', re-coded from society's unwanted rejects into important creatures which were worthy of care. These shifting categories and boundaries were central to the work done, providing the rationale for the deep moral, ethical and personal investment that most of the staff appeared to feel. The animals were central, therefore, in creating and preserving the values that held the shelter workers together; that held the very organisation together.

## 11.4  Final remarks

Animals – at the very heart of the institution – provided the focus for workers to derive a sense of meaning from their time within the shelter. This supports the idea that it is often relationships rather than practical acts that provide the impetus for meaningful work (Pavlish, 2012). The idea that cultural interactions (rather than tasks) play a vital part in creating meaningful work has been supported by a number of other case-studies (see, for example, Stone and Gueutal, 1985). At Caring Companions, however, the most meaningful cultural 'moments' often arose from both human–human and human–animal interactions (Pavlish, 2012). On that basis, it was usual for workers to *contest* boundaries between human and (certain) animals. They did this in a very practical way; that is, through the practice of care. Doing so, workers made a commitment to the underdog by sharing the view that animals were worthy recipients of both their labour and their emotions.

Thus, workers created a 'social world of care' at the shelter that extended across multiple species. This world became supremely powerful within the organisation, serving to remind 'insiders' who they were and why their work mattered. It appeared to us that the ethically charged and emotive experiences of care compensated workers for the lack of career structure, social status and material reward. Yet the occasional periods of tension that arose between individuals at Caring Companions made it difficult to generalise this group as cohesive or universally altruistic in their outlook. The culture of care did not always prevent fragmentation between the workers and their occasionally divergent values. In short, the work was deeply ingrained with human politics which meant that best practice was sometimes contested by those involved.

Counteracting this, however, the unifying presence of animals was especially important to mediate consensus surrounding the ethics of doing good work for the 'right' reasons. As Himmelweit (1999) argues, care work involves a range of motives ranging from 'social obligation, professional service or social justice' (King, 2012: 54) to more pragmatic reasons like the need for paid employment and it is likely that this was the case here too. At Caring Companions, there was often a complex mixture of emotion, moral duty and practical work which was complicated even further by the relationship between human carer and animal 'caree'. In fact, those employed in the shelter appeared to be particularly keen to police the motives of fellow workers, making sure that 'purity of motive' governed everyday decisions. This was an additional form of labour, one which required workers to create and manage shared values of 'good work', 'good care' and – above all – putting the underdog first. Far from being a 'thing' to be looked after, then, these 'underdogs' were the symbolic cornerstone for the cohesiveness of the shelter as a whole. They became the 'cultural glue' that connected employees together (sometimes against management) and helped counteract the ever-present potential for division in their individual motives for work.

In raising these issues (even if only within an exploratory capacity) we are excavating relatively new ground in organisation studies. Human-centred care work has received far more attention over the last few decades than animal-centred care. In fact, the care enacted for other species has received remarkably little attention although in some ways this is unsurprising given that the social sciences in general have a long legacy of a 'limiting anthropocentric orthodoxy' (Sanders, 2003: 406) and a sole focus upon 'the human' (Hamilton and Taylor, 2012). This means that, often, concepts and even *language* are not readily available or amenable to considering non-human others in organisations. We have noted, for example, that in much contemporary organisation theory, ideas about non-humans often relate to robotic, cybernetic, virtual and technological 'others' rather than different species. While the last two decades has seen a small but determined challenge to this state of affairs with the rise of the interdisciplinary Human–Animal Studies and the relatively new philosophy of post-humanism, there are few avenues for organisation studies to unpick the anthropocentric viewpoints adopted by traditional social theory. But doing so would shed greater light on workplaces such as the one investigated in the foregoing account. The idea that other species have a large part to play in human forms of work and organisation is a profound and philosophical issue which has the potential to take us well beyond the scope of the current chapter.

 **REFERENCES**

Alger, J., and Alger, S. (2003) *Cat Culture: The Social World of a Cat Shelter*, Philadelphia: Temple University Press.

Grant, A.M. (2008) 'The significance of task significance: Job performance effects, relational mechanisms and boundary conditions', *Journal of Applied Psychology*, 93, 108–124.

Hamilton, L. and Taylor, N. (2012) 'Ethnography in evolution: Adapting to the animal "other" in organizations', *Journal of Organizational Ethnography*, 1(1), 43–51.

Hamilton, L. and Taylor, N. (2013) *Animals at Work: Identity, Politics and Culture in Work with Animals*, Boston and Leiden: Brill Academic Publishers.

Himmelweit, S. (1999) 'Caring labor', *The ANNALS of the American Academy of Political and Social Science January*, 561(1), 27–38.

Karreman, D. and Alvesson, M. (2004) 'Cages in tandem: Management control, social identity, and identification in a knowledge-intensive firm', *Organization*, 11(1), 149–175.

King, D. (2012) 'It's frustrating! Managing emotional dissonance in aged care work', *Australian Journal of Social Issues*, 47(1), 51–70.

Latimer, J. (2000) *The Conduct of Care: Understanding Nursing Practice*, Oxford: Blackwell.

Pavlish, C. (2012) 'An exploratory study about meaningful work in acute care nursing', *Nursing Forum*, 47(2), 113–122.

Popke, J. (2006) 'Geography and ethics: Everyday mediations through care and consumption', *Progress in Human Geography*, 30(4), 504–512.

Pratt, M.G. and Ashforth, B.E. (2003) 'Fostering meaningfulness in working and at work' in Cameron, K.S., Dutton, J.E. and Quinn, R.E. (eds), *Positive Organizational Scholarship*, San Francisco: Berrett-Koehler.

Sanders, C. (1993) 'Understanding dogs: Caretakers' attributions of mindedness in canine–human relationships', *Journal of Contemporary Ethnography*, 22(2), 205–226.

Sanders, C. (2003) 'Actions speak louder than words: Close relationships between humans and nonhuman animals', *Symbolic Interaction*, 26(3), 405–426.

Stone, E. and Gueutal, H. (1985) 'An empirical derivation of the dimensions along which characteristics of jobs are perceived', *Academy of Management Journal*, 28, 376–396.

Taylor, N. (2004) '"In it for the animals": Moral certainty and animal welfare', *Society and Animals*, 12(4), 317–339.

Taylor, N. (2010) 'Animal shelter emotion management: A case of in situ hegemonic resistance?' *Sociology*, 44(1), 85–102.

# 12

# Where are the alternative organisations in Organisational Behaviour textbooks?

*Anita Mangan*

## 12.1 Introduction

Imagine that you are an undergraduate student about to study a module called 'Organisational Behaviour' (OB). At the introductory lecture, you hear about the different topics that will be covered over the coming weeks. The topics probably include many of the following: organisational culture, leadership, groups and teamwork, the individual, motivation, organisational structure and managing organisations. The module reading guide has a list of textbooks so you browse the library shelves and see multiple copies of bulky looking books. A quick look through the table of contents shows that the same topics seem to crop up again and again in these textbooks. But pause for a second and have another look at the table of contents. Did you ever stop to ask yourself 'where are the alternative organisations in the popular OB textbooks?'

This is not an idle question. If you examine the case studies in these expensive textbooks, which often run to hundreds of pages, you will usually find a range of studies that include large multinational corporations, well-known business brand names and a representative sample of key industry sectors. A review of the OB texts on my bookshelf includes case studies on airlines, technology companies, retailers and banks. The choice of cases are meant to illustrate real life examples of how businesses deal with everyday OB issues and to show that these issues cut across all sectors of industry and different sizes of businesses. Taken together, these textbook examples focus on safe, formalised knowledge about business and they rarely challenge the status quo, preferring instead to offer a sanitised, homogeneous version of the business world. If alternative organisational forms appear at all, it is usually as a marginalised concern, relating to 'new' OB topics such as corporate social responsibility, well-being or job satisfaction. Even then, they rarely take up more than a few pages in the textbook and can easily be missed.

Is this an important question? Alternative organisational forms surround us in our daily lives, yet we have been blinded to their existence, strengths and importance. Whether you are examining co-operative ventures, charities or advocacy groups, some form of organisation and organising is still required for them to function. The fact that these organisational forms are non-profit or outside the mainstream does not mean that they are irrelevant for students of OB; to ignore the diversity and richness of organisational life is to impoverish our understanding of the world of work – both paid and unpaid. This chapter explores possible reasons for the neglect of alternative organisational forms in OB textbooks. Drawing on the idea of 'régimes of truth' (Foucault, 1980), the chapter examines the 'truth' of business as promoted by business schools and encapsulated in the ideals of neo-liberal capitalism. This is followed by a discussion of how alternative organisations could be defined. The chapter concludes by making a positive case for studying alternative organisations, arguing that our understanding of organisation needs to account for diversity of perspectives, the importance of co-operation rather than outright competition, and the importance of making a difference.

## 12.2 Analysing the 'common sense' view of business: A discursive approach

> A discursive approach to the study of social reality focuses on knowledge and language. What can be said is both an indication of social values and a powerful shaper of social action. (Jacques, 1996: 67)

OB textbooks construct a particular view of organisations and organising that both feeds into and reproduces certain 'truths' about the world of business. These echo popular 'common sense' views about business presented in the media and taken for granted by most of us as being how the business world works. These ideas include the inevitability of global capitalism, free market competition, cost reduction, constant change and job insecurity (see also Pearson, Chapter 1 this volume). This section explores how these ideas came to be enshrined as the 'truth' of organisational reality, by drawing on the work of Foucault and in particular his concept of 'régimes of truth'.

For Foucault, 'The Truth' does not exist independently; instead, he argues that truth (with a small 't') is socially constructed and closely related to issues of knowledge and power (Foucault, 1980). Our knowledge of the world is not fixed and eternal; it is constructed by us and must be continually produced and reproduced in our everyday lives. Moreover, Foucault also argues that knowledge is neither objective, nor value-free. All the statements we make (including this one) are closely tied to political positions, which Foucault terms 'régimes' of truth. He defines régimes of truth as 'a system of ordered procedures for the production, regulation, distribution, circulation and operation of statements' (Foucault, 1980: 133). In terms of this defini-tion, knowledge is neither value-free nor capable of increasing incrementally. Rather, it is inextricably bound up with power relationships and the constitu-tion of reality. One has to investigate the 'rules of formation of statements which are accepted as scientifically true' (Foucault, 1980: 112) because for truth claims to become widely accepted, they must be co-opted, accepted and normalised, a process which necessitates exercises of power (Foucault, 1980).

While the language of 'régimes of truth' can seem quite complex, in effect, Foucault is challenging us to think about where common sense ideas come from and why we automatically assume they are true. For example, in the UK we frequently hear phrases such as 'jobs will be lost' or 'firms will go abroad' whenever someone proposes tightening business regulations or closing legal loopholes. Often the statements will be made by respected entrepreneurs or Government ministers, who speak from positions of power and authority. This lends the statements credibility (even if there is insufficient evidence to support the claims being made) and the statements are often presented in ways that suggest there are no other options available. Unless people present a strong counter-argument, the statements become 'normalised', namely, they are widely accepted as true by the majority of the population.

What are the implications of these ideas for our understanding of the 'truth' created in OB textbooks? First, it alerts us to the idea that there is nothing natural or self-evident about business knowledge; theories of organisational behaviour are constructed by privileging certain ideas while ignoring others. Rather than assuming that long-standing theories are still used because they have been proven to work, the notion of a régime of truth alerts us to the pos-sibility that OB theories are 'involved in a double movement of constructing organisational reality and rationality while effacing the process of construc-tion behind a mask of science and "naturalness"' (Fournier and Grey, 2000: 18). In other words, OB textbooks construct a particular view of organi-sations and organising that both reproduces and reinforces certain 'truths' about the world of business. Certain ideas about shareholder value, profit maximisation and the rationality of 'the market' become commonly held and accepted, while alternatives are written out of official accounts of how organisations and organising works. The next section explores this in more detail by examining the role of business schools in constructing and reinforcing received wisdom about organisations and organisational behaviour.

## 12.3 The 'one best way' of learning about business

Management education has long been associated with the US, where the first business schools were founded in the late 19th century (Fournier and Grey, 2000): US universities transformed between 1870 and 1920, gradually switching their focus towards the production of secular, technical knowledge needed in an era of industrialisation (Jacques, 1996). The UK followed European trends in the early 20th century, by treating management education as a set of practical skills to be learned in specialised institutes (Masrani et al., 2011). Management education only started to become part of the UK university system in the 1960s (Masrani et al., 2011) and it took until the 1980s for business schools to become widespread in the UK (Fournier and Grey, 2000). Interestingly, most of the initial research about organisations and organising was conducted within the social sciences, in areas such as sociology and psychology. Over time, however, organisational research came to be concentrated in business schools, rather than across the social sciences (Grey, 2009), leading to a homogenisation of perspectives.

In the case of business schools, homogenisation of perspectives means that discussion about business becomes uniform and standardised. The wide variety of perspectives, theories and alternative viewpoints become condensed into standardised business models and examples of best practice. In effect, management education presents a sanitised, sentimental view of organisations (Grey, 2002) which ignores employees' actual working conditions (Harney, 2009). However, given that modern global capitalism is founded on ruthless competition and exploitative working practices, Grey (2002) asks why mainstream business schools are silent on the issues of inequality and domination in the workplace. The question alerts us to the operation of a régime of truth about business. Certain knowledge is being privileged in a way that constitutes what counts as 'common sense' about business (Parker, 2002a). The role of business schools then becomes one of 'training capitalism's foot soldiers' (Ehrensal, 2001) by legitimating existing business practices and socialising managers (Grey, 2002) so that they can act as ambassadors for market capitalism (Parker, 2002a). The argument that business schools specialise in socialisation and legitimation is a provocative point, one that aims to highlight the political nature of learning and education. These writers are arguing that business education gives students an authorised language to use (Ehrensal, 2001) and the régime of truth associated with this language prioritises, endorses and actively promotes neo-liberal values. Thus, mainstream management education in business schools acts as both an apologist and cheerleader for 'the siren song of the market' (Harney, 2009: 321) by talking about the inevitability of global capitalism, free market competition and the necessity of minimising costs. This critique of business school education could come across as highly abstract and of little practical relevance. In the wake of the financial crisis of 2008 and the ongoing repercussions for ordinary citizens, however, it is important to remember that universities and academics do not exist in isolation and a régime of truth can have real effects. The 'truth' of neo-liberalism espoused in business schools is disseminated, reproduced and reinforced by graduates in their daily lives and through published academic research.

The financial services sector is an important example of a régime of truth in operation. In the UK, as elsewhere, the financial services sector has been regarded as a destination of choice for ambitious business graduates. In pursuing a career in the financial services sector, graduates implement financial models and economic theories that they have learned in business schools (Currie et al., 2010). Although many popular accounts of the financial crisis blame bankers' greed, incompetence and recklessness, or linear, unimaginative thinking (Knights and Tullberg, 2012, Tourish and Hargie, 2012), as Currie et al. (2010: s1) note, it is an 'inconvenient truth' for many business schools that their graduates have been deeply implicated in the financial crisis and it should cause academics to 'reflect more deeply and critically on the purpose and content of business school education', a point also made by Pearson (Chapter 1, this volume).

Thus, rather than focusing solely on banking culture and individual bankers, academic attention has begun to focus on the role of academics and business schools in creating the conditions of possibility for a financial crisis to emerge. In a discussion of knowledge limits and the financial crisis, Bryan et al. (2012) are highly critical of the role of academics and research in finance. First, they argue that academic output has been too narrowly focused, both theoretically and in terms of empirical research. The result is that individual academics have highly specialised expertise, but nobody has developed a sophisticated overview of the field. This is one reason why nobody anticipated a financial crisis happening. More worryingly, it also means that academic explanations for the crisis are also ghettoised; 'each academic affinity group will have translated financial crisis into its own language and explained it to its own satisfaction' (Bryan et al., 2012: 300) without any attempt to reflect on the wider implications of the findings. In addition, they argue that after the crisis there has been too much intellectual score settling between competing theoretical schools, rather than on a search for new perspectives or some critical reflection on academic practice (a point also made by Currie et al., 2010).

Finally, the financial crisis can be read in terms of a homogenisation of perspectives (Grey, 2009) about business. Banks relied on ever more complex mathematical modelling to calculate risk (Currie et al., 2010) and even as financial products were multiplying, alternative financial service providers began to disappear in the UK as building societies started to demutualise following deregulation (Morgan and Sturdy, 2000). With less variety in the market, homogenisation of perspectives was probably inevitable. Certainly, a degree of homogenisation is apparent in the responses given by the UK's senior bankers during the Banking Crisis Inquiry. In their testimony, senior banking executives in the UK often chose to explain their actions using metaphors (Tourish and Hargie, 2012). In their analysis of the testimony, Tourish and Hargie offer a sophisticated account of the complex range of metaphors deployed by the senior bankers, arguing that although the metaphors were a clever attempt to deflect responsibility for the financial crisis, they had limited impact. The metaphors are grouped into four overarching themes: the crisis was the product of the 'wisdom of the crowd', bankers were 'passive observers' overtaken by 'market forces', they were victims and, finally, penitent learners.

Continuing the ideas introduced in the chapter thus far, I would extend Tourish and Hargie's analysis by arguing that the bankers were also enacting the 'truth' of the 'neo-liberal economic consensus' (Currie et al., 2010: s1) that drew on the wisdom of experts such as Alan Greenspan (former Chairman of the US Federal Reserve Board) and assumptions about the inevitability of free market forces. In other words, senior banking executives were drawing on a régime of truth about business that espoused several common sense views about how the world of international finance works. These narrowly defined, common sense assumptions constructed a set of widely accepted rules about business that only began to be questioned after the financial crisis of 2008. Moreover, while the public's faith in the banking sector was undermined immediately after the crisis, judging by media reports (at the time of going to press) of the return of bonus culture in the City of London, it would seem that little has changed in the intervening years and the neo-liberal régime of truth continues to hold sway.

In summary, in this section I have argued that mainstream business school education presents a highly rationalised, functional view of organisations and the world of work. Business school education socialises graduates by providing them with an authorised language (Ehrensal, 2001) and a set of legitimised business practices (Grey, 2002). The key ideas associated with mainstream business education are narrowly focused on neo-liberal economic principles and global capitalism and this is reflected in the mainstream OB textbooks which feature uncontroversial case studies that promote profit maximisation and hierarchical management practices. The régime of truth of neo-liberalism and global capitalism does not allow for cases which feature co-operation, non-competition and alternatives to market capitalism. In the next section, I will briefly explore how alternative organisations could be defined, before arguing in favour of a greater focus on alternative organisations in business school programmes.

## 12.4 Defining alternative organisations

Defining what constitutes an alternative organisation (or form of organising) is complicated. The term is used to refer to a wide variety of organisations that span small, local initiatives to large, national groups. Some are ad hoc with sporadic activity, while others differ from mainstream businesses by being non-profit rather than profit generating. Handy (1988) attempts to make sense of alternative organising by distinguishing between three types of voluntary activities: mutual support, service delivery and campaigning, while noting that there is much interchange and overlap between these categories. Mutual support includes a wide range of activities from hobbies (such as volunteer sports groups or collectors' clubs) or finance (for example credit unions), to health-related support. Service delivery can include counselling, rescue services or family support, while campaigning organisations focus on single issue topics such as human rights, the environment or peace. Other commentators (Batsleer et al., 1991; Butler and Wilson, 1990; Paton, 1992; Courtney, 2002; Davis Smith et al., 1995) have suggested labelling alternative organisations as value-based organisations, the voluntary sector, the social economy and the third economy. More recently, they are referred to as the 'Third Sector' (see Hull et al., 2011). These multiple definitions highlight the diverse and complex types of organisations that can come under the umbrella term 'alternative': frequently there are porous boundaries between them, with individuals associating with multiple organisations at any given time; membership of the organisations is dynamic; they are diffuse and varied with large and small, community-based, regional and international groups all answering to the definition of an alternative organisation (Handy, 1988).

Another way of understanding alternative forms of organising is to compare them with mainstream, for-profit organisations. Courtney (2002) suggests a set of key distinctions related to profit versus non-profit, indicators of success, governance, stakeholders and, finally, resource acquisitions and transactions. Unlike mainstream organisations, the profit motive is not the primary driver of alternative organisations and their level of success is rarely indicated purely by 'the bottom line' (profit). As Handy (1988) notes, in the case of a campaigning organisation, success might mean the winding down of the organisation because the original mission is accomplished. Governance issues are also different because board members are often voluntary, although Courtney seems to assume that alternative organisations will automatically have a board of directors as part of its governance structure. In terms of stakeholders, Courtney (2002) argues that while the private sector often focuses solely on customers and shareholders, alternative organisations often have to acknowledge a broader set of stakeholders because they focus on social and community driven concerns. Finally, in terms of resource acquisitions and transactions, mainstream businesses have a relatively straightforward 'trading relationship' (Courtney, 2002: 47) where products and services are offered and a price agreed. Government funding and private donations are the primary resources for alternative organisations. These distinctions are general and the differences between alternative organisations and mainstream private businesses are not always clear-cut. The variety, size and scope of alternative modes of organising means that some of the organisations are akin to for-profit businesses and have little in common with more radical ventures. However, Courtney's categories can be condensed into two key issues: a focus on co-operation rather than competition and a non-profit ethos that promotes alternative cultures and values than those found in mainstream for-profit businesses.

While the discussion thus far manages to capture much of the richness and diversity of alternative forms of organising, these texts are managerialist in tone and content (see for example Butler and Wilson, 1990; Courtney, 2002; Handy, 1988). The authors offer guides to the *management* of alternative organisations; the subtext of the books is that alternative organisations, and the people involved in them, need careful management in order to succeed in a capitalist, competitive marketplace. Their criteria for success are based solidly within the standardised models of doing business and thus, although they promote and publicise alternative organisations, they treat alternative modes of organising as curiosities that need scrupulous management and scrutiny in case they upset existing, for-profit practices. These are texts written to control the sector, rather than to promote alternatives to mainstream business practices. I would argue that this is a subtle example of a régime of truth in operation; textbooks devoted to managing alternative organisations (of all forms) draw on the norms and disciplinary practices of for-profit organisations to define, judge and co-opt the alternative forms of organising into existing (acceptable and approved) practices. They are examples of how textbooks can be used to constitute a particular form of reality which is presented as 'natural' (Fournier and Grey, 2000) and based on common sense. This is a similar practice to what McGuigan (2009) calls 'cool capitalism'. His argument is that capitalism has always been adept at reinventing itself by absorbing cultural alternatives into the current system, thus neutralising opposition to capitalism itself.

The turn to managerialism is the reason why any discussion of alternative forms of organising needs to consider the political roots of these diverse organisations. Reedy and Learmonth (2009) remind us that the roots of alternative organisations can be found in radical traditions, where people were seeking alternatives to the constraints and inequalities found in society. New forms of organising often developed as socialist, feminist, anarchist or religious responses to the limitations of existing social structures. As such, they were a community's grassroots, collective and political responses to specific social problems identified and defined by the community. For this reason, Reedy and Learmonth's (2009: 242) definition of alternative organisations is explicitly political: 'organizations whose values, purposes and effects provide a strong counter-point to those values normally encountered in business corporations'. In short, they are formed in opposition to the received wisdom that self-interest and the invisible hand of the market is good for everyone. Reedy and Learmonth's criteria are that only the non-capitalist and anti-capitalist organisations should be defined as alternative. That said, they acknowledge that as their argument is explicitly polemical. Their intention is not to close down debate; rather it is to remind readers that alternative organisations have always been premised on the idea of enacting social change through practical action. This is an explicit rebuff to those texts that try to contain and control alternative forms of organising within the established norms and practices of capitalist enterprises.

Alternative organisations are a response to existing power relations and established institutions. They represent attempts to create alternatives to the régimes of truth reproduced and reinforced in mainstream business, alternatives that help to promote co-operation, self-help and mutual concern, based on shared values, rather than profit maximisation and individualism. As such they can be interpreted as examples of people resisting the dominant narratives presented by 'big business' or government (see Taylor and Hamilton, Chapter 11, and Oultram, Chapter 5, this volume). Thus, for the remainder of this chapter, I offer some positive reasons for including alternative organisations in OB textbooks, as well presenting a short case study of the Irish credit union movement (a group of financial co-operatives).

## 12.5 Thinking about the alternatives

Do we really need alternative organisations and organising featured in OB textbooks? It could be argued that this chapter is another example of McGuigan's (2009) cool capitalism, where threats to the status quo are absorbed into the capitalist system and neutralised. After all, this is a textbook about contemporary issues in management, albeit one that is written within a critical tradition. The argument that follows discusses the importance of promoting co-operation over competition, while acknowledging the ongoing difficulties that alternative organisations face. A case study of the Irish credit union movement is used to illustrate this point, showing how credit unions have battled to maintain their distinctive non-profit ethos in a highly regulated environment.

### 12.5.1 Co-operation over competition

Competition is one of the features of neo-liberal discourse. As Knights and Tullberg (2012: 386) note, people assume that the market is 'fuelled by individual economic self-interest' and that the benefits of Adam Smith's invisible hand of the market will be distributed equally. Competition frequently leads to questionable business practices (see Pearson, Chapter 1 this volume) and the inequalities created by global capitalism damage everyone in society, not just the poorest citizens (Wilkinson and Pickett, 2010). There are alternatives to competition, however, but people do not always realise that they are there. In the terms of UK retailing, for example, people might be familiar with the Co-operative Group's shops or the John Lewis Partnership, but since demutualisation and deregulation of the UK banking sector (Morgan and Sturdy, 2000), they may not be aware of the wide range of alternative financial organisations in the UK. Other retail alternatives include community-run shops, pop-up shops and workers' co-operatives.

Studies of alternative organisations can offer examples of groups who co-operate rather than compete, while still managing to earn a living and contribute to the local community's success. For example, Mondragòn is a Spanish worker-owned co-operative organised according to democratic principles, with workers having both the right *and* responsibility to become involved in managing the co-operative (Reedy and Learmonth, 2009). In Japan, following the earthquake–tsunami disaster of 2011, local businesses abandoned the Western competitive practices that they had adopted and returned to a traditional Japanese model of *kyo-jo* (collaborative assistance) with their competitors (Kiyomiya et al., 2013). As Kiyomiya et al. argue, people concluded that the market economy did not work after the tsunami and it led to a realisation that traditional models of co-operation between competitors was both relevant and necessary in order to rebuild the communities.

Granted, not all alternative organisations ventures are successful. Some are deemed illegal (Land, 2007), become politically compromised (Rosol, 2012), or fail and disappear from the records. Even flourishing alternative organisations experience ongoing personal and political struggles (Mangan and Kelly, 2009; Taylor and Hamilton, Chapter 11 this volume). The case study that follows explores how alternative organisational forms struggle to survive and thrive once the founder members move on, or after the initial enthusiasm wears off. This question becomes even more challenging when the existing legislation and regulations do not account for the ethos and operation of the alternative organisational form.

## 12.5.2 Legislating for mutual self-help? A case study of Irish credit unions

Credit unions are financial co-operatives, founded by and run on behalf of the members (Balkenhol, 1999).[1] Membership is based on well-defined categories, known as the common bond, which stipulates that there must be some kind of connection between members. This connection can include geographical locality, a shared workplace or membership of an organisation or club. As non-profit organisations, credit unions specialise in offering financial services to their members, usually in the form of savings and loan accounts. Credit unions are guided by the co-operative principles of equity, equality and mutual self-help. These principles distinguish financial co-operatives from for-profit institutions in several respects. All members have shares in the credit union and voting rights are distributed equally on the principle of 'one member, one vote' (ILCU, 1998: 96) rather than share ownership. Furthermore, credit unions promote mutual self-help through their attention both to members and the wider community in which these members live. Co-operation between co-operatives is encouraged in order to promote collective action and democratic control of the credit unions by their members. Finally, because a credit union is member-owned, any surplus funds generated are returned to members (in the form of dividends), invested back into the credit union or used to promote activities in the wider community. Taken together, these aspects differentiate credit unions from for-profit financial institutions on the one hand and charities on the other; they are non-profit organisations and the principle of mutual self-help requires that members work together for everyone's benefit, rather than simply distributing charity.

The initial drive to form credit unions in Ireland came about in the 1950s as the three founders looked for solutions to the poverty their communities were experiencing (Mangan, 2009; Culloty, 1990; Quinn, 1999). The anteced-ents for credit unions came from an awareness of international experiments with credit unions, as well as domestic experiences of co-operatives. The impetus to experiment with co-operative ideals began in the 19th century as part of an interest in social improvement that had sprung up all over Europe and was subsequently transported to North America. Co-operatives, which were inspired both by Victorian idealism and the rise of trade unionism, were based on the principle of helping the economically weak by promoting thrift and offering loans to craftsmen, farmers and small merchants who would otherwise not have access to capital (Quinn, 1999; Bolger, 1977).

Although the first Irish credit unions did not appear until 1958, several co-operative ventures had been attempted since the 1820s and, despite the failure of the majority of these projects, subsequent social reformers were cognisant of the co-operative ethos. For example, in the 1820s, John Scott Vandeleur took inspiration from Robert Owen's New Lanark co-operative model and created a co-operative village on his estate in Ralahine, Co. Clare (Craig, 1983; Bolger, 1977). The co-operative was forced to close in 1833 due to Vandeleur's gambling habits and debts (Craig, 1983). Nonetheless, the Ralahine experiment was important because it demonstrated that the urge to create social reform was not merely rhetorical but could also be put into prac-tice. A second co-operative initiative in Ireland was the creation of agricultural co-operatives, known as 'land banks', which enjoyed a period of growth in the late 19th and early 20th centuries. The emphasis was on self-help rather than on state aid (Bolger, 1977) as the land banks offered credit facilities to rural populations. Prior to this, the only source of credit available in rural areas of Ireland was from the 'gombeen man',[2] a person who acted as shopkeeper, pro-ducer, buyer and usurer in the community and who usually had political and social influence (Bolger, 1977). These agricultural co-operatives were run on a voluntary basis, interest rates were low because funding for loans came from members' deposits and voluntary work ensured low operating costs (Ivers, 1970). After an initial success, they went into decline from 1910 onwards and were almost extinct by the 1930s (Quinn, 1999).

Although interest in co-operative credit dwindled in the 1940s, communities throughout the country remained familiar with the concepts. Thus, when interest in credit unions emerged in the 1950s, people already had an understanding of community self-help through co-operative finance (Mangan, 2009). The three founder members of the credit union movement travelled the country at their own expense holding information seminars to educate the public about co-operative credit. The Catholic clergy also promoted and popularised the concept (Quinn, 1999). After a decade of intense, voluntary groundwork, enthusiasm for co-operative credit and mutual self-help was widespread and the first credit unions were opened in 1958. In the first six years of the movement's existence, 100 credit unions were established, with scores of study groups also set up around the country (Culloty, 1990).

While interest in credit unions was strong and the movement grew rapidly, the founders were aware of the need to formalise their vision of co-operative, community credit by resolving the credit unions' legal standing. The fledgling credit union movement had no legal status and lack of suitable legislation left credit unions exposed under the Moneylenders Acts, 1900 and 1933, and the Central Bank Act, 1942 (Quinn, 1994). The first credit unions were subject to the Industrial and Provident Societies Act, 1893, which had been enacted to regulate co-operatives and self-help societies rather than credit unions. This led to a trial and error approach whereby members studied the principles of co-operative credit and attempted to legitimise their organisation using the existing laws (Culloty, 1990). This was a short-term solution, however, which did not account for the ethos of co-operative credit and left credit unions vulnerable under existing legislation.

The solution was to lobby the Irish government to enact legislation specifically related to credit unions. This was a challenging task because although the founders argued that legislation was a key factor in promoting nationwide acceptance of credit unions, the movement had not achieved nationwide popularity and the number of members was very small (Culloty, 1990). Furthermore, the experience with 'land banks' less than forty years previously had made people cautious about the value of co-operative credit (Quinn, 1999). In 1957, the founders' persistent lobbying led to the creation of a Government Committee on Co-operation (1957–1963), chaired by the Registrar of Friendly Societies and with Nora Herlihy, one of the founders, on the board (Culloty, 1990).

Nine years later, legislation was enacted, giving the credit unions legal standing in Ireland and adding governmental authority to the credit union concept (Culloty, 1990; Mangan, 2009). The Credit Union Act, 1966, provided for the registration and regulation of credit unions. Importantly, it recognised key elements of the credit union ethos such as the mutuality of credit union members, based on a common bond, and stipulated that each credit union is a separate legal entity. The common bond is a defining part of the credit union ethos because, rather than viewing their members as individualised, sovereign customers (du Gay, 1996; du Gay and Salaman, 1992), the common bond positions members as active participants in a community group. Similarly, it was important that credit unions were legally independent of each other because the primary role of each credit union is to operate within and for a community group, rather than for the credit union movement as a whole. The Act of 1966 also institutionalised the not-for-profit status of credit unions by exempting them from the Moneylenders Acts, 1900 and 1933, and the Central Bank Act, 1942, and by barring them from using the terms 'bank', 'banker' and 'banking' when describing a credit union. Thus, the Credit Union Act, 1966, catered to the co-operative, community ethos of mutual self-help.

Following the example of the founder members, present day credit union representative groups and activities have continued to lobby politicians to ensure that the legislation meets the members' needs and preserves the movements' ethos. Revised legislation was enacted in the Credit Union Act, 1997, which allowed credit unions to offer increased levels of savings and loans and provide additional financial services to members. It also offers legal safeguarding of the credit unions' aspirations for social reform, as it expands the definition of the legal purposes and objectives of Irish credit unions. More recently, consultation on the Credit Union Bill 2012, which was enacted in December 2012, sought to clarify the credit unions' relationship with the Central Bank of Ireland and to balance the needs of community organisations with strict financial regulation.

As outlined in this case study, credit unions are founded on the principles of equity, equality and mutual self-help and use shared community financial resources to offer savings and loans facilities to the community. The ethos of credit unions is that they are non-profit organisations, run for members by members, and with a strong interest in social reform and social justice. This case study examined the historical foundations and evolution of the movement in Ireland, paying particular attention to the importance of legislation in formalising the movement's non-profit ethos. Credit union activists have continually lobbied members of parliament to ensure that their beliefs about what differentiates credit unions from other financial institutions receive legal recognition. Legislation does not, however, guarantee the survival of that ethos. Irish credit unions have faced several challenges in recent years (Mangan, 2009; Mangan and Kelly, 2009); not least the tightening of financial services regulations and Ireland's ongoing economic problems. The experience of the Irish credit unions raises provocative questions about maintaining, reinventing and reinvigorating alternative organisational forms. In a highly regulated sector, how do you ensure that co-operative, non-profit models are given due merit and not undermined by legislation and regulations intended for for-profit business? How do alternative organisations ensure that they address regulatory requirements while continuing to attend to their specific ethos and rationale? How do you ensure that a foundational non-profit ethos endures over time as the alternative organisation moves from the margins to mainstream acceptability? Are successful alternative organisations doomed to failure as a result of being swept into existing systems and structure? Or, is it possible to offer viable alternatives to mainstream non-profit ventures while continuing to maintain a distinctive non-profit ethos?

## 12.6  Interpreting the world from multiple perspectives

In this chapter, I have argued that by including alternative organisations in OB textbooks, we are writing back in what has been written out of official business discourse (Fournier and Grey, 2000). In so doing, we present students with a richer variety of organisations and organising, allowing them to understand the world of work, both paid and unpaid, from multiple perspectives rather than from one dominant narrative. The idea of multiple perspectives is important for many reasons. It gives people insights into hitherto unexplored worlds; opening perspectives rather than shutting down debate. While managers are often heard to praise the idea of 'thinking outside the box', frequently this simply means replacing one set of standard business practices with another set, all of which are based on neo-liberal principles of competitive capitalism. By studying alternative organisations, we can discover a wider variety of responses to specific problems, while also recognising that businesses do not exist in a vacuum, but are embedded in specific, local communities. With a greater range of alternatives to debate, there is a chance that students will arrive at a more nuanced understanding of the different paths available to solve any given problem.

It would be both naïve and coercive to imagine that learning about alternative modes of organising would immediately convert business students into cheerleaders for alternative ventures. However, it is not impossible to imagine that studying alternative organisations would broaden a student's perspective about the possibilities for making a difference. As Reedy and Learmonth (2009: 252) argue:

> Used well, they can speak in accessible ways that directly and explicitly call on us to think of, and practice management differently, whilst encouraging an imaginative

and emotional identification with what alternatives to dominant practices might look like.

Imagining different, better worlds has long been a feature of writing about utopia. Parker (2002b) argues, however, that utopias should be thought of as alternative organisations because they are attempts to rethink the world and solve intractable problems. In making these arguments, Parker is explicitly rejecting the idea that there is 'one best way' for people to organise themselves, either socially or in purely business terms. At the present time of writing (August 2013), there is much uncertainty in the UK about whether the economy is beginning to recover from the financial crisis. Meanwhile, the effects of successive budget cuts made under the aegis of the 'Age of Austerity' are only just beginning to have an effect across the country. Uncertainty is also a feature internationally, with the continuing crisis within the eurozone economies and growing doubts about the previously successful economies of China and India. Amid the daily diet of recession, job losses and cuts in living standards, it is too easy to slip into fatalism and to imagine that nothing can be done and that we are at the mercy of market forces. The lessons from studies about alternative modes of organising demonstrate that it is always possible to make a difference. There are always alternatives to the status quo.

## NOTES

1. Further information about credit unions can be found on the World Council of Credit Unions website (http://www.woccu.org/). Information about the Irish credit union movement is available from CreditUnion.ie (http://www.creditunion.ie/).
2. The term 'gombeen man' is a translation of the Irish word '*gaimbín*', which means usurer (Clinch et al., 2002).

 ## REFERENCES

Balkenhol, B. (1999) 'Introduction: Background and issues', in Balkenhol, B. (ed.), *Credit Unions and the Poverty Challenge: Extending Outreach, Enhancing Sustainability*, Geneva: International Labour Office.

Batsleer, J., Cornforth, C. and Paton, R. (eds) (1991) *Issues in Voluntary and Non-profit Management*, Wokingham, UK: Addison Wesley.

Bolger, P., (1977) *The Irish Co-Operative Movement: Its History and Development*, Dublin: Institute of Public Administration.

Bryan, D., Martin, R., Montgomerie, J. and Williams, K. (2012) 'An important failure: Knowledge limits and the financial crisis', *Economy and Society*, 41(3), 299–315.

Butler, R.J. and Wilson, D.C. (1990) *Managing Voluntary and Non-profit Organizations: Strategy and Structure*, London: Routledge.

Clinch, P. Convery, F. and Walsh, B. (2002) *After the Celtic Tiger: Challenges Ahead*, Dublin: The O'Brien Press.

Courtney, R. (2002) *Strategic Management for Voluntary Nonprofit Organizations*, London and New York: Routledge.

Craig, E.T. (1983) *An Irish Commune: The Experiment at Ralahine, County Clare, 1831–1833*, Dublin: Irish Academic Press.

Culloty, A.T. (1990) *Nora Herlihy: Irish Credit Union Pioneer*, Dublin: Irish League of Credit Unions.

Currie, G., Knights, D. and Starkey, K. (2010) 'Introduction: A post-crisis critical reflection on business schools', *British Journal of Management*, 21, s1–s5.

Davis Smith, J., Rochester, C. and Hedley, R. (eds) (1995) *An Introduction to the Voluntary Sector*, London: Routledge.

Du Gay, P. (1996) *Consumption and Identity at Work*, London: Sage Publications.

Du Gay, P. and Salaman, G. (1992) 'The cult[ure] of the customer', *Journal of Management Studies*, 29(5), 615–633.

Ehrensal, K.N. (2001) 'Training capitalism's foot soldiers: The hidden curriculum in undergraduate business programs', in Margolis, E. (ed.), *The Hidden Curriculum in Higher Education*, New York: Routledge, 97–113.

Foucault, M. (1980) 'Truth and power' in Gordon, C. (ed.), *Power/Knowledge: Selected Interviews & Other Writings 1972–1977*, New York: Pantheon Books, 109–133.

Fournier, V. and Grey, C. (2000) 'At the critical moment: Conditions and prospects for critical management studies', *Human Relations*, 53(1), 7–32.

Grey, C. (2002) 'What are business schools for? On silence and voice in management education', *Journal of Management Education*, 26(5), 496–511.

Grey, C. (2009) *A Very Short, Fairly Interesting and Reasonably Cheap Book about Studying Organizations*, 2nd edition, London: Sage Publications.

Handy, C. (1988) *Understanding Voluntary Organizations*, Harmondsworth: Penguin.

Harney, S. (2009) 'Extreme neo-liberalism: An introduction', *Ephemera*, 9(4), 318–329.

Hull, R., Gibbon, J., Branzei, O. and Haugh, H. (eds) (2011) *The Third Sector*, Bingley, UK: Emerald Publishing.

ILCU (1998) *Standard Rules for Credit Unions (Republic of Ireland) Registered under the Credit Union Act, 1997, affiliated to Irish League of Credit Unions*, Dublin: Irish League of Credit Unions.

Ivers, J. (1970) *The Further Development of Credit Unions in Ireland*, Dublin: University College Dublin.

Jacques, R. (1996) *Manufacturing the Employee: Management Knowledge from the 19th to 21st Centuries*, London: Sage Publications.

Kiyomiya, T., Masuda, Y. and Hayashi, S. (2013) 'Collaborative assistance (Kyo-jo) in recovering business under the crisis situation', in Numagami, T., Fujiwara, M. and Little, S. (eds), *APROS 15 Conference: Re-Covering Organizations*, 14–17 February 2013.

Knights, D. and Tullberg, M. (2012) 'Managing masculinity/mismanaging the corporation', *Organization*, 19(4), 385–404.

Land, C. (2007) 'Flying the black flag: Revolt, revolution and the social organization of piracy in the "golden age"', *Management & Organizational History*, 2(2), 169–192.

Mangan, A. (2009) '"We're not banks": Exploring self-discipline, subjectivity and co-operative work', *Human Relations*, 62(1), 93–117.

Mangan, A. and Kelly, S. (2009) 'Information systems and the allure of organisational integration: A cautionary tale from the Irish financial services sector', *European Journal of Information Systems*, 18, 66–78.

Masrani, S., Williams, A.P.O. and McKiernan, P. (2011) 'Management education in the UK: The roles of the British Academy of Management and the Association of Business Schools', *British Journal of Management*, 22(3), 382–400.

McGuigan, J. (2009) *Cool Capitalism*, London: Pluto Press.

Morgan, G. and Sturdy, A. (2000) *Beyond Organizational Change: Structure, Discourse and Power in UK Financial Services*, Basingstoke: Macmillan.

Parker, M. (2002a) *Against Management: Organization in the Age of Managerialism*, Cambridge: Polity Press.

Parker, M. (ed.) (2002b) *Utopian and Organization*, Oxford: Blackwell Publishing/The Sociological Review.

Paton, R. (1992) 'The social economy: Value-based organizations in the wider society', in Batsleer, J., Cornforth, C. and Paton, R. (eds), *Issues in Voluntary and Non-profit Management*, Wokingham: Addison-Wesley Publishing Company.

Quinn, A.P. (1994) *Credit Unions in Ireland*, Dublin: Oak Tree Press.

Quinn, A.P. (1999) *Credit Unions in Ireland*, 2nd edition, Dublin: Oak Tree Press.

Reedy, P. and Learmonth, M. (2009) 'Other possibilities? The contribution to management education of alternative organizations', *Management Learning*, 40(3), 241–258.

Rosol, M. (2012) 'Community volunteering as neoliberal strategy? Green space production in Berlin', *Antipode*, 44(1), 239–257.

Tourish, D. and Hargie, O. (2012) 'Metaphors of failure and the failures of metaphor: A critical study of root metaphors used by bankers in explaining the banking crisis', *Organization Studies*, 33(8), 1045–1069.

Walsham, G. (1993) *Interpreting Information Systems in Organizations*, Chichester: John Wiley & Sons.

Wilkinson, R. and Pickett, K. (2010) *The Spirit Level: Why Equality is Better for Everyone*, London: Penguin Books.

 **FURTHER READING**

Foucault, M. (1977) *Discipline and Punish: The Birth of the Prison*, London: Penguin Books.

Foucault, M. (1980), *Power/Knowledge: Selected Interviews & Other Writings 1972–1977*, Gordon, C. (ed.), New York: Pantheon Books.

Foucault, M. (1982) 'Afterword: The subject and power', in Dreyfus, H.L. and Rabinow, P. (eds), *Michel Foucault: Beyond Structuralism and Hermeneutics,* Bristol: The Harvester Press.

Foucault, M. (1990) *The History of Sexuality Volume 1: An Introduction*, London: Penguin Books.

Gutting, G. (ed.) (2005) *The Cambridge Companion to Foucault*, 2nd edition, Cambridge: Cambridge University Press.

Nealon, J. (2008) *Foucault Beyond Foucault: Power and its Intensifications since 1984*, Stanford: Stanford University Press.

Phillips, N. and Hardy, C. (2002) *Discourse Analysis: Investigating Processes of Social Construction*, Thousand Oaks, CA: Sage Publications.

# Epilogue: Reflections on practice

*Phil Johnson*

If management theory as taught in universities does not translate in a meaningful way into the workplace, it remains just that: theory. As an abstract model, blind theory can present a simple world, whereas the workplace – as evident in this book – is both complex and messy. There are many benefits, both to students and society, to be gained from a degree, and a crucial one for employers is that they expect graduates to be able to apply what they have learnt to the workplace for the benefit of both parties. As an experienced manager turned teacher, I have seen this from both sides and it is now my daily job to demonstrate to students that though simplistic approaches to the imposition of theory are of little value to organisations, there is nonetheless significant value to be found in the appreciation of appropriate concepts. My own Masters studies (undertaken whilst holding down a full time senior management role) helped me to look at, and respond to, the workplace in new ways. I do not claim special status in such a revelation; as I have seen years of students since acknowledge a similar dawning of understanding. As one postgraduate student once said to me as she graduated, 'I always knew *what* was going on at work, now I understand *why*.'

As a practicing manager in a famously 'paternalistic' company, where paternalism manifested through uniquely impressive staff benefits including very extensive (and expensive) staff training and management development, I was subject(ed!) to many hours of 'one size fits all' management 'solutions' that would allegedly transform both my performance and that of my team. As my experience grew, it became increasingly clear to me that much of this received wisdom was a waste of time. Not that the theory was wrong as such, but as Kelemen (Chapter 2, this volume) argues, it is not able to deal with ambiguous, realistic work situations. There was a lack of recognition that context, understanding and interpretation are crucial.

As Pearson (Chapter 1, this volume) points out, the unthinking, uncritical acceptance and slavish adoption of pat explanations can have far-reaching consequences and I have seen for myself that a simplistic assumption that people's motivations can be represented neatly by one or other of McGregor's (1960) 'Theory X' or 'Theory Y' categories, is at best not very helpful and ultimately patent nonsense. Yet the multitude of textbooks produced to educate business school graduates worldwide have unintended consequences, as such simplified ideas become the basis for informing mainstream management. As Pearson states, 'business culture, corporate law and management theory, are not independent of each other, but interact in the way they shape business practice'. Mangan (Chapter 12, this volume) argues strongly that this connection is a good reason to worry about the lack of alternative organisations and differing ideas presented to students. People, organisations (which are people) and society (which is both) are simply too complicated, unpredictable and changeable to be pigeonholed by the broad brush of convenient or popular management fads.

Many of the contributors to this book raise crucial issues about management in the contemporary workplace and offer contrasting examples of good and bad practice: for instance, many people are looking for a great deal more than just a salary from their work. I would cite Emery's farmers and Oultram's apprentices (Chapter 6, and Chapter 5, this volume, respectively) as such, who evince a fierce pride in their work and a loyalty to their craft. However, Hamilton and McCabe (Chapter 7, this volume) offer us a Dante-esque picture of 'Farmstock' as a Fordist lower circle of Hell where privileged and distant managers preside over highly qualified vets who are legally barred from exercising the full range of their skills, and silent and soldiering manual workers whose work rate is set by the speed of the line. This offers us a snapshot of a successful company based on practices that many thought had died out (in the West, at least) decades ago. The classic stance of orthodox texts suggests that 'Farmstock' should not work. As an outdated and crude 'solution' to the motivation and productivity of employees it ought to have been replaced by more subtle and benevolent forms of management. It is clear that not only is this not the case, but that in this modern incarnation it is thriving and patronised by the big supermarkets. How different is the position of Farmstock's staff, relative to the immigrant labour force of the early 20th century (as addressed elsewhere in this book)?

So where does this leave us? For me, the value of this book lies in its refusal to accept simplistic solutions: there simply are no 'one size fits all' answers and we will all become better academics, teachers and managers if we recognise this.

What I find reassuring is that, within this challenging collection, we can identify key themes that – when critically considered within the specific context
of any individual workplace – can be genuinely helpful. For instance, recognition that *in most cases* people at *all* levels of the organisation really do take
pride in their work, if allowed to do so by company culture and structure (or
indeed, sometimes in spite of these). Some of the proudest and most committed workers I have come across in my thirty years in business have been
amongst the most poorly paid: clerks, warehouse operatives and cleaners,
and managers would do well to remember this.

Senior management's responsibility is not simply to lock themselves away
and think lofty thoughts of short-term shareholder returns. It is their job not
simply to set the organisational strategy in the ambiguous context of government interventions of whatever kind, or what Mintzberg (1979; 1985)
would call the 'messiness' of day to day life, and Schofield (Chapter 10, this
volume) underlines: 'events in the real world can't be timetabled', although
this is difficult and important enough. Such immediate problems might need
immediate responses, yet the role of management and of those who study it
is so much broader, since the impact of organisations on our lives and societies can be so great. Irrespective of size, sector or industry, could it be management's place to help build an environment (a 'culture', if you will) within
which people are enabled to be the best they can be? 'Farmstock' pays, but
how successful could it be given a more enlightened management approach?
What might happen if a competitor with a different management mindset
were to move in? Could it be that some organisations are doing far more
than just fulfilling what they see as their obligations to society? Could it be
that – to come back to making the theory real and relevant in the workplace
– they are actually attracting staff, at all levels, who see life as much more
than 'Theory X', to the benefit of both the organisation and society, presenting a virtuous circle that goes beyond the bottom line?

Just as, in my experience, the short-term benefits of overbearing management, or the popularity of weak or laissez-faire managers seem appealing,
I would like to think that exploitative and outdated management practices
– whilst undeniably often effective in the short-term – will not deliver
viable and sustainable businesses in the longer term. What will happen to
'Farmstock' when a more enlightened competitor appears? And what are the
social dangers of ignoring the skills and experience of trained experts, simply
to pursue a cheaper labour force? More importantly, the long-term impact of
failing to highlight to our students the relevance of context, of understanding the limitations of theory and of the politics of its interpretation may
come at great cost. Such a naïve approach not only sells the discipline of

management short, but also does our students a disservice when forced to confront a messy and uncompromising world.

In the end, management skills are life skills and I believe that a critical approach to received wisdom such as offered in this book, combined with a commitment to treating others with respect, form the basis of good theory *and* good management.

 **REFERENCES**

McGregor, D. (1960) *The Human Side of Enterprise*, New York: McGraw-Hill.
Mintzberg, H. (1979) *The Structuring of Organizations*, Englewood Cliffs, NJ: Prentice Hall.
Mintzberg, H. and Waters, J.A. (1985) 'Of strategies, deliberate and emergent', *Strategic Management Journal*, 6(3), 257–272.

# Glossary

| | |
|---|---|
| **abattoir** | a building or place for killing livestock |
| **agriculture** | farming, the cultivation of crops or rearing of livestock |
| **ambiguity** | the simultaneous presence of multiple valid possible interpretations or meanings |
| **ameliorate** | to lessen or soften the effects of |
| **anachronism** | inconsistency, usually an idea or object which seems out of place or from a different historical period |
| **anarchy** | the absence of formal regulation or authority |
| **anthropology** | the study of humans, particularly tribal societies |
| **anthropomorphism** | to attribute human-like characteristics, impulses or behaviours to non-human entities |
| **apprenticeship** | a system of training where a novice or beginner spends extended time working alongside an expert in order to learn specialised skills. Traditionally associated with craft occupations such as carpentry or metalworking |
| **aristocratic** | with noble characteristics |
| **autonomy** | the freedom to regulate one's own actions |
| **axiology** | the study of, or beliefs about, what is valuable or worthwhile (may refer to ethics) |
| **benevolent** | well-meaning, acting for the general good |
| **bifurcation** | a split into two paths or sections |
| **biography** | the story of an individual's life history. Literally, life-writing |
| **bureaucracy** | the administration or organisation of activities by strict task divisions and clear hierarchies |
| **capitalism** | the organisation of society based on private ownership to promote the accumulation of material wealth. **Industrial capitalism** is the combination of economic organisation of capitalism with mass production of trade goods |
| **catch-22** | a direct contradiction between different rules or expectations |
| **coding** | the labelling of data according to distinct themes; |

| | |
|---|---|
| **coding protocol** | a standard set of identification and labelling systems for analysing data |
| **coercion** | the use of power to force individuals to act in a way which may not necessarily be in their best interests |
| **cohesion** | for strong bonds to be evident between persons or actors |
| **community of practice** | a group of experts or fellow practitioners who may not work for the same organisation, but share common expertise, information and insights to support each other's work |
| **consumption** | the use or absorption of a product, often used to refer to the purchase of goods or services; **consumer society** a society dominated by the importance of the use or absorption of products |
| **corporate social responsibility** | a term widely debated, this broadly refers to the engagement of organisations in matters which are considered external to the functional operations of the business, but may be argued as the moral duty of the organisation to a broader variety of stakeholders |
| **critique** | the identification of limitations among a set of ideas or beliefs or the identification of flaws in a logical argument |
| **culture** | a term used to encapsulate a wide range of behaviours, interpretations, rules and attitudes within an organisation or group |
| **curriculum** | a course or planned schedule of topics. Plural: **curricula** |
| **determinist** | to presume something is caused by the actions of another agent or system |
| **dichotomy** | the separation into two (usually opposing) concepts or frames of analysis |
| **differentiation** | the identification of key distinguishing differences between groups or individuals |
| **dignity** | intrinsic worth or value |
| **discipline** | commonly, self-control. Often the term discipline is used in everyday language to refer to punishment as a response to 'bad' behavior. Foucault wrote extensively on the relationship to explore relations of power and forms of control, and the term is often used in academic writing to refer to this work |
| **discourse** | in everyday use, discourse simply refers to general discussion and debate. However, scholars tend to use |

the term in combination with the work of Foucault, to refer to the combined systems of knowledge and power embedded in everyday language from which we cannot escape

**dissociation**  to distance from, to emphasise a lack of connection

**economically solvent**  having enough funds available to meet debts

**economics**  the scientific study of business transactions, predominantly the exchange of money for goods and services through markets

**emancipation**  the promotion of equality through distribution of rights or wealth to those without them

**embodiment**  the embedding of concepts or attitudes in materials or in the human body

**enactment**  the manifestation of something in behaviour

**enterprise**  the undertaking of a new project or business where there may be risk and/or uncertainty; **enterprise discourse** the frequent occurrence of an ideology which positions individuals as agents expected to be engaged in and responsible for personal enterprise

**epistemology**  the study of, or beliefs about, what we can know and understand

**ethic**  a rule or system of rules of conduct determining good behaviour. Sometimes used to refer to particular virtues or morality; **work ethic** the rules of conduct determining good behaviour in work activities, often refers to the Protestant work ethic depicted by Max Weber

**ethnography**  a method in social science based on participation and close observation of the research participants in their own environment; **ethnographer** a researcher using the techniques of ethnography

**exploitation**  the division of effort and reward in an unjust manner

**globalisation**  the increase in worldwide connections, systems or ideologies

**groupthink**  the psychological tendency for a collection of people working together to promote similar ideas and silence or ignore alternatives in order to maintain the group

**heterodox**  different or alternative. When used to describe academic literature it describes theoretical positions which differ from the majority of work

| | |
|---|---|
| **hierarchy** | vertical relations of function and authority within an organisation |
| **homo œconomicus** | an idealised model of human behaviour which assumes actions are determined by rational evaluation of the costs and benefits |
| **ideology** | a system of beliefs about the world |
| **incomer** | non-native resident, may be used as a derogatory/offensive term |
| **individualism** | an ideology focusing on the promotion of the individual as the most significant entity of value (rather than the family, the community or other social unit) |
| **individualisation** | the phenomenon of the individual being presented as increasingly more responsible and accountable for the events of their own life (rather than chance, luck, the effects of economics or any other external factor). Developed mainly in the work of Ulrich Beck and Zygmunt Bauman |
| **instrumentalism** | to focus on the means of obtaining an outcome over the outcome itself, may refer to an overemphasis on people as mechanisms of production |
| **intensification** | the increase or concentration of; **work intensification** an increase in tasks during an allotted period |
| **kite mark** | a mark of recognition or accreditation from an awarding body usually indicating the achievement of a registered standard |
| **labour market** | the collection of people readily available and willing to work for wages |
| **lateral** | horizontal; **lateral thinking** to approach from an unusual perspective |
| **liberalism** | an economic perspective which advocated freedom of economic activity from state interference with trade or individual business, commonly held until the early 20th century; **neo-liberalism** a revived approach to liberalism which allows for limited state regulation and is often critiqued for suggesting the state should protect only the interests of business |
| **marginal** | the periphery, outlying area or edge, often used to describe the limits of acceptability; **marginalisation** the act of highlighting something as less acceptable or normal, nearly unacceptable |
| **mediation** | the use of a third independent individual, technology or organisation to convey information or organ- |

ise action between two entities, e.g., their discussion was mediated by telephone

**migration**   the movement of people from one nation state to another, often in the search for a better quality of life; **immigration** the process of entering a country in order to live (and work) there; **emigration** the process of leaving a country in order to live (and work) elsewhere

**morals**   beliefs about good or virtuous behaviour, usually upheld as such by a community or culture; **morality** to act in accordance with morals (opposite: **amorality**, to act contrary to moral behaviour)

**mutual**   for multiple persons to have the same relationship or opinions to each other, often used to describe organisations structured on a communal basis or for the equal benefit of a community

**mythology**   a set of stories or legends common to a particular culture

**NEET**   abbreviation for 'not in employment, education or training'

**normative**   idealised (in pure conceptual or abstract form). May also refer to a typical or normal set of ideas or perspectives in a given culture or society

**ontology**   the study of, or beliefs about, what exists

**orthodox**   ordinary or mainstream. When used to describe academic literature it describes the theoretical position of the majority of work

**paradox**   the co-existence of two or more logical inconsistencies

**participant observation**   a technique commonly used in ethnography where the researcher engages in the tasks of the participants as well as observing their behaviour

**paternalism**   a style of management that emphasises management's right to decide how best to ensure their employee's welfare. Often associated with the Quaker-owned businesses of the early 20th century

**phenomenon**   a set of observations or logical evidence which represents a puzzle or a problem for interpretation. Plural: **phenomena**

**positivism**   a scientific ideology which assumes that what can be known and what is are the same, i.e. there is no

|  |  |
|---|---|
| | reality which cannot be known given appropriate methods |
| **postmodernism** | a reaction against the principles of modernism. Often used to refer to an ideology which emphasises the limitations of rationality or models of rational behaviour |
| **prank** | a practical joke or trick, usually directed at an individual |
| **prestige** | high status |
| **problematic** | puzzling, inconsistent |
| **pseudonym** | a fictional name, often attributed to research participants in order to protect their identity |
| **real economy** | the part of the economic market which is comprised of extraction (primary industry), manufacturing (secondary industry), distribution and non-financial services (tertiary industry) |
| **rhetoric** | the art of speech, particularly of persuasion; **rhetorical question** a device to highlight an author's point, usually a question which does not require a response from the audience or reader |
| **rite of passage** | an obligatory act or process whereby individuals are accepted into a group or society |
| **ritual** | a sequence of symbolic acts. May refer to everyday acts which are regularly repeated by an individual and which may have a symbolic edge; e.g., His morning ritual of coffee and a newspaper was interrupted |
| **sexism** | to behave as if one gender or sex of person is of less intrinsic value or lacking in capacities |
| **solidarity** | unified feeling or action, usually based on common interests or loyalty |
| **stakeholder** | a person or organisation with a vested interest in the outcome of an organisation's activities. May refer to shareholders as well as outsiders to the organisation |
| **stigma** | the persistent attachment of negative associations to an entity |
| **subsistence** | the minimum requirements for living, the action of living on the minimum commodities or pay |
| **taint** | negative associations, usually from contact with a substance or category condemned as bad or taboo |
| **telework** | abbreviation of telephone work, but usually used to refer to any sort of work mediated by technology |

|               |                                                                                                                                                      |
| ------------- | ---------------------------------------------------------------------------------------------------------------------------------------------------- |
|               | often undertaken at a distance from the employer's premises                                                                                          |
| **uncertainty** | confusion over valid interpretation or meaning                                                                                                      |
| **value**     | esteem, social standing, worth. Can refer to particular ethics or virtues upheld as particularly good or important. May also refer to monetary value or price |
| **victim**    | someone who has been negatively affected or harmed, usually by the actions of an outside agency                                                      |
| **virtue**    | a universally good quality attributed to an individual's character or behaviour; e.g., honesty, charity                                              |
| **vocation**  | a career or occupation for which someone is particularly talented or committed to                                                                    |

# Index